ZEN HANDBOOK

A Westerner's Guide to Awakening: aphorisms, essays, fables, jokes, poems.

Other books authored

_____

Temple of the Origin, Small Press, New York, 1991

A Portrait of the Artist as an Anthropomorphic Genius-Machine, Novatrix Library, New York, 2002

On sale at Amazon.com and selected book stores

ZEN HANDBOOK

Zen

Aphorisms,

Zen

Essays,

No-mind Zen

by **Peter Jalesh**

Novatrix Library

101 W, 55th Street, Suite 7D

New York, NY 10019, USA

Published by Novatrix Library
101 W 55th Street, Suite 7D
New York, NY 10019, U.S.A
Phone: 212-247-6808; Fax: 212-582-6535

Copyright © by Boris Musteata, 2004
All rights reserved

By the same author:
Temple of the origin, a phantasmagoric novel
A portrait of the artist as an anthropomorphic genius-machine, a novel

Library of Congress Cataloging-in-Publication Data
Musteata, Boris
    Zen Handbook Zen Aphorisms, Zen Essays, No-mind Zen
Writers Guild of America, East
WGAE AFL-CIO
Musteata, Boris
    Zen Aphorisms, Zen Essays, No-Mind Zen
    Reg. No. R13855-00 on 09/24/2003
ISBN 0-9717487-1 3
    1. Zen Handbook

Art Cover: Peter Jalesh, *Untitled*, 2000, acrylic on canvas, 6 ft.x11 ft.

To my daughters, Oana-Maria Voichita and Natalie Marie-Christine
and to my ex-wife and dear friend Elena-Dana Comnea

Motto:

If you are a monk this book is not for you. If you're a layman you could start your Zen experience of emptiness from a variation of Wittgenstein's utterance about the world:

"The world *of Zen* is both, what the world is and what the world is not".

If you also succeeded to erase the above duality you'd discover another way of knowing;   you'd be able to "see" a world that lies within the real world and yet beyond discrimination – a permanent and unified universe – the Emptiness.

CONTENTS

Preface

Zen has been in vogue in America for more than half of a century. It started with the excitement generated by basic books signed by D. T. Suzuki, Philip Kapleau, Trevor Leggett, Alan Watts, Christmas Humphreys, Thomas Cleary and others, and continued with an enormous interest in specialized Zen books. Anthologies of koans, exegeses on various Zen schools, books on Zen art and literature, philosophical and psychoanalytical interpretations of Zen tried to gratify those demands. Colleges and universities introduced Zen philosophy in their curriculum.

In the Western intellectual process of Zen assimilation - other Eastern directions of thought - such as Tao and Buddhism, have been incorporated under Zen umbrella so that gradually any Zen label was considered to be a Zen product. In fact, only a few Zen books are written from the proximity of a true Zen philosophy.

Lately, the interest in Zen reached a new peak. To some, Zen is not seen anymore as a narrow intellectual pursuit, but as a practical mean that could improve one's life and experiences that eventually bring about the awakening.

By reviewing all the existing books on Zen I found out to my surprise that in majority they are either translations of Chinese and Japanese original texts or compilations of already published materials.

In this respect the current book approaches Zen from an original viewpoint. Rather than using known quotations from existing Zen books and therefore repeating what had been already said, it provides original thinking and explores in a practical way the evolution of Zen "understanding" based on my own experiences. The book goes some way towards clarifying some Zen fundamental questions, though, by observing what Zen was to my own development, it directs attention to the problem of how and what Zen could accomplish for one who embarks for

Zen as a life time practice. By virtue of the fact that the book originates from within an individual experience of awakening outside of the Zen establishment it is doubtless the most accessible and reliable guide to anyone who'd like to approach Zen outside a Zen dogma, while being obliged to live a normal and responsible social life.

Zen Handbook consists of essays, aphorisms, fables and poems never published before.

The short essays delineate the main Zen concepts, including commentaries of practical values regarding the koan approach, meditation and breathing. The introduction is more or less an overture to the language that Zen uses. Its purpose is to make Zen accessible to an intellectual understanding and also to provide an evaluation of various Zen experiences and their possible outcome.

The middle part of the book consists of almost two thousand aphorisms, fables and notes that are touching, reviewing and refreshing most of the principles found in Zen. This part of the book is an extract from 1,300 pages that I have written from 1975 to today. Upon selection, some of the early written material had to be modified and corrected to fit the later writings as far as writing style or Zen understanding are concerned. The interspersed notes within the aphorism chapter are retracing the progress or the regress of my awakening experience.

Due to the fact that the written material was produced on an extended period of time, some of the Zen concepts are subject to multiple aphorisms, though each of them are setting a different tone and "understanding" of Zen or belong to a different form of expression.

A few notes are written in contempt to the orthodox Zen, and needed as a moral support to those who think that Zen, as a science of freedom, allows dissent.

The third part is a Zen poem with a Biblical twist. Zen and Haiku poetry represent already assimilated creative forms into Western culture. The poem, called *Inner-mind Zen, outer-life...* consists of typical Zen poetry in a mix with invocations of love (a Zen muse would be an oxymoron) and longings for a simple life that seems always to belong to the past, until the awakening happens…

A short glossary attached to the end of the book provides short definitions of other Zen or Buddhist terms used throughout the book.

Note: I practiced Zen from 1978. My Eastern Philosophy based experiences originate in 1975 with Hata Yoga, followed by Raja Yoga and Bakhti Yoga that evolved by the end of 1977 into Zen. I began writing about various Zen subjects in order to feed or to register my own Zen experiences. My only Zen achievements occurred in 1982: a Samadhi incidence that, two days later, was followed by Satori. Both events lasted less than a couple of minutes. None of those experiences repeated since. I kept having various moments of elation that resembled Samadhi, others that I could call revelations, though none of them were as powerful as the 1982 events. There is well known that Satori is one of the most elusive events. What it gives to those who experience it, is an overwhelming illusion of mind merging with the whole universe, of a body-mind getting dissolved in the universal emptiness. The other side of the token is that - in real life - one might understand the essence and the invariance of the whole universe through every day's life and practice.

The Author

Bio: *PETER JALESH*, born Boris Musteata in Romania. In 1960 he graduated from the School of Cinematography. In 1965 he received a MS degree in Nuclear Physics from the Polytechnic Institute, Bucharest, followed by two MA degrees: in Linguistics in 1970 and in Philosophy in 1974, both from University of Bucharest. He began his writing career in 1958. He published several volumes of poetry: *Menuet* (1968), *Poema* (1970), *Poemele Marii* (1975), *Cintul Etern* and *Poema Dacica* (1977), *Luminile de dimineata* (1978, a novel - *Vinzatorul de memorii* (1978), a volume of modern poetry translated from Russian, other translations from universal symbolist poetry. From 1970 to 1979 he wrote scenarios for animation and documentary features, commentaries for radio and television shows. In 1978 he translated B. Malinovsky's *Cultural Anthropology*. In 1972 he became a political dissident and spent the next years under the surveillance of the Communist Secret Police (Securitate). Before escaping to U.S. he was subjected to numerous coercive interrogatories and tortures.

In 1979 he asked for political asylum. He became an American citizen in 1988. Since emigration he published seven books on subjects related to IBM computer software, and two novels, *Temple of the Origin* and *A portrait of the Artist as an Anthropomorphic Genius Machine*.

Major one-man art exhibitions: *"Quasi Still Life Series"*, 56 abstract paintings and drawings, Deep Space Gallery, 11/1996, New York, *"Abstract Endings on Large Canvases"*, abstract paintings on oversize (11 ft. to 25 ft.) canvases, Pearl Gallery, 02/2000, New York, *"A Retrospective of Quasi-Action Painting"*, 82 old and new abstract paintings, Mercedes-Benz Showroom Gallery, 02/2003, New York.

Essays

The Way of Zen

The way of Zen could be easily understood in a fleeting moment of innocence. Thus, a Zen text should begin with affirming this innocence and also saying that – unfortunately – its text is nothing else but a deceit. Why so? Because such a text should be understood only as layers and layers of uttering surrounding a "core of emptiness"… Language has limitations when it tries to describe facts that are beyond comprehension and as such it would have to define Zen as a "philosophical impossibility". Fortunately we encounter a similar approach to language in any religious text. Though, in contrast to a Zen text a religious text is richer in superstitions, miracles, supernatural events and utterances that are sold as immortal or absolute. To a devotee a religion promises to provide a way to liberation through unabated faith in God and through its customary religious practices – prayers, meditation, masses and so on and so forth. If Zen is another way to attain liberation could we use a narrative to define what this liberation is and what a Zen devotee should do to attain it? Most of the Zen books are clear and explicit on both issues though non committal. An example from astronomy that shows how a noncommittal definition holds grounds and become committal is the definition of a black hole. Zen, the Way of Liberation, at its core, could be compared with such a cosmic entity that concentrates an enormous absorbent energy and yet allows an infinitesimal amount of radiation to escape its trappings. For Zen, this small amount of radiation is the human language with its shortcomings trying to describe the impossible – what the Way of Liberation is, what is the Enlightenment, what is Realization? In terms of these "Zen essentials" we still use words. A Zen text book or manual is nothing else but a collection of various expressions trying to deal in a hypothetical way with the unknown, which by its very nature resides beyond one's intellect. A hypothetical way to explain the unknown may never get satisfactorily resolved. And this lack of finality arises out of every author's definition of the awakening or the enlightenment: it is like trying to trap the infinite in the narrowness of one's mind. But what else is the Way of Liberation if not just that? What about the traditional Zen texts or Sutras? Aren't they just passages used to draw the gradual path a Zen pupil should follow to attain awakening? What about a Koan? A Koan is a rigidly build fable that doesn't allow its ultimate meaning to surface until one succeeds to penetrate its crust and have a glance at that "ultimate truth within". To get there one uses language and intuition - as opposed to language and reason used in the normal process of knowledge. For a human being – Westerner or Easterner - a language gives meaning to what one knows or experiences. Obviously there are limitations in understanding some aspects of various cultures and a translation of an entire culture in terms of the other is difficult or discordant when attempted. But I think it isn't true that such a process creates insurmountable uncertainties and inabilities to live the experiences of another culture. In human terms such a divergence could be yet beneficial. And this is the point I'd like to make about Yoga, Zen and other Eastern practices borrowed by the West. I even suggest that the Westerner's "inadequacy" to approach Zen using a non-Oriental mindset could result in a different liberation experience altogether. Zen offers just a method among others in which the intuitive power of interpretation turns upon itself and through reinforcements gives way to the liberation process. In fact in a common Zen practice the mixture of intellectualism and intuitive progression must be subtly divided into a) what is understood as Zen meaning and b) what escapes the interpretation and dodges the intellectual process. The later acts as a noisy background in which one's intuition keep floating. A Zen adept should have the capacity to allow this noisy background to widen and so help the intuition to prosper. There is some "myth" present in relation to any utterance, no matter how simple it is. The insistence of the Western philosophy that an expression is nothing else but what it is (what you see is what you get) describes in reality just the surface of it all. Well, to make it short, the idea is to read texts that increase this noisy background where the "thinking" process is merely intuitive and unsuitable for abstraction. Sutras are a good choice for this purpose. The aphorisms and Zen poetry quoted in this book try to supply other means to stimulate the intuitive process. What else a Westerner can do? We can't make a Westerner think in a Chinese, Korean, Japanese or Indian way. Since defining the Way of Liberation is considered an impossible task in any language why not trying to "feel" it as imperfect as it may come out through language? I began my Zen this way, trying to extract from books any mentioning about awakening, Satori and Enlightenment. I couldn't eliminate the uncertainty of what really such an experience could mean. Also I took the mystery surrounding the subject as being an attribute of any unattainable goal. Though I kept reading passionately and then rereading books by Suzuki, Allen Watts, R. H. Blyth, Christmas Humphreys, Mumonkan, Dogen, and others, I had to overcome disappointments and failures, some perpetrated by my life style in which there was no place and time for Zen and Zazen to take over. I found that the texts that had relevance in my efforts to get "there" where those that quoted abundantly the primeval Zen masters. This "intellectual" process began slowly to work inward. Sometimes I literally felt that I was making huge and sometimes threatening leaps towards awakening. Of course, as one might expect with Zen, the delusion was as valuable as the real event. Koans reading were another intellectual pursuit. For me the Koan practice was wrong as I stubbornly tried to discover patterns of coherence in its chaotic maze. Of course I found some stories conspicuously empty of interest, other imperfect or so limited in their suggestive means not to deserve any further inquiry. Mu was and continues to be the most intriguing Koan though in its simplicity it looked like something communicated plainly. What I learned early on was that what is communicated unequivocally has to be discarded. Knowledge as far as Zen goes should be anticlimactic. The same approach I used when a certain Zen utterance gave me the impression that I successfully deciphered its meaning. The idea is that when a meaning of an expression is successfully grasped the expression – as far as Zen is concerned – is dead. Now, there are limits in what one can express in order to suggest a reality beyond comprehension and without retorting to metaphor. Though, in a common language, metaphors could represent a powerful linguistic tool to push the knowledge into a "comprehensive impossibility". Some of the aphorisms try to do just that: using metaphors to pull the intuition out of its unknown territory and make it do some Zen work.

A popular koan: Mu

Most of the people that tried to attain enlightenment and want to do it fast – just to have a taste of it – are using an "initiation" koan called "Mu", otherwise known as "Chao-Chou's dog". The koan is extremely simple and nothing special should emerge from either reading or "understanding" it. The koan's lines are also not helpful into creating that particular puzzling story that eventually gives to the reader some way to look at it as a detective would, decoding the intersecting meanings and so trying to go beyond the common sense and find a clue, which in the case of a Zen pursuer would be that precious awakening cookie. This is the koan's text:

A monk asked Chao-Chou: "Does a dog have Buddha nature or not?" Chao-Chou answered: "Mu!"

This dialog took place in Chinese. "Mu", in Chinese means "is not, has not". If one asked this question in English the answer would have been "No, it has not!" and the story would have ended there. Well, it can't happen so fast in an Eastern world and that's the reason books on Zen flourish. Curiously enough for Mu koan almost all translations kept Mu as the answer as if Mu was some kind of dislocated word (from Chinese to English) that needed to be (un)grasped in its original Chinese sounding to be of use. The sophisticated westerners pay attention to what sounds exotic and so Mu emerged as a transporter of some guaranteed but hidden promise to a quick awakening. It felt easier for one to "cut off" the understanding and shut off one's mind by using Mu instead of "has not". Mu seemed to connect one directly with a Zen higher ground. Mu was able to generate that stream of intuition needed to break the language barrier and to guide one into a mind trap: a trap where one has to experience the unintelligible, mysterious and impossible task of "knowing" the unknown. Called the Gateless Barrier, Mu promises an experience of immediate awakening when allowed to burn in one's mind free of any mental effort to see it, perceive it, comprehend it, discriminate it, or even – in a subtle way – extract it as the essence of what originally meant "has not" ("has"). Mu is neither "has" nor "has not", and in a more profound way, it is neither question nor answer: *missing* Mu in its becoming undergoes a transformation in which the whole context of the koan falls into an impasse. That, eventually, shows to be the Gateless barrier that one should penetrate. I'd advise those who want to practice any koan to choose a Zen school for such experience due to the fact that in this aim to break through barrier strange things might happen, some of them being just distortions, aberrations, surrealist "disorders", hallucinations that have to be guided towards the right path. The work on Mu could last a life time. Zen talks about various planes or degrees of realizing Mu, as if one could experience the noness (oneness) of Emptiness in progressively deeper states of the original Whole.

Practicing Zen

_____

Practicing Zen means a lot of things. Firstly, there are a lot of Zen schools; mostly are old but carefully filtered by excellent teachings, a good number of them providing real guidelines to awakening. Anyone trying to start practicing Zen should question thoroughly his/her affiliation with the method provided by a school or another. What is essential in practicing Zen is to find a method that is intellectually stimulating, that seems to be suggestive and sympathetic to your thinking, and that lets your imagination struggle pleasantly while trying to experience the unequivocal Zen. This principle works in the same way as it does with any religion: a prayer you dislike cannot help you reach God while - on the contrary - a pleasant prayer could help you see God before you least expect it to happen. The school or method you choose should fit your level of awareness and yet appear capable to give you enough room to grow and acknowledge your intermediate achievements. The text used for learning and practice should be clear and definite though not simple. The complexity of the Zen text is important in order to maintain that feeling of an indefinite resolution that a practitioner needs to struggle with in order to achieve noticeable progress. Personally I encourage an intellectual approach to Zen at the very beginning. With this in mind any important new "Zen concept" – such as emptiness – should be analyzed so as to become an element of one's normal cognitive experience. Through this intellectual approach one should gradually open his/her mind to the intuitive reading. Zen poetry, Zen aphorisms and Zen Koans could help this process a lot. After an intensive intellectual practice one could easily feel that he/she could perceive things differently and that the most benign daily experience gets enriched. To say that from the very start one should use a Zen way of reading as opposed to an intellectual one is like trying to implement the most difficult stage in Zen practice before even the practice begins.

Intuition

As people experience Zen they realize that, piece by piece, their thinking gets subtly stolen by an unknown force and digested by a newly found inner mind that exists in the deepness of their being. Once this subtle development (awakening) is ascertained it opens the door to an internalized and yet unresolved meaning of reality. Even more Zen makes one aware of a total different mental state of affairs than everything else one felt as being mental before. This feeling of a different mental state gets augmented and becomes dizzying and slightly delightful. One might find himself/herself getting trapped deeper and deeper in this practice and feel that in that state of awakening, the known and the knowing - even if they seem absurd - don't need a confirmation from the real mind and its senses. It is as if a different reality on a different plane emerges through a "mental" devise we call intuition.

What is intuition? You would have to use the intuition to find out what the intuition is? It is for sure an indefinable kind of instrument used by one's mind to be aware of truths beyond a rationalized knowledge. As such the intuition is older than reason and rationalization and so it holds an eternal and universal eminence. The intuition reads the indefinable, the ineffable, and the inexpressible. It resolves contradictions and the opposites, dealing with illogical and irrational in terms of a direct knowledge. Since this direct knowledge goes beyond rationalization it may disagree with what the mind asserts or argue about. If it always agreed and could be verified and confirmed as valid by the mind what would be the purpose to have an intuition after all? Mind knows about a relative reality, intuition brings forth the absolute one. From the intuition point of view the reason is a dead form of knowing used by us to go on with our everyday experiences in life.

Though, if rationalization or reason is called positive-thinking we can't say that intuition is negative-thinking, for the "reason" that intuition goes beyond the mind knowledge. Also, I state, the intuition occurs on the universal plan rather than on the individual one. This last sentence may sound mystical and so it needs an explanation. If the whole universe is a compound of matter, energy and information the intuition works at that subliminal state of the universe where a point (any point and every point) reflects all the possible states of the universe. Such a reflection is unlimited, unobstructed and as synchronous to the events as it is required. Some people have more intuition than others. The awareness to the existence of the intuition and a daily exercise to keep it awake could enhance its power to the point where one can live mystical experiences while still being able to cope with the normal life. Some psychologists explain the intuition as coming from an unconscious layer of the brain where a fuzzy network of synapses could suddenly apprehend at moments of fortuitous happenings revelatory truths. Chose whatever definition fits better your way of thinking. For me it is obvious that once we would be able to define what the intuition is, we'd also be able to use it more willfully to create ideas of relevance to itself. Some of the utterances in this book are intended to be used as a means to enhance the awareness towards intuition and to give it a good food and allow it to grow.

The three phases of Zen

Zen practice has three phases: I) Preparatory phase, working with Zen inwardly in order to prepare for awakening, II) The Awakening, III) Returning to a life of Zen after being awakened. Phase I is characterized by a deep interest (sometimes passionate and obsessive) to get awakened. It is a difficult period in which Zazen or other methods of meditation and breathing are employed in order to get to see what the enlightenment produces. During this period one's mind supplies the proper attitude towards its own role – to know – and establishes the limits within which it can function while letting gradually the intuition to take over. For instance, the effort of a Zen student to become one with his/her koan is a process of subtle subversion of the mind, and at the same time an effort to coerce it to play. Any other thinking is suspended in order to allow the koan to penetrate every pore of the mind and eventually overwhelm it. Phase II is the sudden enlightenment. This phase might be preceded by light Samadhi moments where the universal unity and the feeling of perfection of the world accompanied by a blissful peace of mind and body and a boundless happiness may occur. Those Samadhi moments are good signs that the brain works in the direction of enlightenment and should not hamper or disrupt one's effort to complete his/her work to achieve full enlightenment. Phase III is the return to reality, that is, life, family, obligations, responsibilities, job, survival. One's daily approach to life including feelings, moods, attitudes seem slightly different. There is going to be a period of adjustment when as one looks at ordinary things like bread, flowers, birds, etc. he/she may feel a hidden joy sweeping all over his/her entire being. The end of seeking is the beginning of searching. Once awakened one seems to understand how the whole universe works like a well tuned organ. Every simple atom is a messenger. Emptiness is lettering every microscopic stain showing what direction it should follow. Cows graze here, butterflies look for flowers on the beach sand… Gradually one would know that the brain doesn't want to venture further anymore. In fact, the feeling is that the brain gradually and steadily regains control of the "old" world, which looks less and less ineffable and mysterious. It looks like a return from a long convalescence that was full of wonder and miracles.

Emptiness

A simplified model of the world could be described as follows: The Universe is made up of energy and information. The information is organized as an infinite network of interrelated equations. The equations generate matter. The matter manifests itself as forms. The forms interact and create life. The life evolves into mind-life. The mind-life is a battery of energy and information.

As one could see in such a model the common denominator of all utterances is emptiness, that is, emptiness is behind each of the previous assertions. Does anything else "exist" clear of emptiness? Probably not! Then the "essence" must be nonsense, that is, some mental need to believe into a solid ground under one's mental feet. If the universe is the creation of intelligent equations the question is how these equations came upon to exist? As one tries to capture a sense of it, the "meaning" shuns away from one's mental view. The task of enlightenment is to make one a participant mirror within the universal network of equations. At the moment the enlightenment sets in one becomes a pure reflection of the emptiness. Forms shows then as the projection of the emptiness into one's mind. Matter and its attributes become a "conditioned emptiness" that creates transient constants. That's why an object cannot be another object at the same time. That's why an attribute (such as white) cannot be another attribute at the same time (such as blue). Knowledge tends to organize and classify the transient constants into categories. At the atomic level this conditioned emptiness vanishes, that is, all manifestations of emptiness such as movement, position, matter, time go back to the equations substratum.

Philosophy as known by westerners assumes that the world has some reality and that the mind (a function of the brain) is the only way to know it. Oriental Philosophy considers that mind and reality are the same and at the extreme that mind is the creator of reality. The world needs either a physical commitment (Western) or a metaphysical one (Eastern). The fact that emptiness is assumed to be a perennial presence in the universe and regarded as preceding anything else leads to the belief that emptiness is kind of an omnipresent "life form" that originated all and is the finality of all. What one's a sense perceives – phenomena – are nothing else but the manifestation of emptiness. This manifestation can take elaborate forms that become so complexly interleaved that it makes difficult to one to see in them the presence of this fundamental ground that initiates all phenomena – the emptiness. The mind is in part responsible for such estrangement. The irony is that the more the rational knowledge advances into the territory of phenomena the further the mind moves away from the original source of truth. The history of humanity proves that this is an inescapable route. The conflict with the human natural development occurs in those Zen doctrines that stipulate that natural knowledge (physics, astronomy, philosophy, natural sciences, etc.) has no value as far as truth goes; it means that the world of perception, representation, taxonomy and thought - the entire human experience – is void, since it doesn't designate in any way the relationship with the original base of all that exists – emptiness. It sounds agnostic and tactically leads to agnosticism if not corroborated with a post-awakening Zen conjecture that says – no more no less – that the world is what the world is, a perfect manifestation of the emptiness as seen. All the philosophical concepts rejected as knowledge get reunited in ONE: ephemeral is also eternal, the infinite and a grain of dust are alike, life – though nothing but an illusion, a Karma given wonder, the order of nature – gets a compassionate color, time has only present tense (though Karma acts on past wrong deeds), the space becomes the emptiness's "undistinguishable" boundary.

Zen Upgrade

There is impossible to say farewell to the old traditional Zen and embark onto a new Zen Enterprise, trying to upgrade its principles and philosophy so that it can be made part of a modern integrated culture. One could easily recognize that there are some practical Zen inadequacies that have to be resolved to make it a vibrant and widely accepted practice. The most important concern is the lack of any contemporary link between our modern life and the old Zen schools. It could be true that such an antiquated and anachronistic science or endeavor may still hide in its natural and human universal context a transcendental core that is equally cognition, revelation and permanence. By stating that a new Zen school has to go a step further means that any Zen teacher of these days should try to create a new Zen approach in order to help professionals to use their western knowledge fruitfully while approaching Zen. A teacher should understand that a Western intellectual has to discard a truckload of knowledge in order to approach a teacher. On the other hand to read Zen as anti-Zen is still a Zen reading. To use Zen and its beyond-the-realm-of-knowledge principles in order to get a mystical experience is still Zen "reading". I used the word mystical in the sense that a Zen realization is not entirely reasonable, that is, it involves sometimes an "illegitimate" contortion of logic for teaching and a "direct experience" of a metaphysical reality for acting. For a westerner - common knowledge (common life) and Zen experience will be thoroughly entwined. In this respect Zen realization will always be conditioned by one's capacity to play the "Zen game" of detachment and eventually freedom from cognition. Zen teaching should throw a rope bridge that could gradually pull the student into the world of pure and immediate consciousness.

Zen writing and the aim of it

What Zen stands for – nowadays - to a westerner? It stands for lots of things, though none of them resembling the original Zen or any of the new Zen schools that evolved from it in China, Korea or Japan. There are two Zen modes that a westerner could approach: one is literary Zen or philosophical Zen (therefore intellectual in nature); the other one is traditional Zen that entails meditation (Zazen) and koan "resolution". The intellectual Zen is helpful to those who don't have time or application to pursue Zen as a discipline that eventually might lead to one's enlightenment. No one would argue that the amount of Zen texts that spawned upon all the intellectual levels of the Western world shows that the interest in the "empirical" Zen is prevailing. As an intellectual pursuit, Zen literature is considered helpless to those who want to attain awakening (enlightenment). Zen poetry has a special place in this prejudicial judgment. Some old and new Zen schools take as their aim poetry as means to express the level of one's (un)-grasp of the ultimate truth. On the other hand, the refusal of poetry as a Zen messenger is due to the fact that wordy expressions of such an ultimate truth are tainted by duality and discrimination, which are part of the reasoning makeup. To expand on this, I could say that words are "perceptual carriers" and so they identify only the reality that could be known through perception: to Zen, such a reality is empty and far from being part of any truth. Since to Zen the reality – phenomena – is an illusion, its essence is empty. The theory of emptiness as the ultimate reality points the world – as we know it – beyond any beginning and any ending. If one's mind is able to disregard the manifestation of emptiness within the infinite world of phenomena and collapse it in a point of no-time-no-space where there is nothing else but un-manifested emptiness one might free himself from the burden to take this world seriously. If one considers that what reason takes as truth is non-truth and that "truth" resides somewhere else – neither in the knowing nor in the knower – one may find worthy to spend a lifetime just to know what "this" is? Some people get disaffected because they can't "catch a glimpse" of this notion of emptiness and make it part of the daily picture of life. On this regard Zen poetry and Zen aphorisms could be of a great help.

Zen training

For a Westerner, Zen training should be given in several acts, where awakening could be part or not of a finale. First act is to read one of the fundamental Buddhist texts – a Sutra for instance – where the essential concepts used in Zen are introduced from multiple points of view and so create a plurality of meanings that a mind could easily absorb as subjects worthy of interpretation. Usually such texts are a mix of fairy tales, metaphors, question and answer plots, aphoristic utterances, etc. Sometimes difficult to read to a Westerner, such texts have the advantage of lacing the reason with intuit traces that even in their emblematic and unresolved state are ready to bear fruit. This is the main difference between reading an original text as opposed to a speculative one. A speculative text provides definitions of terms and explains what the original text tries to put into words. Here again we'd have to make a clear distinction between the moment in history when the Sutra was written and the modern reader, nevertheless taking into account the differences in history and culture, if convergent or divergent, that makes such a reading more or less significant to the reader's insights. A fundamental concept such as emptiness would for sure be initially understood as coming from the outside, as any other concept coming to live for a while into the angle of reason. One might recognize the meaning and use it with no concern that it became another concept to be used to express ideas. That's when Zen aphorisms and poetry come into place. Just as the reminder to those that are taking the emptiness as part of their common world in which life is the main principle: the modern man knows more about emptiness from physics, microbiology, astronomy than any other human being or Buddha living on the planet Earth ever before. Though this "grasp" of emptiness is on a tangible plane it helps the modern man reasoning metaphysically. Such knowledge could prove to be vital to imagination. It can be used and interrogated upon whenever one's thinking is bound up with the awakening process. The traditional Zen is full of prejudices that in essence say that: a) either one lives by the understanding of all and so he/she could never attain realization or b) one gradually reduces his/her knowledge to a condition of total detachment from the world – all attachments are reduced to the point of extinction – and suppresses the act of knowing in order to attain the supreme experience of awakening. The first result of the later is that one begins to "perceive" that things, facts and events are just a fleeting manifestation of the emptiness and that the whole nature is ephemeral, impermanent and doomed to enter into all states of endless transformation. Simple elements of knowledge enter such an altered state and make use of it to integrate the whole universe as a whole. For instance, anthropologically speaking leaves fall, snow falls, water falls, etc. What are all these to a crow or to a dog? What about blooming? Or of the tall grass loaded with dew? What to a human mind is submission to phenomena is for an insect a flickering insight. A flower flooded with bees, grasshoppers taking a dew bath… Zen asserts that for the mind that is seeking mountain is not yet a mountain; river is not yet a river. Look past the infinite that is given! As you become a bee searching for a flower or a grasshopper hopping through the ebb of grass you'll get it: a thin stock of goodies given away each season: don't miss the elements: Bamboozled…If these examples look ephemeral then it is more difficult to one to look at the whole cosmos – in its historical concreteness and stability and see it as being impermanent. Another doubt raised by Zen relates to concepts (words) and the reason using them to compose utterances. Why not seeing – one might ask – the emptiness in its manifestation and the knowledge that unfolds in one's mind from it as recognition of the emptiness' intent to make itself known as such-ness? By allowing one's mind to attach concepts to matter and facts the emptiness directs one's intellect into knowing the plurality of the existent, be it micro, macro or the hidden-unknown. The pre-given emptiness is worth of discovering but, isn't it what life is, as it flows, outlined by empty aspects that get assimilated into knowledge as well as becoming part of the human history? Understood as such, emptiness doesn't become a special concept itself that one has eventually to get rid of. I wouldn't be surprised one day to find out that concepts like liberation from birth-and-death cycles, the eternal life, the ultimate truth and the awakening are all products of some universal sequence of codes that the universe used to guide us towards seeing the multiple folds of the same reality.

Aphorisms, notes, fables, jokes, Zen poetry

---

1.   An object can't be spoken. A fact cannot be told. Though one ought to take both into account when in doubt.

2.   The quandary of Zen logic: using words means discrimination; discrimination means "not being within truth". What's being within truth? (Don't open your mouth: needless to say a word). Could you feel it in your guts? If the gate opens there pass through! If not, wait in front of the gate like a bull: seeing but not seeing, knowing but not knowing… Crack the gate open with a shout!

3.   Emptiness permeates the living as living permeates Zen. The question is what emptiness needs to manifest itself. Zen's answer is Zazen.

4.   Expressionless means "lacking an expression" but not a meaning. By the same token emptiness means empty but not void.

5.   The baobab tree is too old to count seasons. The green landscapes are all gone. Thousand woods became ashes. To escape this call one has to use no eyes and no ears. Chase dogs with no nose searching for a prey…

6.   Satori is the vibration of the universal life into one's mind.

7.   Zen joke: Listening to Zen imperatives: attention, be aware, drop your ego, wipe out your attachments, look into your true nature, show respect to Buddhas… Then you read the Zen masters and find out that Buddha is a dried shit stick.

8.   As I woke up from Satori the first thing I saw was my cat sitting on the window pane: still trying to catch pigeons…

9.   The intellect is the extension of the language and the knowledge is what one's a brain stores as a combination of words and punctuation signs that provide the meaning of the observed reality. If a reality exists beyond this intellectual interface then the intellect is an imperfect instrument. To say that "I don't know if what I see, hear, and feel is true" so that one would have to wait for awakening to give one a confirmation is not practical. The practical approach is to accept openly that what you see is what you get and avoid interpretation. By accepting things as they are, you act like a free mind, neither attached to that, nor separated from that.

10.   Emptying one's mind as one would do with a basket…

11.   Knowledge of emptiness preserves the beauty of every living moment; (I wanted to write "of every everlasting moment).

12.   Saying that emptiness preceded everything is a "true" statement. But, weren't we supposed to get rid of so called "true" statements altogether? Though a statement may be true try not to go near it with your mind.

13.   Tranquility when one lives is more desirable than the one that comes after…

14.   Last night I had a malicious dream: a grass blade with its power of deception was separating white from black, noise from silence, good from bad… I had to zap it: the world stayed untouched and in its place, unchanged and pure, as I used to carry it in my mind - while a child: a nameless world, as I learned lately that it should be.

15.   The wolf's howl and the dog's bark. The celestial chariot docks between the village and the forest. In the clearing the metallic eyes; on the street the dogs' restless bark is not a secret anymore. Long columns of snow kept returning to my memory… Stillness and silence, while howls and barks go on…

16.   In the water tank there is a gold fish, swimming… If the fish needed your mind to acknowledge that it exists, it would be dead by now…

17.   When in the magical silence you hear the chorus of icicles stirred by the wind in the winter garden…

18.   Empty and emptiness: this is what intuition sees everywhere (where perceptions and consciousness see a "relative reality"). Unborn and beyond dying: that's what intuition thinks about mind (while the relative mind thinks that mind is one of the states of the "impermanent" existent). Ultimate truth is beyond causation: that's what the intuition determines as being the ultimate case (while mind is using causation to look into action-reaction phenomena). When duality is wiped out there is no perceiver and no perceived: individuality becomes null and void, the self and the other become one: whose intuition is getting those insights? Whose mind echoes the intuition's findings?

19.   Emptiness is seen as colored in black. In reality in every color one could see the emptiness in manifestation.

20.   Words are empty, so don't let them enter your mind. They should resonate in their emptiness as if they were voiced by a wooden gong…

21.   A life's harvest: seeing through stars while day-dreaming on a lonely chair.

22.   To practice, pain seems to be a better occurrence than pleasure. That's because almost everything else seems to be part of the dual world except the pain. When you have it you know that it is not an illusion as you merge and become one with your pain. Behind the pain there is a booth where Buddha takes notes as to your Karma. He's also one with your pain. In Zen the knowledge of what-pain-is is vain and the presence of Buddha is never mentioned. Is the pain empty? Meditating on this while sitting in Zazen could be a real nuisance.

23.   The story of a singing ant that built a house in a deaf ear.

24.   Life looks like a reward for one who dies. Last night he could still hear the wind and the thought that he didn't capture enough of it made him bitter. In life terms, wind is still an angle to measure the living. A certain measure…

25.   Sometimes simplicity is as obscure as complexity is. In search of truth one needs to watch a balance.

26.   Self is a subcategory of natural things, so it is part of the relative world. To look into your true nature you'd have to drop from your mind your-*self* together with the whole-world-*self*, as they appear through "understanding". Then you, as "knower" will merge with the "known oneness" world - that is - you'd be able to look into your true nature which is the true nature of all things. It is called no-ness of emptiness.

27.   Mind, suddenly still, sees the world in an unspeakable way.

28.   Man's awakening doesn't change nature but makes life more accountable for what it is.

29.   How in a Western world can one get rid of conceptual thought, then of speech, then of actions – good or evil – that produce Karma? The only way out would be to live in compassion

for the suffering of all beings and forget anything else in the process. A pure light flashing in your brain is more transitory than the grace felt while helping an ant to get out of a slippery hole.

30.   A spider web collecting dew is a void bound manifestation. How would a spider web look in an unbound manifestation? No spider web, void in the clear.

31.   Zen Irony: Fundamentally Karmic conditions have created fertile soil that allowed potato to flourish. Fundamentally potato had never been farmed, so nobody had ever had a taste of potato.

32.   Words may carry the mind away…

33.   What is the Way? The eyes can't tell you where you go. Clear your throat and tongue of all pronounceable words! Sun's shining madly through one's tongue cannot rattle anything about. A roaring infinite sends a soundless message: Listen! The damn teapot is full of fire-flies. What is pointing to is what is pointing at? Mountains seem lighter than a feather as it lasts. No choice to make in this endless nothing. Trying to unstuck your mind from the endless emptiness. Absolute laws ruling on relative mirrors. Tasteless, soundless, fragrant less, colorless, formless water. Wordless prophecy. Being abandoned by the owner the world puts its face up for sale. By preaching emptiness a hunter catches a spoiled fox. You left your legs behind and "surprise"! Last night the wind bent the poplar so low that it touched the bottom of the ocean. Scratching with a nail the surface of a star. The white clouds of the absolute have twin-white-clouds in the relative: (that's the absolute, what you get there, dressed in a relative robe). Letting unfinished words to be shown on flashcards. Some blossom burns to ashes. The blind who finds its way home using a flashlight.

34.   What is useful is more beautiful in Zen than beauty itself. That's why white rice is used for eating and flowers are used in contemplation. Although, meditation in front of a bare wall does justice to both…

35.   Truth is transparent, knowledge is cloudy…

36.   Every Zen awakening is different. The circumstances that help it happen and the indecipherable elements that are essential to it are so diverse that to design a method that would work for everybody would be a difficult task. Zen schools though tried to do just that though. For a Westerner the idea that awakening could be attained in different ways is encouraging. The easiest way is to learn how to exchange a thousand thoughts for none.

37.   An eye becomes image; when the image sees that - it is already too late: dew becomes pearls; snow has a second coming and birds wait for a wink, knowing how their flight might be answered…

38.   Does a snake have a Buddha nature: don't bet on it if you don't want to be bitten into?

39.   Think of what is unborn, incessant and inexpressible as a subtle odor less incense that penetrates the whole universe. In the fierce fire of the universe at birth birds were laying eggs, trees unfurled their leaves, clouds moved with the wind striving to reach the sky. The incense is now felt more in the flowers bloom where it miraculously labors.

40.   To give is to receive. Giving is one of the awakening calls… What is the receiving?

41.   An impure enlightenment means an impure Buddha-nature experience. A snow remains to be seen as a relative happening and your mind is still mirroring it as "white icy crystals

reflecting the moonlight". Who's that tongue waiting in the middle of the road to melt a flake? After an impure awakening one cannot see Buddha-nature of no-mind, no-tongue, and no-flake. Though, the snow falls ringing now loudly and - on your tongue - a flake reflects more moonshine than ever…

42.   Saying: "The light of a lamp is different than the light of a moon". Cut your tongue and examine again…

43.   I didn't talk for almost a week: feeling the tongue getting cold…

44.   Emptiness making faces at us: which one is the original face?

45.   How to design a weevil: make a red round shell spotted with white dots and stuff it with a tiny moving body.

46.   The rewards for your efforts to get awakened may come in the shape of a goat with a huge udder bursting of milk. You have two options to choose: If you milk the goat you lose. If you don't milk the goat you also lose. Now that you know how things are once you see the goat - don't wait - kick the goat as hard as you can, whoosh her away. The key to the story: When you make progress on your road to attainment the relative reality is going to tempt you again. If you get a taste of it you lose; if you get tempted but don't get a taste of it you also lose. You'll have to get rid of it, to kick the "goat" and send it back to her pen).

47.   As you crush grapes with your feet, you crush a smaller truth that becomes a larger truth when the wine pours.

48.   If I was a fox one day I'd expect to see God coming out from behind a bush and saying: there is a river in the valley and as you walk past the big rock you're going to step in a pool of water

where I trapped a fish for you to enjoy. Unfortunately, I'm not a fox.

49.   A thousand cubic miles of emptiness can accommodate a thousand cubic miles of phenomena.

50.   Getting deeper and deeper into Zazen: Still the world looks the same. A mental gazing at your mental gazing? What a treachery! And getting deeper even more while knowing that eventually the whole universe won't emerge alive out of it. We're sort of Zazen people and sort of Buddhas, though one short moment of awakening could change that forever...

51.   Cut your understanding and deliver the first and last word that there was. It is the one that sounded before things began to be brought forth? Far in the future when the last candle would die and the trace of the universe would be wiped out, forms, colors, sound, movement and mind... Silkweed silence...

52.   In a transient world leaves outnumber mountains. In a transcendent world mountains outnumber mountains...

53.   If everything that the language constructs is illusion, the road to enlightenment is an illusion also. To rise to it one has to go back (physically) to the beginning of the universe where there was no right and no wrong. The path of speech was man's fall from Heaven. Interrogate...

54.   In sleep a butterfly dreams about a pond not invaded by frogs, contrary to what a frog may dream of... This might show how sorts of phenomena – dreams in this case – are empty to their core.

55.   Instead of asking what awakening is, just do Zazen and you'll get it... Zazen is made for people to meditate, to cleanse their mind of consciousness. One could see the emptiness in the making while watching the world coming into being... It is no

more than "what is not", replacing gradually "what is". A living emptiness is an oxymoron. Though, after awakening that's what it looks like. Then "a living emptiness" stops being an oxymoron.

56.   Zazen: Mirrors have been compromised by lines in the glass. That's why the mind should take every moment and object as they happen to come by. A short journeying makes a long sitting enjoyable.

57.   This head start is for those who know some truth, though it should be reviewed after all the intellectual stuff had been exhausted and done with. *Buddha and the Holy Grail are empty; mind is empty; language is empty; seeing, hearing are empty "feelings"; "feelings" are empty; within a perfect clarity of mind nothing could be taught; the simplest word opens the gate towards the least known; knowledge savings point into a wrong direction; you're getting a better answer if the question is not asked; the ultimate is the first anterior to nothing and in between there is nothing to be preserved; everything can pass through this gate but the reasoning mind…*

58.   What kind of reading of a Zen text could let one penetrate the truth? There is neither reading nor failing to read. And there is neither comprehension nor let go. An open-ended reading might do it if the reading manifests itself. When you start reading open an accolade… Where are you now?

59.   To be a bat, never to see the moonlight, like a blindfolded prisoner sensing the road but seeing nothing, anywhere. The above statement may sound abysmal, though the true Zazen is nothing else but that.

60.   A lone tree on a mountain peak. Like the moon on a starless sky… Name the thought! A lone thing but thousand arrows pointing at it. When crows fly on a hot day a dash of wind values its weight in gold.

61.   Projecting reality is like mind using a boomerang.

62.   Moving between relative and absolute I had to trade my own eyes for a pair of no-good-no-bad glassy eyes. All points of space and time got gathered there. Getting back to the relative world I traded back my neither-good-nor-bad eyes for my own. I wear them now though I see as if I wear the others.

63.   Sky broke, light broke, water broke and there she was: the mystic moon, on all sides of the world…

64.   I bow to the bamboo wall that resonate like a bamboo; a bow to the sea wall that resonate like a wave. What stands will stand forever. What floats will be stripped of standing even when it stands. When nothing moves, nothing stands! When nothing stands, nothing moves!

65.   A dragonfly howls when the wind blows, a firefly howls when the moon shines.

66.   Being thrown in the vastness of radiant space with no thing to be seen anywhere. No thinking, no remembering: the mind seal is the seal of the mind. To see again you'd need eyes as you return.

67.   Could mind be understood as a human treat? You can't point at it or touch it with your finger, though you sense it and by sensing it you think this is satisfactory. What is mind? Who is mind? (Who is mind sounds religious!) Zen wants to think of mind as being virtual - a vibration of the infinite mind "within". No gaps though, no walls, not the slightest possibility of distinction between a mind and another, between a mind and the infinite field of the universal mind.

68.   Life is packed with phenomena: seeing them empty evens out your walk through.

69.   Purifying your dual reading by letting the emptiness check on each meaning that raises its head: kick it, make it duck!

70.   As you awaken you get all possible answers with no questions to ask. Your eyes stay wide open while your mouth falls in a deep sleep: no lips movements, no tongue to keep your teeth wet. "The Great Mouth of Tranquility yawns about the Way!"

71.   Incessant, that's how life is… Though waters look still, they unfold waves (as trees unfold leaves and birds unfold wings). To a baptized Zen, every moment that lives has its own godliness…

72.   When a question cannot be asked the answer doesn't get thrown out.

73.   Emptiness escorts the impermanence as the impermanence returns to emptiness. Since a thing has a form and the form is impermanent this implies that the thing is empty. Empty is everything else that is not permanent – such as matter. And the same logic applies to life, cosmos and everything else. Since everything in the universe is impermanent it means that the whole universe is empty. So, the only permanent thing is the emptiness. Mind seems to be an exception: neither born nor meant to die. Though, *presence of mind* is clearly an attribute of the living only. The essence of mind is the "emptiness' state of mind".

74.   The limitless vision of the ultimate truth is obscured by the discriminative process of knowing.

75.   Emptiness: As dust rises with the wind, the dust and the wind are one. So the dust tells the inside story of what being a wind is like. As the wind dies the dust doesn't die with it. It becomes clay. So the dust tells the inside story of what being clay

is like. Then the rain erodes the clay and carries the dust to the river. So the dust tells the story of what being a river is like. Then the river carries the dust into the wide ocean… The mind is like that dust: carried through states, telling stories…

76.   Never forget to let your ego sleep at night if you stay awake. An ego without sleep is like a sick tiger: anger would never calm it down, agony would never make it draw back to its senses.

77.   Reality becomes foreign to the mind when one separates words from their "resemblance".

78.   When an eye opens up the reality moves forward and stops at an optimal distance. When an eye closes down the whole universe flies back to heaven.

79.   Riding a boat on the infinite ocean waters man thinks of being bounded by birth and death. As he gets enlightened the infinite outside becomes the infinite inside. In that sense who's riding the boat and who's the ocean?

80.   It is true that reading Zen and then reading more of it is not going to enlighten anybody. Though you'd be better off reading it rather than not. Practicing Zazen and keeping the practice steadily needs will, time and strength to fight doubts and disillusionment. Do not sit against your will. When you sit, remember that you and the world are mutually needed. Do it for your self, do it for world-self! And remember: seek within…

81.   What Zen does is to educate us in knowing that where our life is – is where truth should be found. Just try to separate your life from words…

82.   Emptiness redux: In the midst of everything, everywhere and yet impossible to be seen. When a stone with heads talks to the moon, muscles of iron seize the world flow. Thoughts that

don't have an object, reflection that doesn't come from one's mind…

83.   Water – but no boat. Boat – but no water. Very much as everything else in life.

84.   Karma might give us some leeway to fight against the evil.

85.   Clouds are falling, sun is rising! Cherry trees are bearing flowers… That's a typical Zen landscape. Meanwhile a spade of grass is denting another spade of grass: the stealth war… As one would have never thought, not every Zen happening is painful…

86.   Take a trip into your childhood and forget your life that lies in the middle. Your childhood knows the Way…

87.   That moment the silence was so thick that the river stopped flowing; the burning bonfire froze low; the Mountain and its peak became hypothetical. The slightest sound would have awakened all. Though, not the silence.

88.   The original emptiness was a non causal world. In such a non causal world a casual chance seems free of Karma. In that original world Karma itself was an empty thing as anything else. In order to manifest itself in the world of phenomena Karma has to have a beginning, to be born. When Karma comes into existence? It is born when an initiating act creates a deed - creates Karma. Then Karma behaves like a thistle, attached to the body responsible for the act until it gets emptied out through rebirths. Since a deed is created even by an *intention* to act it means that Karma applies only to living bodies, which have intentions and perform volitional acts. *If one has to clean himself of Karma and so become free from the cycle of rebirths, he has to abstain from creating both "good" and "bad" deeds. Another Zen quandary!*

89.   Ice coated birds in the stillness of a crystal like tree. (Far away from here there is a hot summer day in the making).

90.   A mind that is "absolute" is as nonsensical as an emptiness that is "relative". Only the manifestations of the emptiness are relative. Clinging to one aspect you can't see the other. Though clinging to breathe you might succeed to see them all: You can walk Buddha's Way only while living…

91.   The difficulty to get awakened is that feelings, perceptions, mental activities and consciousness are not one. To sense the universe as one – one has to shut down all four "living aggregates" and use the fifth one – intuition – to get there.

92.   The life call: Stop doing Zazen! Do just the opposite: live your life fully with no regrets, no grievances, no repentance. The emptiness that gave you the current living form has more insights than what you'd discover by doing sixteen billion years of Zazen. Though, by doing Zazen and getting awakened it's like getting impregnated with permanence. Who wouldn't like to be everlasting?

93.   There are so many things whose names I don't know: they bring about a suitable universe for enlightenment…

94.   Still doing Zazen after so much sense of loss? What seems near is far; but what is far is not as far as your delusion. For what is far is near…

95.   One gets reborn in multiples and multiples die in one.

96.   MU means "does not have" in the sense that when the eye sees right "it does not have" to take what is seen as what is known: birds dropping cannot be confused with snow flakes. It may sound funny but when the Zen eye sees right they are the same.

97.   A child clings to his mom as a phenomena clings to its essence.

98.   If one thinks having a viewpoint about enlightenment – in some mysterious way – it means that one doesn't have a viewpoint at all.

99.   The nakedness of nature is harmless even when a word turns to be meaningful…

100.   Awakening warning: "Never to see the world as is again!"

101.   If the "I" becomes "not-I" who's getting enlightened? Either "I" engages in the process and does something to this end-result or "non-I" takes over when the result occurs. Though, after the result occurs who's in charge? It is some remnant "I" that while watching puts some relative color on the absolute revealed… <u>The otherness in "I" is always watching!</u>

102.   The otherness of "I": This "I" stands for the principle of "I" rather than the "I" attached to a person…

103.   The absolute: "Pretty much it goes like this and right here!"

104.   When you end your seeking the universe embarks on seeking you.

105.   The way to God is guarded by people who forgot who they were. You may ask what they are guarding. They're guarding the way one can seek God.

106.   If something has to be acknowledged, there is somebody that has to acknowledge and then somebody to acknowledge to. The rule is that those who acknowledge loose.

107.   Zen joke: "The thinking comes from God. The words are a devilish business".

108.   Where nights die away and days shine…

109.   The thing that would transcend all things in the universe would be featherless. IT would be either a dead fish or a moribund fox. (Buddha crossed out… This drum had been whacked for too long. Shattered sutras spreading the sweet smell of faltering flame…)

110.   The doubt that the world is real is one thing. The doubt that you're real is another thing.

111.   God was sober when he created beauty and drank when he created ugliness. Who knows? He may have hanged by a rope around his neck when he let ugliness go. Zen though sees everything as being perfect. God's work could be a matter of misinterpretation.

112.   If a river flows here and there it doesn't mean that it flows everywhere.

113.   Even the simplest thought has God in it.

114.   To choose awakening out of a multitude of your life outcome and to find out that the only way to alleviate your pain is by rationalizing it, by making your suffering part of your life, as is… For the whole humanity is even more so. Suddenly, in your suffering, you might see God.

115.   The bats – with their ultrasound sensors – must be part of a different Zen sect. An aphorism using ultrasound would be: neither seen nor heard, but ultra-sensed…

116.   Zazen: The mind starved by lack of thoughts is ready to meet the emptiness. The departed thoughts look like crows resting in line on an electric wire. A girl sings: her song irrigates the universe…

117.   During a good season a bee doesn't have any time to spare…

118.   Truest enlightenment comes through compassion, charity and moral merits. For when one's body goes one gets to live the ultimate truth anyway.

119.   In Zen - tears never carry a feeling of guilt. To understand Zen compassion, watch a summer rain shower. It may look as a short happening since it is beyond epics.

120.   You can't do Zen just because you like the act. That's attachment, craving, addiction, and so on. Don't do it as a pain inflicted act either. Your mind should behave like oil on water: not dissolving but always in a merging state. When awakening comes there are no more distinctions: oil or water will be as the hollow state of the universe.

121.   Seeing with the clarity of mind that the lights passing by are leaves silenced in their fall by enlightenment. Though nothing is to be expected to happen, they keep falling.

122.   The formless happiness of seeing.

123.   Ascetic in a mountain retreat: In monasteries monks do Zazen. On the fields farmers keep an eye onto their crops. Prayers

would be really nothingness if the monks wouldn't have anything to eat. Cleaning rice in the morning, eating cold barley after the last bell.

124.   Rejecting a word for a more suitable one I forgot what I was going to say. That shows how difficult is to describe what awakening is.

125.   The rusted nails are rising above the floor, like the crows scattered by the wind touching a barren tree. (Crows – what a marked cliché! Though nails seem like a fresh start for an old hammer).

126.   Nothing and nothingness makes a snowflake look unnatural.

127.   The spiritual merit of a donkey carrying loads is as invaluable as the load it carries. Same is true for what burden an enlightened mind carries. Empty yes! Even when it has the weight of an iron mountain.

128.   A firefly caught in a dew drop sees a ten fold magnified emptiness.

129.   The intuition: to know without knowing the knower and the known. If a phenomenon is an impermanent deceiver, its essence is a perennial truth. For the sake of the example, when a plate breaks, its essence stays untouched, though its phenomenon spreads in multiples.

130.   Knowing but not "knowing": using words to make sense of things as opposed to going on the opposite direction… Things-left-to-introduce-themselves…

131.   Sunken fire… Ashes scattered around. An owl cries near a fresh tomb…

132.   The salt is salted and the sugar is sweetened. As you fast those ideas are hiding away. What about eye-fasting, ear-fasting? Who's watching over your senses while you're fasting?

133.   Even a shadow has two twin parts: one is called phenomena, the other is called essence.

134.   No matter how far and how deep you go with your Zazen if the awakening doesn't happen, don't despair; it should happen. If it doesn't happen during this life time it should surely happen during the next one. If it doesn't happen during the next several lives then obviously you'd have to start Zazen all over again, from the very beginning.

135.   If a thing faces north but goes south it must be a river. Mountains are different.

136.   Raising and bowing when Buddha shows up: bowing and sitting when Buddha leaves.

137.   Don't hurry to get there. Once you get through, hurry up! If answers are provided questions seem simple. Moon emerging like Buddha's eyed original face.

138.   When the moon is high the tides are low. When the sun is high the tides step aside.

139.   Enlightenment is a problematic occurrence. Attain it carefully if you cannot afford to attain it otherwise.

140.   A featherless bird has a Zen nature in the sense that it puts one's thoughts about birds into Limbo...

141.   You can't speak of Nirvana without Karma: So, an assault to one's consciousness comes true when Karma is ready.

Fundamentally speaking, nothing is to be seen: the window opens to the emptiness...

142.   The songs of the childhood are not the same. It looks like they became charmingly dumb while aging.

143.   Enlightenment: Mourning the world that passed away while the tea is still in the making. Calling the dog to keep a living company around. A tea leaf for a bark…

144.   Life starts awake and ends in sleep: If every day we knew where we were… The old harbor is seeing new boats… Although, they follow the same century old stream from the North shore to the South shore…

145.   Love is born, hatred is learned…

146.   Thinking of non-thinking is still thinking. Not-thinking of thinking is still thinking. Emptiness opens to a full view when the notions of thinking or non-thinking are wiped out.

147.   You don't have to penetrate the clouds if you already fly above them. Though, as a shepherded would say, the right pace to climb a mountain is the pace of a goat. By going too fast you may encounter there things not well done, illusory bodies coming to challenge you, some of them difficult to handle. Though if you don't have the choice of going back you'd have to treat them with a no-spoken kindness. They're going to confront your duality. To show that you're not conditioned stand still! They'd barely notice that you're part of a birth-and-death world. Eventually they'd leave. That would in fact happen when you'd let them go. Be brave! Once there, a ticking heart or a dry shit instead wouldn't make a difference.

148.   To see the truth in every single thing and fact is a gift that comes with liberation: merits abolished, ego – like a shadow rubbed out by the darkness, attachments weakened by poor

nourishments, ascetic deeds carried out even while asleep. Then, the light from the world beyond words comes into plain view.

149.   If concepts are false and things are true – it is the in-between world that matters. If things are false and concepts are true – it is the in-between world that matters. As soon as the in-between world shows through, there is nothing one might call false, there is nothing one might call true…

150.   The wind of life blows! The wind of death blows!

151.   The mind is no longer there. The reality is no longer there. To call this a situation is to admit that there exists some knowledge of how one can live through it. If it is conditioned by any context it can't be used. If it is not conditioned, walls of essence would instantly vanish in a tiny hole. The immediate state after: the mind is there, the reality – no more of it…

152.   This rock felt the sun's warmth for ages. Now it drinks the same rain drops as I do: pearls in a leaf cup. The rock said something. I wonder: why don't I need anymore an interpreter?

153.   As the seen returns to its source the mind forgets what seen is. Shining beyond senses though not adverse to the act of thinking. A bird in flight is neither arriving nor departing. A formless and clawless lion trying to make a scratch on the original mirror. Overflowing oceans reach the mountain peak. No more ground to return to, no more roads to walk on. No more embodiments! No traces onto the surface hollow or into the deep.

154.   Understanding Zen reveals the meaning of Zen. Living Zen enables the meaning to manifest itself. When understanding and manifestation cease to become known, the ultimate bliss emerges…

155.   Zen upgrade: The door was changed but the entrance remained still too narrow to let a bull's tail pass through…

156.   It must be lonely on a mountain peak. The valley surroundings swell with life and noise, flowers are crowned, orchards blow their fragrance, stones stumble into the water, birds shine – as if the outer nature doesn't care what the inner nature is. Tears flow on your cheeks as your tongue cannot fulfill its righteous task of saying words. A goal of enlightenment makes sense if it is part of the purpose of living. To suppress birth and death one must race back to the origin of the universe. And even there…

157.   A doctrine or a dogma is like a mill of tongues adding to the core of banners fresh remnants of interpretation.

158.   Passions are wild horses. Once they're gone they become wooden horses. You still can ride them but arrive nowhere.

159.   Pointing to the leaves not yet created by the next spring is like entertaining an illusion. That's how mind works anyway. Pointing to a mind wrought reality that is not there, like the absolute or even simpler phenomena of the mind, like seeing…

160.   How could you explain that emptiness is empty but not void while phenomena are void but not empty?

161.   What's new doesn't have resemblance. Journeying over eons there is nothing seen as new. Therefore new has resemblance. A true eye knows that "never" is "always". Suspicious about this logic? Present, past, eternity belongs to the original emptiness, the owner of all. When moon goes home it goes there. The sound and feelings and consciousness go there also. If we steer clear of nothingness the origin has no name so it cannot be called new. Though the tiny blooming acacia bushes are new every single spring.

162.   You cannot separate the speaker from his speech…

163.   If you look at an object with your mind and then look at the same object with a no-mind involvement how those two views differ? A flower that beautifies a tree will be seen exactly as it is. Though, the view without bonds is not used to listening to a buzzing bee.

164.   Eat Zen, raw and bare…

165.   The Doctrine of the Mind: The in-sight "knowledge" that the Emptiness teaches the mind.

166.   The sight is "what it appears to be…" What about "what it appears to be"? What is it? A hand for the mind is like a handmade glove perfectly fitting the hand… But, what is the hand?

167.   I used to sleep with my thoughts around. Not anymore… Did they go away, I wonder, or they just stopped to rap? Even this question seems inscrutable. No more words sprouting. Wind mills grinding silence…

168.   Only a well tuned mind could hear the moon banging on the wooden gate. Though, when loud enough, even a deaf ear can hear it.

169.   Gaining reality, loosing eternity.

170.   To Zen, to liken a womb with a grave is almost common sense. Babies turned mummies turned babies. Also, to Zen, the antinomy of truth is time… To be born just to fulfill some Zen rites? What a bore…

171.   Non-Zen paradox: to see the universe beyond the reach of reason while reasoning on it.

172.   Angels could pass through walls and yet bulls cannot pass their tail through a window... What words deceive, mind conceives...

173.   When a secret eternal word is passed in a whisper from a mouth to an ear there is no sound-to-sense that counts: with no understanding in place, an arrow passes through the mind: as the mind reaches out, the emptiness draws closer. I'm talking about being at that state of mind by now.

174.   Noisy like a magpie, silent like an empty nest.

175.   For each clay pot in the making, a flower in the waiting exits the emptiness. The pot master is choking dust for thousand of years. When he talks he can't make pots if the pot is not in the talking. One day, by mistake, his finger pierced the pot's clay. "I penetrated", he said. The pierced pot looked like a dead dog. The master threw it back into the trough and mixed it with the unformed clay. This year the market for pots was flourishing though no pots were ever sold. Next year, who knows? If you carry too many you break too may. If you carry a few you might not break any though you may not sell any. In the wake of a great expectation carrying loads is neither a guarantee of success nor a reason for failure. Walk the True Way with the feet of no return and you'll see through it.

176.   Sleep is to the sleeper what koan is to Zen. That's why you'd have to be one with your koan if you want to put yourself through.

177.   It's out of the ordinary that words that – *when pronounced* – resemble reality, could direct the mind into knowing the expressionless world from beyond...

178.   Never leave your thoughts linger longer among dead thoughts. This remaining-riddled mind…

179.   Playing with a weevil in my palm: what it means when we say "letting go!"

180.   The main Zen principle is to use your intuitive senses when practicing. Try treating all different things as alike and all things alike as different. The later is easier since one has to do what one has learned in a lifetime: to discriminate. The earlier is more difficult. To escape the limitations alter the game: treat all things alike as same and all different things as same. Remember: **A** immediately follows **A**, **B** immediately follows **A**.

181.   Zazen: Ears are always open to realization. Eyes are half closed.

182.   So far as I could see there are Buddha faces everywhere. The sum of all of them makes up the universe. Though they appear as being identical, they're neither definite nor indefinite: like a bull and a fly, like an elephant and a butterfly, like a dragon and a fire-fly…

183.   Clothed in dead thoughts mind keeps talking to itself. Chasing chimeras…

184.   The plum blossoms are bloodless. The snow caped peaks are mindless. Buddhas are selfless. In accordance to the old texts plum blossoms on a mountain snowed peak go back to the beginning of Buddha nature.

185.   Awakening: like the patience of light encountering a shadow.

186.   Silence is the perfect exile for one's words.

187.   Zen about reasoning: "The word was born so that smoke could explain what fire is".

188.   Thought and mind are like a glider approaching the mountain. If it hits the mountain – lots of debris. A little breeze might push it out of course. Though, glider or fly, let them fly, don't kill them. Cutting the mind road means letting them pass by, letting them go…

189.   The formless fish jumps from a formless lake and gets caught by a formless bird.

190.   Looking for essence after finding that Phenomena are empty. Eventually finding that the Essence is also empty. It is just the mind; and to the mind - *thus*.

191.   It is easier to fail! Wouldn't be nice if in this world it would be easier to succeed, instead? But then, the word "perseverance" would be an oxymoron.

192.   Letting go is either pushing it away or getting out of it… To get out of it is easy to understand, but difficult to do.

193.   To find what a ride is in the riding…

194.   I never knew that horses shed tears. The whip stirs their strength though the pain devours their pride. Old soon, it will be left free to roam the grass field: working hard for a happy retirement.

195.   On one hand a Zen pupil has to be aware of each lived fact (sensation, perception, and feeling, thought) while on the other hand he/she has to let it go. Knowing and not-knowing, grasping and letting go… Would I still be able to recognize while letting go the fact that I let go as a fact? For instance, as I eat and let go is the food still recognizable as food, is my taste what I

think my taste is, or all those depend on my intuition to make a sense and no-sense out of those things? Let's say that my ultimate awakening occurs while I'm eating an apple: is the intuition-seen-apple still an object of desire (taste, smell, image) or my apple is going to borrow some universal aspects to itself and move together with my hand holding it into the realm of absolute manifestation, a world in which nobody feels, thinks, (or eats, for that matter)? Literally, as the awakening allows the universe to manifest itself in the hollow consciousness teaming with intuition what is an apple in this becoming? *An apple.*

196.   Being essence makes anything else "essence": no parts, not the slightest degree of separation. Gaps are matters fabricated by the mind. By not dwelling on anything your mind closes the gaps, and knocks down the thousand walls between knower, knowing, knowledge and known.

197.   A letter in the spirit of the common sense: "Who can smell a flower can smell a sewer also. Who can hear the silence can hear a scratching noise also. The range of sensation is so vast that one can't find a name for each "feeling instance" encountered. That's why the division of sounds – for instance – in pleasant sounds and unpleasant sounds is suitable though the two partitions so defined are sharing boundaries. In some way pleasant-unpleasant, sounds like the opposition between bad and good, (pleasant and good being desirable, while unpleasant and bad being undesirable). Now, Sakyamuni used a flower to entice a response of the awakened among his disciples. Wasn't this a "desirable" choice? It seems to me that "what is pleasant and desirable" makes one's mind more fruitful. Same judgment applies to good and evil. To come to the essence of one's mind one has to renounce to judge things as being good or evil (duality). Though one of the principal Buddhist moral principles is to perform good deeds for the benefit of the suffering mankind. That shows another explicit choice between good and evil. Then what about

the environment designed for the Zen apprentice's dwelling? The incense burning (pleasure for the nose), the bell and the chanting (pleasure for the ear), the wine sprinkled antics (pleasure for the tongue), and also the punishment-reward game to reject or approve one's progress on the Way (pleasure for the mind), aren't all those *pleasure-instruments* used to persuade an apprentice that the Way has a pleasure-colored-way to the rider? One would have to cut those attachments though some infinitesimal attachments would have to be kept and exert a pull on one's mind! Those measured desires still don't leave - during Zen training - much room for compassion. Then, with the enlightenment – an arid and uncompassionate mind – penetrates through the "great death" and rides the "unbounded stillness". The countless forests of phenomena freeze. In a state of stupor the mind sees the supreme chamber of spirituality, the universe wearing the lit shroud of the original ghost. Big deal! Once seeing it how could one still look at the being and not realize that the living is in fact the only supreme spirituality; and that understanding is meant to inform the universe that yes, the truth had been grasped in accordance with what is given as truth in front of one's mind. It's true that there are myriads of mental states to be explored. With honesty, with the mind at peace and with measured attachments to desire one could explore what is inner and what is outer, without encountering too much of a hindrance; living while guided by morals one can achieve happiness for himself and for the whole surrounding world beyond any Zen awakening".

198.   The clawed thing one calls a cat is a two fold thought: one of the folds involves a mouse.

199.   As I get carried away by my thoughts somehow I get back to the same point; my mind is there, shining like a moon-pearl under the cold autumn water.

200.   A thought clinging on your mind: how do you transcend it? Even what one usually calls "a transcendent concept"?

201.   Mind... Wrong-Mind...No-mind...Right-mind...

202.   No remaining self? What a to-become-cold-world is given to us to live in? A self at large meets a mind at large? How come? The water is already wet when one thinks of it. Isn't the self there when one thinks of himself? Too many Zen paradoxes could make one overlook the surrounding reality. One of the realities is that I'm writing now. Another reality is that you're reading now.

203.   Awakening: one acquires transcendence by performing a transcendental act.

204.   A dead horse doesn't fear the whip of the coachman. In other words – talking about mind – an armored dead horse can't be brought into battle... Letting go knowledge! A dead horse is questioned by the coachman: "What is Buddha?" The horse doesn't move its lips. Now watch, if it didn't talk it may be bloody alive and well...

205.   When one asks "What is Buddha?" one may come up with various definitions and be tempted to interpret them by using either one's intellect or one's intuition. If a true picture of one of the living Buddhas would exist around, the question would have an answer. The questioner though doesn't ask who is Buddha but "What is Buddha?" This question cannot be answered using an ordinary language as one may think. If one thinks of it being an inward question it means that it doesn't need an answer from the outside. In the language game there is the one who asks the question about some concept – in this case Buddha – and the one who gives the answer. Some questions can't get an answer even if the answer originates in the deepest realm of one's intuition. Whoever accepts to answer such a question seriously is a man outside of the Zen realm. Whoever answers it in a humorous or paradoxical way, usually far from the context of Buddhas

themselves, tries to keep himself clear of any intellectual involvement. The best action you should take when one asks you "What is Buddha?" is to kick the questioner's ass and send him to Hell. Though more polite approaches vary: you could just slap one, you could break one's bones, you could shout, you could scream or - if the question is asked at dawn – you could jump on a fence and crow like a rooster.

206.   The strenuous effort of the mind to disengage itself from the knowledge process creates a fertile inner vacuum for awakening.

207.   A body language is more appropriate to Zen because it can't say too much.

208.   The rose is a form of emptiness. The carnation is another form of emptiness. Mentally one may choose the rose as a form of emptiness versus carnation. Having an unbound mind – and as far as emptiness is concerned – one doesn't have a choice.

209.   Zen joke: To get rid of good-evil duality you'd have to do bad things while intending to do good and vice versa. Why don't you start now? Go to the street and as you see a needy beat him up to the pulp.

210.   A drifting wave is freer: white foams rocking the harbor… How your ashes would look going uphill, moving back, washed and cleanse until they shine? Bone ashes ready to be mixed with wall paint: it seems, waves are getting taller every year with the crescent moon getting nearer…

211.   Zen redundancy: There are no holy truths! But you could recognize one if it awakens your mind. "There are no holy truths" is just half of the story. Not only that there are no holy truths. If there are any you cannot tell… If there are not, you still cannot tell. No matter how far it goes the mind returns to itself. Seeking truth one seeks oneself. Thus, mind heaves truths of itself, never

attached to outer, never clinging to inner. In that sense there are no holy truths - though you cannot tell.

212.   The compassionate look of a Buddha's statue. What can you make of it? The rain vanished leaving a rainbow in the sky.

213.   Zen awakening is a marvelous deception: delusions, illusion, paradoxical logic, metaphors – all are the offspring of the desire to abolish the "obvious reality". The mind whipped by emptiness and forced into submission. Tell me what you want to see? Is this emptiness? So clear in its own cloth, the obvious reality marches crowned with frosty mist.

214.   Every word has a redemption value: the thing it names… Though, there is no beauty in "beauty" and no ugliness in "ugliness".

215.   Each time the sun comes down the darkness unfolds. No more sights, just the whistling wind. If you could see this in a plain light the baobab tree is going to bow to you. The baobab tree is your resemblance, of course.

216.   Zen is like an ox among oxen. A birth in a bone-and-flesh body, a sweating life spent in silence, a death in a bone-and-flesh body. The only awkward thing is its head, for it thinks that that is the one that doesn't do the thinking.

217.   If you want to see the path while practicing Zazen you'd have to learn how to oil your lamp.

218.   People are phenomena. That's why they can't be part of anyone else's story. That's why group Satori will succeed only when jack asses, calves and moutons would be able to sit in Zazen.

219.   Japanese Zen to Americans is what the American atomic bomb was to Japanese. If you can't swallow this, what do you think your silence means? If emptiness generates pain and suffering one should rather use Zen as an alternative weapon? Did Zen ever cut an umbilical cord? Did it ever kill? Delicate lotus flowers kept captive in muddy waters: That's what Zen looks like to the Western world.

220.   To do "bad" to destroy "bad" you'd still have to judge which "bad" is better so you'd fall again in the quandary of good versus bad. To do "good" to destroy "good" wouldn't make sense even if you judge a "good" being less good than the other "good". With an unbound mind, bad seems to be a suitable companion for good, and both seem sacred. Mind says that even sacred – they can't dwell together. Also, it says that contrary to good and bad, a good doer and a bad doer look alike. The moral is that bad and good can be judged only in action. If there is no doer there is no bad or good to be done. Then to do bad to destroy bad when no bad is done is mindful; and mindful is to destroy good doing good. If you read carefully this text you'd see that beyond the void of sense there is a mountain of Karma.

221.   To be able to reach the original form by other means than comprehension and still be able to know what is right and what is wrong is an example of impure awakening.

222.   Sometimes bells pay dues to Karma too: they crack…

223.   Rabbits are not dogs and dogs are not horses. At any rate what is not still proves to be what it is and what it is proves to be different. This is how a relative reality is described using rabbits, dogs and horses as examples. What about reality while talking about stars that get born every day in the heaven? That's like when you try to hit a ball that's too high: you miss it but you know that it was there…

224.   When at night pain changes in dreams I either get bitten by dogs or thrown by a rocking boat into the rapids. Somehow I know that I dream and that the pain is an illusion...

225.   Joke: he got awakened while eating. Deep ingrained in his throat the doctors found a grain of rice.

226.   Body is a vehicle that sustains the mind's vehicle. When you travel in Zazen one vehicle carries the pack of goodies for the other vehicle. The awakening leap empties both packs: thousand smiles crowned by a laughing. Is that all?

227.   Living in a temple you do what is needed for the temple to be hospitable. Living in nature you let nature do the work for you. No rules mean universal rules. Universal rules mean no rules.

228.   Zen persuasion goes like that: At the beginning of the universe there was emptiness. Whatever was born from this emptiness is empty as well. To go back to this original one has to let go the relative world of phenomena (forms, facts) - in reality an empty space - and the mental world of understanding (perception, feelings, language, utterances) – in its outward appearance an illusion. Obviously if the outside reality is empty a mind doesn't have anything to reflect upon and so it stays also empty. Since both realities are empty there is no difference between the world outside and the world inside so the "two" worlds go back to their original face as one: emptiness, and only one. Zen is one of the methods that could help those who pursue such a philosophy to attain it, that is, to become aware of the truth that indeed the whole universe is nothing else but a pure and clear emptiness in which everything – if there is anything to talk about – resonates at unison...

229.   In mid-step the road looks longer...

230.   The knowledge of pain makes suffering easier. That's why some knowledge should remain un-cleansed by a Zen experience. Should we loose suffering we'd lose our after-Zen compassionate voice.

231.   A Zen eye can see a fly flying, as its true nature/ And a spider knitting a web as a Karma spy/ While the web is miles away but ready for business/ The fly's true nature is to get caught in it and eventually die…

232.   When failure is not an option the success tends to be mediocre.

233.   Emptiness and the mankind history: pure grains of ashes that mix with water so swiftly that one cannot trace a line to differentiate what is water from what are ashes.

234.   Everyday practicing your birthrights and postponing the ultimate treat…

235.   A sparrow flies to the sky and then withdraws. Her daily errand… At night I listen to her uninterrupted song sounding like a baby cry: being, being, being, being, being…

236.   On the front porch my mom planted Zen flowers. Since they are unborn they don't need to be watered. According to Zen customs my mom is pruning their formless blossom in the summer, trying to see if it's true what sages say: that this year plenty of seeds would be empty.

237.   Drenched in the illusion of a morning meditation I see the world standing still – though flowing – image after image; it is as if the world is living within me, over and over again… Lifting my eyes I could let it go though I'm afraid that it may never return.

238.   The bird from the cage flew away. The gate was locked, the lattice was tightly knitted. One takes a note of the tiny feather… Zen teaching: Learn how to fly out of a cage; learn how to fleet from a prison…

239.   Every chore is a moment in the becoming. Every thought is a moment in the being…

240.   Early morning when the rooster is crowning/ You can hear the mountain train whistling/ Then the dogs start barking/ The sparrows follow chirping/ And suddenly, all become so quiet/ You can hear a snow flake melting in the air… *The moral: Don't let your thoughts get stirred by what you hear; cut off your thinking, "cut off your ears…"*

241.   A practical advice: Sit patiently in Zazen. When you're not doing Zazen, knock the world out, kick ass… Then again, sit patiently in Zazen… Obviously this is an advice to those that don't love Zazen as much as they love to live in this world…

242.   Anti-Zen note: "Against one of the most respected Zen principles a word spoken – any word – carries with it more compassion than a myriad of koans. Even in a cynical utterance tears flow, laughing swells, birds follow a speeding ship hoping to lend on it and rest".

243.   To point at the invisible pigeon that passed through in a flash flight the universes before any being was ever born…

244.   A monkey bouncing on a net resembles a child. When a child is bouncing the net is bouncing also.

245.   While living - your life comes and goes, comes and goes… You just don't know it…

246.   I slept the whole day but then I stayed awake the whole night. The sweet things taste sweeter at night. Then I had a day dream that I still remember: I was carrying a bucket full of sparks which I took in my dream as being my remnants. I think this is really what life is: carrying bits and pieces, odds and ends in your mind-body from a destination to another. Why would ever end?

247.   The teacher says: "Now put your eyes back on in your skull to see". You can't hold the seen and you can't throw it away. The principle says that you should burry the seen back into emptiness. The practical thought says to keep the seen at handy. If everyone is Buddha, what is the seen without a seer?

248.   A mind at rest brings clouds to a standstill…

249.   Sitting in front of the mirror you contemplate its reflection. If you see none it means that your attachment had been successfully annihilated. If you see an image it means that you are sitting in front of the mirror…

250.   Anthropologically mindless? Impossible…

251.   Autumn's late flowers: white snow within…

252.   With the eyes slightly open and cast down I could see the reflection of the peak onto the floor. Slowly, my mind surrenders to the peak's glow and falls asleep. When the bell rings, my mind freezes. Pitiless bell: among forgotten things I saw Buddha slowly combing-out the peak of the early snow… (A true self is awake at all times, even during times when the entire universe rests…)

253.   Remember: the ear used to hear is the same ear used to listen, and the eye to see is the same eye used to peek.

254.   It would be nice if the moment of birth would hint to another moment of birth and so on. Unfortunately once you're born you race to die without the knowledge of the dying.

255.   Understanding your true self and being compassionate about.

256.   The floods stopped short to reach the pine forest. The waters are now quiet and cloudless. I could see the spider web drowned by the window, intact, as if interlaced under water. But the spider is gone. I hope it went up onto the roof. If it perished who's going to take care of ants and mosquitoes while I snooze in Zazen?

257.   Buried deep, the white bones of Buddhas…

258.   The beginner's thought: independent of perception.

259.   Heartless nature: to give tongue to a creature and as a result to frame its mind into a faulty talking…

260.   Mind is a careless vagrant. Neither kept in a leash nor left to run uncontrollably through the void. That's how it works: when mind thinks of salt, the mind is salted. When mind thinks of water, the mind is wet. But this is still looking as if the mind was connected to particulars. The indiscriminate way would be: when mind thinks of salt it is salt; when mind thinks of water it is water. Zen goes a step further: when mind thinks mind acts: the rest, all those abundant phenomena are a noisy background emanated by emptiness.

261.   If the mind is left to dance it would know what dance is. Once it starts reasoning the dance goes away.

262.   If mind stops being an insider (as opposed to reality being an outsider) the merge of both is like lightening: a lifetime knowledge withdraws. No affinities to boil, no congealed thoughts

to melt. When reality absorbs mind there is no more path to choose, no more tongues to arouse utterances.

263.   Flakes of emptiness in the morning glow...

264.   Genesis is made up of thoughts. Using an open mind as a shelter to nothingness one can catch a glimpse of the universe involved in its most intimate labors.

265.   Carrying out the act of compassion towards the whole universe! Big words, pure and empty.

266.   As is the eye so is the seeing: pristine mystery.

267.   The water dried up but the river of dust keeps flowing. Ice it if you can with no help from the vanished water.

268.   An atom is tasteless. A molecule is also tasteless. At what stage in the natural structure taste becomes apparent, sight becomes clear, and hearing becomes discernible? Science knows the answer, Zen intuition does not. And the emptiness doesn't care. My question is: is intuition making a mystery of well known facts?

269.   As a moment arises, it goes. As it goes, it arises. And what one has in mind yields to mindless.

270.   It is not the same for the man in the saddle as it is for the horse under the saddle. If the horse hits the road blind and deaf there is no way to seek. If the rider hits the road blind and deaf there is no Way to be missed.

271.   To bathe in a summer breeze: echoes of unity in separation...

272.   Striving for pleasure is worse than striving for understanding, though both spread out thin your true nature.

Except when plenty of leisure time and future are given. Fortunate are those who do nothing, neither think nor meditate. Living like a leaf in a forest, like a rock on a mountain. Neither trying to see the clearing nor to climb up with the purpose to reach the mountain peak.

273.   Attachment: To be oxen but desire to be the chief of the herd.

274.   "Give up on this life!" Easy to say it than to do it. I prefer to yawn when hearing this sentence, usually at night, when any other sentence is silenced. But then, as the objects of senses go to sleep – my mind goes away, soars into emptiness. Sometimes a dream comes along knitting phenomena out of emptiness. If I lived my life with virtue and without cravings, my dreams would be like compassionate stories that come true. If I didn't have enough food or clothing my mind would not flow away, knitting opulent dreams with feasts and fashion parades. Living in a capitalist world the only holy practice one needs is to relieve his/her ego by killing the pride and then work compassionately the daily slavery while measuring with modesty the food intake and the fashionable clothing. After one passes away - in the black tent - one is going to see lots of silenced people ready to meditate.

275.   In life, moments-that-have-been depart in tears. That's what a true self never sees.

276.   Is the smell projected by the nose on the outer reality? Why would then seeing be a projection of the eye? Or the sound a projection of the ear? You could imagine mountains covered with fragrant flowers and you'd not have a smell of any. To have a directed mind means to be focused on reality. When the mind travels through a cloud of incense even the view and the hearing

become part of it. Above a thick forest the sun doesn't care to answer to the wild cock crowing.

277.   On a positive side of a negative saying: an eye for an eye is like seeing what it is seen...

278.   The field of awareness: nearing the contrasts, freezing the arising fires. No gaps! The infinite "all inclusive" down to the virtual nothingness. Is the "virtual one" indistinguishable from one's true nature?

279.   The riverbed is bare: the water expired but its howl still wanders about...

280.   "Who" am I is more important then "what" am I. Though at the origin of time "what" came first and enveloping everything else. Thinking how "who" came to fit like a soft glove "what's" shoes.

281.   As my wife and I were walking by the subway station we saw a naked homeless sleeping on top of a gutter. "Did you see that?" my wife asked. "He's tired..." I said. "Look again", she insisted. I looked back. "I see", I said. "What did you see?" my wife asked. "He's even more tired than I thought..." I said. "You Zen dog!" my wife said. "Having skin deep enlightenment and trying not to see it", she concluded.

282.   A whisper is pacing a tongue silently...

283.   In the spring time the window becomes wider, the sun looks like a spread over the shallow heat. Climbing up my leg, I witness the first living stuff. Flowers don't have thorns yet, butterflies fly with no direction in mind. Beginning is always like a foal that never felt the bridle-rein.

284.   They said it was going to snow today, the first snow of the year. From morning till night, being seated on a chair, I waited

in front of the window to see it happen. It didn't snow. As I turned the lights off I suddenly understood what first snow of the year meant if either snows or not.

285.   An accomplished desire – thousand sorrows to the mind...

286.   Drops falling in a pond are not identical to those falling close on. Falling in a pond is like virgin echoes merging with virgin sounds, like wool growing silently on a sheep, like kisses immersed in neglected kisses...

287.   A mind chasing a fly may end up caught in a spider web.

288.   The warrior came back home: burying a hatchet, using a knife to hack a root...

289.   The only thing that remains pure is the self. A heart is just one's self reverberations...

290.   A dual horse that passes though a non-duality gate still exits as a dual horse. I wonder what kind of horse wouldn't...

291.   In search of what's right I found what is wrong. Like two drops of ink of different color dripping in a glass of water: they blend, they mix, and they're undistinguishable.

292.   Zazen: Eyes stay half open when clouds pass by/ In front of the moon./ You think: On full moon nights roads are more slippery.../ Two guests both fell and vanished/ Nobody would ever come in, no event would ever be attended...

293.   Today cannot reach tomorrow. If past and present exists, future is just a presumption. So is what we know as opposed to

what we're going to learn. Time is indivisible only if it is future. So is our learning.

294.   A round mirror doesn't show a room round. A square mirror doesn't show the horizon square…

295.   Zen: out of simplicity, find eloquence…

296.   Though the pain seems to go away/ It is felt when one exercises desire./ Karma is like a spinning vulture, close watching in silence/ A sweet rabbit searching the ground for carrots.

297.   The perfect cry of an owl: "O"

298.   Through the hole of a needle the whole universe could pass back and forth. Wandering cows, as many as the drops of water in a cloud, swell as they pass through. The native emptiness is still unknown to pathfinders…

299.   If you come too late excuse yourself for coming too early. In a wrinkle of time the teapot gets cold. The host says: You can smash it any time you fell doing so. No anguish though: experiencing a pot getting cold? The host says: Ice for the finest guest…

300.   The mind wonder: an unsung melody could be heard; an unpainted image could be seen.

301.   One thought for one act…

302.   Once an act is committed its thought runs away.

303.   The universe is wired to burst into phenomena. Armies of phenomena die in battle. More armies are brought-in to fight. The everlasting battle of the impermanence…

304.   The fisherman doesn't understand what the fish is saying… As water recedes and the river bed dries up, both of them understand. Water is much needed for the act of fishing… Fish are just extra…

305.   As usual means new and unusual. Here is how you could create a usual thing: descend on the bare ground and as you touch it you'll feel from head to foot, that fundamentally usual and unusual are one.

306.   A Zen world is uninhabited by humans; flowers and bees, straws and crows, sunrises and roosters… It gives to the human mind the right to see but not to live… (Those empty ponds where the moon drowns and dies are the origin of a Shakespearian like question: " Why forms abound and essence is what it is not?")

307.   Untraceable waves…

308.   To talk or to listen? A bell sound doesn't gather dust.

309.   The stealth awakening: like a bird dropping… Its fall hidden by leaves. Once it hits the target - the smell everywhere…

310.   I saw a cormorant swallowing a fish bigger then his body. His neck got severely enlarged. That's how larger phenomena like you are swallowed by smaller ones – like Zen. Time is made not to cease, space is made not to end. Though, even the smallest fly can swallow them wholly…

311.   Because of too much light the tree behind the window looks lifeless…

312.   When one coaches his "I" to become a "non-I" there is a moment when neither I nor non-I are manifest. Though, most of the time neither would manifest without the other.

313.   Enlightenment is not suitable to those who ride on the back of an ox named ignorance...

314.   There were myriads of confirmed live manifestation of Buddha and miracle stories abound about it. Though, when the universe went dark some other day, people looked for lamps and flashlights as their guidance.

315.   The brain never stops its words-mill. The immaterial knowledge makes a desperate attempt to be recognized as a mirror of reality.

316.   As the fog is born and dies with the first sunshine so does a moment of living; interrupting my obedience to Karma I didn't behave well today. As the day passed away I heard a crow at dusk: Karma, Karma! An ageless song, I thought...

317.   Though every infinitesimal thing is the centre of the universe, there are those that yield the way to others that will see the way longer...

318.   In logic you can follow traces back and forth. Surely this is not the case when awakening happens...

319.   In order to go north you have to turn your back to the South. As you go north you see the North. Since you can't see south how on Earth you still know where South is? (This is an example of how knowledge drops data in the process of seeking a higher truth...)

320.   Karma is beyond causation. That means that what is happening to you is not determined. Same goes with good and

bad and God and your head. So! I brought this topic out here for you to show you that you should behave.

321.   At the center of it all, a frosty breath…

322.   How come that the nature evolves onto creating more pleasurable things (fruits are sweet, flowers are beautiful, landscapes are magnificent, etc) that entice desires? Isn't it unnatural for Zen to appeal to one's mind to cut off desires? If a tree wouldn't know that its fruits are sweet who else would ever know? Tasting, if allowed would be an option.

323.   A path so narrow that a flake of snow can't get in but large enough to allow cause and effect swing together. What was yesterday there - all there was - was still there… Including the untainted mirrors of the emptiness…

324.   Seeking eulogy on a death bed: what a waste! A marble memorial with a gold coffin inside and daguerreotyped portraits sequencing a life that is gone. Then letters from fans still pouring long after you're gone. What a waste, what a waste…

325.   The morning moon is crowning the Northern hill. The sparrow's chirp sounds flat. Hopping over gaps and stopping and hopping again! Shadows cannot be trusted…

326.   Suchness is beyond speculation. Though one knows that the universe is made out of unprintable layers of knowledge, layer after layer after layer hanging at dawn like a silvery mist, well bleached and sanctified…

327.   Thoughts lay buried in previous representations. They have been carelessly gathered in a cylinder like vase, left open…

328.   Life is an expression of birth. Death is the dissolution of any expression. Once birth occurs death is a definite thing. If birth doesn't occur death is an indefinite thing.

329.   Worthy to be thought: the present… Worthy to be seen: the future…

330.   A moving tortoise is hiding emptiness under her shell; her movements unfold the void's manifestation; her shell shows the imperturbable aura of fathomable bodies; tranquility is seen further on – out of her stepping forward into the void.

331.   Knowledge: To conceal the truth in the mere expression of what truth could be…

332.   A bird's mind dwells upon something and a dog's mind dwells upon something else. They don't know their mind. But you, if you want to see your mind, you should stop it dwelling on things. Beware: dwelling upon nothing shouldn't become a knowledgeable thing or you missed the point.

333.   Be hard as far your practice goes and soft as far as your practice doesn't.

334.   Good or bad, black and white – and any discrimination of sorts – have to be called off, for the quest of awakening to progress. Though, before one attempts to do that, one should know that implemented as a Zen law, ethics are still a condition to awakening. This is to be sure that awakening is not exploited for illicit spiritual trafficking and that, after it happens, the trumpeted compassion that would help alleviate the suffering of every being holds true.

335.   I quite forgot that the unseen is part of the seeing…

336.   The only way to know for sure that you passed a true awakening is to realize that you truly became an infinitely compassionate self.

337.   Doing each thing as if the ultimate truth is watching you from inside…

338.   Barefoot walk creates barefoot thoughts: neither a word, nor a feeling…

339.   The emptiness is neither white nor black, neither fragrant nor odorless, neither hard nor soft, neither noisy nor silent: but when it manifests itself it is all of the above and all in-between and all out-round about.

340.   Did you wash your cloth today? Wash and fold…

341.   Summer grass knows no haste: patches like pillows under one's foot. Killing an ant in a moment of innocence…

342.   A fox hissing: hailstones are raining with a warlike echo, and then withdraw. To let the fox pass…

343.   To the center-that-holds the horizon is not forgotten.

344.   Flowers witness it, bees witness it, and snow flakes witness it – a wasted journey. Unutterable beginnings with no returns…

345.   What implications would an individual awakening have upon the world as it is seen?

346.   Is intuition just a way of looking at reality or the "new reality" that is subject to intuition forces us to adapt out language to it, replacing "looking" (which is observing) with something else

(?) deprived of sense, feelings, representation, thoughts: one could say "the intuition penetrates the wall of knowledge to reach the one-ness" and that's what we fully understand. Since we understand that how could we think that intuition would ever overcome the reasoning?

347.   Awakening is not giving you new eyes but a new way of seeing.

348.   Empty space honors the arrival of objects…

349.   Mu! You can't imagine two objects living within such a short syllable. If it can accommodate an object this object should be small and empty. Furthermore, indeed, such a small object should have a clear texture though completely transparent and be neither cold nor warm. If you think that the previous statements are not correct say "No!" If you think they're correct don't say anything because Mu is going to speak to you if you do. Mu would say: "It's just so! It's just so!"

350.   In a lie there is a lot of truth. In a truth there is not a bit of a lie…

351.   The wood scent travels valleys and hills. No need of wings to do that.

352.   Teaming with Mu then letting Mu take over. (Lending your body and mind to a hound searching the emptiness for an ancient bone).

353.   Echoes are calling, but nobody is around to answer…

354.   Closing the mind curtains you could develop a picture of your world within the universe. Opening the mind curtains you could see that your world and the universe are one.

355.   The only difference between sea waves and ocean waves is their placement.

356.   If enlightenment would be obvious people who talk would listen.

357.   Barefoot, searching the riverbank mud for worms... (Rising up its head, sliding back into the hole...) Today Buddhas are guarding their side... Sleeping birds, everywhere...

358.   A frozen fire...

359.   Does awakening have any meaning? If it is meaningless why is it taken as a goal? If Zen is called a spiritual practice what is so spiritual about it anyway? What about those that don't get awakened? Are they failures of a spiritual quest? No. And this is why Zen has an escape gate: everyday life is Zen; every dedicated thought to an act is Zen. As opposed to no-thought, no-act, no-life – as the world could be described after passing the gateless barrier. Stunned...

360.   Self authentication of Satori instead of a Zen Master's authentication is like saying that water is cold since you tried it. Though, you know the water for what it is, while Satori is a kind of water one cannot "know". In life some events are confirmed by witnesses when the subject of the event may have not been aware of it. This could mean that if an event is unthinkable self authentication of it is false.

361.   The clouds could not be heard. Neither a sword would make them moan, nor would the innocence make them laugh. The sun penetrates them through: nothing else would do...

362.   Did the crowing of the crow say anything? "I'm flying on the right side of a muddy road..."

363.   Not even to a mirror red is red and green is green. How then it would ever be possible for a mind to perceive the true color? Like silence having various degrees to each ear so the color has to the eye.

364.   Does the mind depend on objects of thought? If yes, then if we avoided, pushed or eliminated the objects of thought, mind could become a pure territory, a beginner's mind: sightless dark, hearless silence, stillness everywhere. Mind as vast as emptiness is.

365.   When one hears "a string of stars aligned at the horizon" the hearing and the view get together. Mental stuff is the only weight that one carries in the pilgrimage. If the mind is in "open-gates state" the whole universe comes into clear: water is floating, skies are expanding. Obeying or refusing is not anymore in one's power. Otherwise, every day is what we can make out of it to get us going...

366.   The incessant motion ceased. The frozen river melted. What is inside your mind now may return later: what is outside your mind now will never be the same. Ripples of thought like water transcending fire...

367.   Old proverb: "No malady could touch the self. Though a malady could architecture its pass on..."

368.   The moon lets the white dove hide under the snow undetected. Even the dove's cries sound like falling cotton in the snowy air.

369.   What is intuited is also left as food to logic. For otherwise we'll all be Zen masters: letting the mind go and create the world for us.

370.   When the mind becomes virtual the reality stops flapping its wings.

371.   The essence of the mind and the essence of reality are the same. The moonlight irrigates the darkness. Under the feather weight of the emptiness the aura of a weightless mind.

372.   Watching the sky while sleeping on the roof I found that stars don't fit within a world that could be exhausted. I could say something like star number one, star number two, star number three, etc… I could see this as an opportunity to live there where thoughts are lingering and where either living or getting awakened is an act of making a complete inventory of the reality.

373.   When you understand, the river is flowing, the smoke is rising, and the wind is gliding; the fundamental knowledge, though, ends all these: icicles hang on the intertwined creeper, although, the pitiless summer is setting still…

374.   What the intuition does is playing with the unthinkable.

375.   To senses the emptiness is a distant land though the senses are empty.

376.   A white fox enters her den. Another white fox comes out. After last night's snow the moon shines over the unmarked hole. Like everything else around here, there is neither a point of departure nor a destination.

377.   The silence in the mountains is different than the silence in the meadow. One is utterly high, the other is utterly low. The magpie, draped in green, flies by unnoticed.

378.   The relative world cannot be a good food for the intuition, but – as the enlightenment goes – the absolute world could be a good food for the mind.

379.   A small thing doesn't make the universe look smaller.

380.   Unaccustomed with the concept of anything that could be nameless… Though, what else is "nothing"? It's really nothing so far as it doesn't carry its own name "nothing"…

381.   Even modern cats have diversified their meow beyond the animal innocence against the belief that all species have acquired their tongue "free of discrimination". A black fish in black water or a green fish in green water would starve a fox to death…

382.   In Zazen one has to suspend his mind work. If the world - as we know it – consist of thoughts, one has to disallow thinking to occur. What is left in one's awareness is a mysterious way of the mind to deal with an indefinite and indeterminate reality. No thing is mentioned by name, and a thing is neither good nor bad.

383.   Think this: this lake never reflected a red moon. How to explain phenomena that originate in your mind? Aren't the mental things also phenomena that you can watch as if reflected in a hand mirror? The occasional outburst of egoism is what makes a red colored moon not to be reflected on all lakes that there are out there… Same works while seeing dragons traversing the clear sky or horny cocks crowing the national anthem…

384.   What is this nostalgia to call back in one's mind the very beginnings? It was always the beginning with its never ending…

385.   What a wonderful idea: to sweeten the ocean waters so that children can enjoy swimming…

386.   Thoughts rising and falling: If this is "It" I overlooked "It" before. If this is not "It", tales of many give meanings to a few. The weather is too warm for sledging…

387.   What one can never weight is the mental gain. In the autumn – twilight leaves are carried by the wind until they reach the water surface. They all then sail. Till when? Not way of knowing…

388.   If awakening is individual and unique how is it possible for anybody else to confirm, validate, accept or deny it? I mean, guidance is one thing. But to validate an experience as complete awakening means to make objective an experience which by its own "substance" is the intimate revelation of the universal IT which is everlastingly hidden and unknown to others but to the enlightened one. And isn't the confirmation of such awakening an act of mounting on a pedestal an ego (I) that by previous experience should have been reduced to nothingness?

389.   The stillness of the altitude: one bird in its flight and the whole pledge gets broken…

390.   When enlightenment pierces through the wall of ideas the wooden head's memory springs up: Mu!

391.   So many ways to know and so many ways to be awakened. Though, a compass shows always North!

392.   No need to explain Nirvana: a brief breeze tears off curtains to let the path irrigate the whole reality: it plunges you in it and it's already vanishing. The only way to sustain it is by entering the void without any attempt to give to the reason a place to hang on. Sometimes this becomes a matter of life and death.

393.   Emptiness gave birth to mind in the hope that mind would acknowledge emptiness. Reality's tentacles are hindering one from realizing that: hic et nunc: you're here and now! So is emptiness.

394.   The essence of the mind is to look into the essence of reality. Aren't they identical?

395.   What one can find in an emptied mind? Everything seen as anew: the new pair of glasses drowned in the black ink.

396.   Satori makes reality bloom. Afterward the world looks like a blossoming tree: busy bees roaming around. Though, watch out: underground, foxes hide in their den; above vultures rove in the sky...

397.   Time of unutterable measure, space of unutterable measurement.

398.   Some words need a handle like a watering pot needs one. A handle for an unmovable thing that still lets the water flowing...

399.   A raw peach tastes better than a raw fish! That's knowledge. And that's how we realize that a thing unheard doesn't teach you much.

400.   Sleeping awakened is like dreaming of insomnia while in a deep sleep...

401.   Zen saying: The difference between a bovine and a non-bovine is that what-is-not defines the terms for what it is.

402.   The truth is... What is the truth, one may ask? The truth is... Something could be told about it and something more could be left out. But remember, medicine cannot be taken by a doctor to heal a patient's illness...

403.   The echo knows better the truth than its original sound does.

404.   If a Zen cure to life was no-life then I'd prefer to-live-my-life-as-a-hot-passion to awakening. Though if a Zen cure to life is more-to-life I'd have to temper down the passion while it is still lingering there, in my body-and-mind. Passion dwells in the world of phenomena. You drop body-and-mind, you drop passion. To drop only one of them is not enough. To drop both is difficult. Do passion with no lust and Zen with no longings and you'll be okay.

405.   Do Zazen with the patience of a bird hatching an iron egg.

406.   Having a short life to accomplish all: patient but not lazy, impatient but not in a rush…

407.   To see the life as a living truth you'd have to acquire a special relation between your mind and your living, called prajna. The ordinary life will become your Zen teacher while walking, working, preparing a meal, going to sleep. Your life and Zen will become one.

408.   What's there? A hill born wind…

409.   Mind is the originator of the world. In this respect void has mind also. As an acquaintance to the living, mind becomes a hindrance: The indiscriminating mind of emptiness became the discriminating mind of the living. What does it mean that the end of discrimination is the end of suffering?

410.   Zen: a sweat shop…

411.   Cleansing your mind of any imprint and then opening your eyes to a sight of innocence.

412.   By locking your jaws or cutting your tongue you'll starve the talking but not the thinking. So, leave things where thcy are. Thousand scarecrows will attract more birds than a good designed one. If you think that you know how to make such a scarecrow don't try to be stylish. For birds, the "World?" And "The Way" are both simple matters.

413.   When a thing decays, its name decays. A blade of light can uproot a Blackened Tree.

414.   To be awaken and not seeing the light. Being asleep and taking it for granted.

415.   Using finest China to serve Japanese tea: what a historical treat…

416.   Becoming one with the universe and thinking how imperfect the universe is.

417.   The way to enlightenment is like a dirt road in a boundless forest. If you miss an exit to a clearing you'd have to go back to that exit and try to take it again. How do you turn around? You turn carefully, trying to remember the road based on internal motions: there is no ear to hear a sound, no eye to see a sign…

418.   Successive facts are the result of a continued and unobstructed possibility.

419.   Welcoming the incoming hunter season with a charged bow… Echoes of foxes hauling, birds crying, deafening noise of falling stars… Their bones known only to God…

420.   When the enlightenment emerges there is neither entrance nor exit: the end of searching, the end of seeking, and the

end of the world. It delivers one's mind from reason and one's eyes from seeing.

421.   The preconceived ideas are like shadowy nets thrown upon reality: as if silence could be taken out of a noise…

422.   A pyre for egos that left their owners and forgot their way to return…

423.   Everywhere the illusion of reality and the reality of the illusion: which one creates the other? A half-way bridge looks at the other half-way of water.

424.   The forth eye trying to see what an ordinary eye sees while avoiding the signal from the third eye. Things are vanquished shadows of thoughts. And thoughts are not what one would think, but what a thing could call attention to in a short blink.

425.   A log hides claws of fire though it cannot defy the snow.

426.   To deliver one from understanding a teacher could either say a thing that would start one's mind's work afresh or say nothing to slam out one's mind. The first method is called "seeding"; the second method is called "un-seeding".

427.   At night, clouds move apart, darkness comes into view.

428.   The mind got forgotten and the wall of knowledge was reduced to rubble. Man and wind in a brotherhood appearance… On the way back, clear clouds unravel the new moon…

429.   If you see God in a cow shit God doesn't get offended. You may get offended because of your limitations. What is

unlimited is all encompassing, that is embracing everything: that includes cow shit, horse shit, etc.

430.   Life, a fault of breath… Shiny drops of dew on the lake's mirror. Things and words unconditioned by one's self…

431.   *A new cast of a dice, a new Buddha is coming into view.* Even if the whole world was a continuum of Buddhas, no Buddha could be known (seen) through knowledge (casting a dice). If mind is the source of all Buddhas, then mind is the whole world. Therefore, again, at each new cast of a dice a new Buddha is coming into view. Buddha is mind, mind is Buddha.

432.   Clear your mind of knowledge and wisdom altogether. Stand like a newborn in front of the unknown. Easier to say than to do: that's why the mind invented aphorisms in the first place.

433.   The enlightenment is not an event driven by my self (inner or outer). Though I tend to relate all things that are happening (out or in) to myself (I); the awakening is in fact a total depersonalization. What one experiences then is being looked upon by the universe that assembles itself as an immediate insight. For the subject experiencing awakening it is as if the meaning had been brought up by a "miracle sight".

434.   Stillness is a Zen bluff… The only world that exists is made out of actions, movements, transformation. Ah! If you asked what the very first action-movement-transformation (that preceeded everything else) was you must use your immortal eyes to look and your immortal ears to listen: Zen tales could help just a little…

435.   The autumn fires dies down: it gives to a crow's tongue reasons to crow: "I'll crow though I'll not be heard!"

436.   The million folds of the wind and the moon's halo…

437.   The foothills are whitened by the fallen cherry blossoms. Throw the time away, watch the uninterrupted blossom.

438.   Walking across the mountain bridge I gather neither ice nor fire. With the river floating past my eyes, the peak looks like an unattainable illusion.

439.   Known facts: the stillness of knowledge.

440.   The incessant sound that only an ear could make cease…

441.   The egg-laying and the egg-hatching! What a mysterious way to bring into being BEINGS.

442.   Karma: People who are killing insects are going to be eaten by dragons.

443.   In Zen-schools pupils who understand are penalized. Not answering to teacher's inquiries is considered an act of merit.

444.   The start of each snow and the dogs howls… At night, they'll all be covered in white: silence, pierced by the flakes, icing…

445.   The muffled sound of the moonlight climbing up the hillside…

446.   Satori: the frog sang it, the falcons sang it. It even emerged from the throat of a dead fox. With the day never turning to darkness you don't need to pound anymore at foreign gates. The endless walk is finished. All the doors are wide open.

447.   If you know yourself you don't care what you are in the eyes of others. Mountains and rivers follow the same philosophy.

448.   Humiliation is a condition that one needs in order to adjust his humbleness. For it comes usually when humbleness has long been forgotten. Same rule works for any happenings we call "negative": guilt, remorse, sin, pain, and suffering. All those are closed in Karma's accolades while each of them is breathed differently. Non-attachment is the cure for all. When the sources of attachment dry up the infinite reservoir of tranquility comes into clear view.

449.   To understand the nature of the mind – the mind itself has to travel beyond comprehension. How a mind does that? Snows of faded blossoms dampen on thousand mountains. Mind cannot enclose what the infinite discloses. An open mind, a flash and an inexpressible sorrow.

450.   In Chinese listening and smelling are expressed by the same word. Listening to a smell would be interesting. Same would be to smell a sound. Going further we could listen to a color (some colors are quite, others are clamorous) or see a smell (the smell of a rose becomes a rose), etc. It shows that the senses can slide one in each other. Listening to a smell though seems more than any other on the void side of the world.

451.   Truths that words keep only to themselves when not uttered…

452.   To judge a grown up vegetarian from the point of view of a Zen cow is like giving a prize to a child for not killing butterflies. The truth is that if it is for feeding humans, a dead cow could mean a lesser Karma than a dead butterfly. Necessity is moral: naturlich to mensch.

453.   Smashing a Buddha's statue is an act of disobedience and courage. The act doesn't have any consequence except that it may haunt you and kill you while asleep.

454.   Ending thinking on a reflexive note: about thoughts –
put any contradictions to rest; about morals: following the
positive, meeting the negative without arguing; about the sparrows
chirps at the window: slamming the gate is of no use. My skull is
like an old grave: bare bones vacancy…

455.   What is mortal wants to be a deity. But deities don't
exist. Therefore what is a mortal longs for immortality? The whole
human history is like that: trying to fill the ocean of happiness
with tears…

456.   A woman moving a comb in her hair: ravens, crows,
sunburn marches, darkened drizzles… As the comb clings to it,
the mirage flees…

457.   Doubts make certitude starve: the war upon ideas amidst
faded words and utterances. Chocking ideas to find the true self…

458.   Hell bound, heaven bound… Once it's dark it can be lit.
Once it's lit it can be darkened. What a lousy thinking: clutching
either one or the other while both are hauling the burden of void
afterthoughts. A consecrated mirror to burnt insights…

459.   The universe may have never had a beginning, and it may
never have an end. The mistake of the mind is to contemplate the
eternal and the infinite using an ephemeral and limited mind. For
instance, the mind could say: "when all light is gone and all noise
is gone" sounds fitting for the beginning and also for the end of
the universe. Human perspectives describing before-birth and
after-death situations might never apply to the universe. That's
why even if enlightenment is an interesting experience it will never
lay a hand on *THE UNDERLYING UNITY OF ALL THAT
EXIST OR NOT.* As long as mind works lips tend to talk. If
heart stops, mind stops. Only then you can talk as if you were
alive: tell us all about the ultimate truth!

460.   If you plan to become Buddha you'd have to get dressed in black robes, straw sandals, to speak softly and to mind your own business. The way to awakening is a private business. People talk about the flower of the youth and the fruit of the elder. What about the smoke of the departed? A black robe can't hide it…

461.   Enlightenment and death are interchangeable. Though after one is enlightened one still lives. In an analogous sense emptiness and relative reality are interchangeable.

462.   Confronting the limitation of any human experience Man invented God.

463.   A wordless teaching is worth a cow dung coin.

464.   Life is like an apparition in the mist. You get near it, it runs away. You move away, it follows you closely. The universe looks like a reminiscent dream in which you got lost. After the enlightenment the meaning of the relative world becomes crystal clear. Enjoy your common way as if it was The Way. And if you had a choice, choose to live.

465.   Some people are born Buddhas. Others are born to run for cover while seeing one.

466.   A spotless mirror reflects better a spotless mind.

467.   A bull's tail that passes through a window generates Zen controversy.

468.   I wonder how many people who preach the awakening got awakened. Americans tend to add some excitement to their boredom. So they import stuff, in this case Japanese. What's Zen? A "mind" version of what Sushi is to food. Compared to a regular food what Sushi tastes of? Nothing. Same with Zen: it teaches one "nothing". On the contrary… What's really rewarding is that an

American society made for consumption wants more (and more diverse) "nothing" in its mind storage.

469.   The arriving coffin is for the departing body. An empty box to hold emptiness.

470.   When the sun comes back every morning it is a new sun. An absolute sun shows up only once during a universal lifetime.

471.   The essence has to return to phenomena to show itself. That's why sun shines, metals melt and water flows. As the phenomena return to essence sun's shine becomes dim, metals don't melt, water stops flowing. Some while back (16 billion years ago) the sunlight was just a poetry theme. As a result everything else was…

472.   At a wake the mourners' duty is to weep. As they leave the wake, they go partying…

473.   Don't despair: where chance chooses a few, the unseen Heaven chooses many.

474.   The irony of Zen is that if you don't get awakened you really get "nothing" out of Zen. If you get awakened you get a crowned version of it.

475.   An absolute ocean could hold only absolute fish.

476.   At a Zen center somebody proposed to raise money and build a Zen monument. It was agreed that the monument should be a pillar. Eventually there were not enough money to build one and a tree was plated instead. It dried up very fast. The gardener chopped its branches and trimmed it to its naked trunk. The trunk was left to rot. A pillar!

477.   He ate his mind while meditating and found it tasteless.

478.   Flies roaming around the head of a Buddha disciple.

479.   Interlocking causation is like intercourse with no participating bodies.

480.   Monks: They're still playing like kindergarten kids do, kicking each other, shouting, screaming – while Buddha comes around to watch: "Bring him a chair!"

481.   On the pilot seat there is this one who forgot almost everything…

482.   Emptiness: the true nature of reality is like soap wash. While the soap is used to wash it vanishes into the gutter.

483.   Grotesque joke: What's the difference between a cow (vegetarian) and a lion (non-vegetarian, I suppose)? One of them is the source of red meat to the other. In Zen all things are equal, though it seems from the late example that a cow is less equal to a lion. After awakening though, if you know what is what, they are all equal in their emptiness. That is the cow is the lion and the lion is the cow.

484.   The body of chaos has more hands than Buddha's. Some apprehend some let go! What's the ocean if not a big lake?

485.   You, who have known what awakening is, tell me what kind of rice would you like to eat after you die?

486.   Without minding, without saying, without seeking not to…

487.   When I see I think with my eyes, when I hear I think with my ears.

488.   When the time comes for me to go, I wish I could see again the unreal world of Satori: wrapped in translucent white, an old man, on the road to liberation, keeps jumping over imaginary rocks and thorny bushes towards the infinite ocean.

489.   To life a fly murdered in Tokyo reverberates in the wings of a fly that copulates in England.

490.   Giving to a beggar a handful of change: "It's too much!" he says.

491.   Words that awaken: "Wake up!"

492.   With appropriate training the-"I" could be that beast that would eat your Ego.

493.   The inevitable mistake is to question It. The mistake to be avoided is to answer it.

494.   Zen joke: Greet your neighbor by simply saying "Good morning". If your neighbor doesn't answer your greeting he is probably following a different Zen school of thought. The enlightenment though may come out of you both, equally.

495.   Beyond birth and death the sky will be blue, the pee will be yellow.

496.   When the awakening is happening the time and space stop flowing. Then, as the six senses come back and you open your jaws there is no word you could use to describe what you just missed…

497.   The stone Buddha was broken by the last earthquake. People get enlightened just by glancing at the stone fragments.

498.   Everyday, at about ten o'clock, the sun wipes out the shadows on my lawn. Grasshoppers know that: I see them hopping towards the backyard bushes.

499.   The call of a bird-body addressed to another bird-body…

500.   Nights are more of a nothing than days are.

501.   The absolute reality one strives for can be foreseen by means of detachment and withdrawal. The illusion arises from slowing down the mental activity to a halt. During such short moments some people apprehend the world beyond discrimination. Those moments should be taken as signs of grace. That's a way to put a label on what realization is not.

502.   Suzuki says: "When no thoughts are stirred within yourselves, no faults are committed anywhere". How beautiful and how masterly expressed! No thoughts – and Buddha emerges! There is no doctrine, no dogma, no philosophy, and no principle within all above that would ever beat the deepness of this utterance. But I wonder: if thoughts were stirred within ourselves would there be any faults committed anywhere? The only fault I see is that "thoughts were stirred within ourselves".

503.   Awakening can change the way one looks at life. What seemed to be a moonlight hue proves to be afterwards just a moonlight hue. Minds are all holly. Those sentenced to permanent sufferings are the only Buddhas. The rest, I mean awakening, the enlightenment - are just low mental creations.

504.   Lost completely, found completely…

505.   Koan: Sitting in one of the corners of a small room you could see in one view the other three corners. As the room gets larger you could see in one view only two of the three corners. In a very large room one could see in a view only one corner.

Question: while sitting in one of the corners of a room when you could see clearly in one view all the four corners?

506.   After he got robbed of awakening he stole a priest robe.

507.   The universe has big holes where not even nothingness could fit in. Emptiness though can be found everywhere.

508.   Not holding on to anything is letting go of everything. No thing remains grounded. Processes are neither determined nor reasonable. Mind rests comfortably on an empty pillow. But like the red sparrow prescient of every nest around - as she flies up and down - she always return to what she calls home.

509.   If Buddha is mind, mind is "thus". Is no-mind "not-thus"? But no-mind is no-self. Therefore no-mind is "thus". When Buddha is mind "IT" is at the same time no-mind.

510.   The true way is the unchangeable view of what tomorrow is.

511.   Mind and Brain: What water is for water-balloons?

512.   A horse tailed mule is equal to a jack-ass tailed mule. Yet, if you understand their differences you lose.

513.   This bowl of emptiness is like a spotless snowfall: as you seek a meaning the snow melts. What a rain-bow, what a miraculous rain-bow: building things anew every single instant.

514.   Winter Sun: A white fox bakes on a stone. The breeze scatters the fresh snow about.

515.   By attaining the true way the untangled drums got muted and the blow of the sticks froze still before the beat. If they'd ever

resume their beat it will be neither loud nor quiet: the dimmed echo of the forgotten past.

516.   A fly flying and a crow crowing…

517.   Zen joke: "Zen could be found easily in a hair rather than in a clock. Firstly because a hair is not made out of parts assembled together to show time. Secondly because the hair grows while the clock doesn't. Though, if the clock would know intimately how it produces the measured time, one would find in a clock more Zen".

518.   If the true (absolute) world is not the (relative) world we're living in, it means that there is no true world in the relative world. A relative world is made up of parts (things and facts). An absolute world is made up of all and everything comprised in one: nothingness.

519.   Where is that simple Way which in old days awakened so many? And where are they all? Magic over the mountain peak: birth is painful, life is suffering, and death is swift. Past – as silent as the moonlight. Crows fly across the snowy fields. If one day emptiness would become the truth of the whole world, love would flourish; compassion would never be put to rest.

520.   Story: "Things are not going well with my Zen neighbor: his dog died of old age. When something bad happens to my neighbor he starts greeting me and my life gets infused with mercy and compassion though I don't really know my neighbor. I heard his Zen daughter saying: "Dad, you promised me another dog. We'll name him like the last one we had before…" Her Zen dad says: "We'll not name him. We'll just watch him playing, eating, and running after pigeons: he shall be doing the same thing as the other one did, being with us for a while before passing away. No name though…"

521.   To ferry oxen is my job. If they drown, this is their Karma job.

522.   A painted Buddha looks better than a Buddha carved in stone. At night nature doesn't use colors and the moon penetrates the lake waters. At day colors are lit in front of the stony Buddha. Bang-bang sounds are heard. Sun doesn't penetrate the surface of the lake water. A gardener with a green hose washes the Buddha statue of life and death.

523.   In the world of relative knowledge what is contained looks at what contains it and vice versa. At the beginning of the world this separation didn't exist for the contained and the container were one. First stage in Zen is just to put this unity back into place.

524.   Being carried in *Mother Nature's* womb for eons and still not being allowed to call her by *name*...

525.   There was a cloud she had never seen and the river stream was new also. And her longing for them was centuries old. As she flew between the cloud and the river she could exclaim: "I'm a crow!" This story reveals the limitations of certain living beings to let the "I" go.

526.   Satori: If you got it don't keep it. If you didn't get it keep it until you get it again.

527.   The past brought forward is felt as grief. No moon seen throughout, no light. The eternal and immortal wind blowing through a sand castle...

528.   No remembrance to hold, no remembrance to let go.

529.   The weightless wing of the primeval light: nesting shadows. So many instances when the emptiness returns unchecked to emptiness and then comes back again in the guise of new phenomena. Neither the sky was touched nor did the clouds scattered. Mind: a frustrated explorer. Coming empty handed – leaving empty handed.

530.   The world seen by container and contained is the same if they sail as one. *Joke: The eyes of a duck (contained) are seeing the same world as the duck is seeing (container).*

531.   The dissolution of the relative reality in the eyes of the enlightened... What does it mean? Firstly, it acknowledges the emptiness. Secondly, it acknowledges that the relative reality was born there. That is, instead of rejecting the relative reality it acknowledges it as a loss...

532.   Piano lesson: where fingers play mind rests. Keys and strings fill the emptiness with flakes of echoes. Listening detached: neither to make sense out of, nor to keep it flowing...

533.   What emptiness is to one is emptiness to the other. Just the form of seeing it is different.

534.   If mind is no Buddha you must light a lamp at mid-day to find the Way. Beside your mind there is other mind. Then there is the eternal mind. The eternal mind is neither your mind nor other mind. There is one mind only that comprises all minds. When mind is empty the ventriloquist universe impersonates Buddha. Then mind-as-Buddha is riding the primeval ox on its home-coming day.

535.   Warning: The unknown may come to confuse you under the form, shape and appearance of "what's known". Be careful; don't lose the opportunity to smash the bowl.

536.   The eye can see everything around but not itself. Except when it is mirrored. The mind's eye can see everything, but not itself. Except when it is mirrored. Where mind's eye gets mirrored? To see this you'd have to stop rationalizing.

537.   The whistle of the tea-pot: the sound of a ready-made ceremonial. The daily haste is put to an end bringing forth the immortality.

538.   I wonder how much of direct awareness one should use as opposed to intellect in every moment of ones' life! If we keep a child in his initial awareness for the rest of his life and away from feeling, perceiving and knowing he may feel at ease in a cave and its surroundings but not in a society. To see the autumn leaves turning from green to yellow and then to see them back to green in spring, gives one a deep insight of what life means when Zen calls it *no birth-no death*. My humble and of course, wrong impression, is that Einstein's Theory of Relativity is Zen also. Van Gogh is Zen. The Titanic is Zen. My mom is Zen also.

539.   The sudden appearance is the result of one's practicing. Shaped into a mountain: all trees scorched to ashes. On the mountain tip, an early snow is sign of an unfulfilled prophecy.

540.   What is born will die. What is not born yet will be born. There are no extras. So many Buddhas, so little time…

541.   Choosing a Zen path while you're a stone is easy if you don't start walking the Way with a big mouth and saying big words or letting go with a loud laughter.

542.   When wings unfold they show their function. Sitting on a branch a bird looks like part of the sea of leaves. As autumn comes, leaves are falling, birds are falling. Mind seems not to see

the difference though the bird could distinctly be seen on the barren branches.

543.   The well-tuned universe was custom made for a drum-less ear.

544.   That the truth of Zen is equal to the relative truth doesn't bother me. What bothers me is that the truth of Zen is equal to the relative truth. The above tautology is not a mistake. It is just what Zen is.

545.   To be on a cliff alone: your eyes hung over the blue dark valley. A wind-scented fog roams around like a messenger of the unknown. The ice covered cane became an impediment to the climbing.

546.   Not dependent on words but playing with poetry. Somehow the promise holds if you don't draw to near...

547.   The innermost self lives unaffected by events. In Satori one can feel its presence and sense that it has nothing to do with one's body. Something feel sad about that lurking inside the only thing that remains intact as one lives or dies, is the part that we barely know anything about.

548.   To live in the vastness of space and time, not to be entrapped. One hunter – thousand tigers... One tiger – thousand hunters... All happen here though it seems to happen in a far off place...

549.   A moon has no clue about the fox howling in her den, or of the owl crying non-stop on the holly tree. If a moon awakens there is no hole one can hide, no birds could fly to safety.

550.   Pupil: "The emptiness is just another thing..." Teacher: "Yes! But it is a thing you don't have to think about!" Pupil: "How I can refrain from thinking it?" Teacher: "You need

practice…" Pupil: "Then which is better: practicing thinking, or practicing non-thinking?" Teacher: "If you don't watch an apple falling, it will always fall in the right place…"

551.   Flowers are a good offering when emptiness comes into being. The richness of seen and heard is gone. Blossoming is seen though there is no seer. Finally the sculpted Buddha can have an ordinary dream.

552.   Shooting straight: the bird on the ground lies still before you lift the trigger.

553.   The only reincarnation one might be able to talk about is through DNA – on which one may find inscribed names of one's ancestors down to some mileniums back. Interesting memories may surface if one could get back to those primeval times, thousand and thousand of years ago. One day I succeeded to go there: harsh life, lots of pains, suffering and lack of hope. My advice: don't go there! Awaken your mind to the present time. Listen to the moon ascent, its light wrapped in even more light…

554.   When the breeze blows the sparrows swell.

555.   A circumference can be stretched out to encompass the whole universe. Inside the circle the inner plane of empty radiance. Outside the circle the resplendent plane of outer radiance. A bird flying in and out of the circle wouldn't be aware of the difference.

556.   The traceless time! With every wink the clothed gets naked and the naked gets clothed. As time stops mind sees the uncreated… If afraid of ghosts, dare not look…

557.   Mind travels only when it gets out of sight…

558.   Pure intuition is the intuition not affected by thinking. In a pure intuition state, neither things nor thoughts appear: the relations between things and thoughts are dropped also. Instead, when using pure intuition, one is in a waiting state for the incidental awakening to occur. "Liberated from thinking I could see clearly my original face before the entire universe was born: spitting phenomena, ingesting essence".

559.   Cold doesn't have any consequence to coldness.

560.   Habits of language: keep going is like keep staying. A Zen law validates this. If you limit your mind to the relative reality you'd either go or stay. The absolute may free your mind from seeing movement where movement is not. What about staying?

561.   If you build a temple for your mind, remember that cupolas are always empty.

562.   Acting according to ethics may suddenly open one's eyes to a mystical experience. Not thinking bad-good is a way to eliminate the contradictions of the mind fighting opposite categories. Doing good and not bad is a Karma thing. The same mind that in Zazen suppresses differentiation and discrimination is the bearer of one's morals. Think that all things and thoughts are equal. But when you act follow the ethics path.

563.   The ocean bowl: emptiness in the form of a fish soup…

564.   A runner keeps running in his dreams.

565.   Cleansing the amassed dust from all corners of your mind. Knowledge is an affliction that shuns the grace. Sweet ashes blown away. The inner window renewed.

566.   For wine distillers water is an uncolored liquid used to wash grapes. That's why, as simple as Zen is, to enjoy its taste one needs to use sutras as his drunken escort…

567.   A mountain could hold so many climbing feet. Though it allows on its peak only a few. If the peak was like a flat field sheep would go their first.

568.   Dharma is the pillar of two phenomena: body and mind. But mind is Buddha, body is not! Then, guess who's talking! You'll hear this question if you don't know the answer… Buddha's body lays buried far away from his mind.

569.   I understand that a moment of eternity is the eternity of the moment. What about those moments that had never occurred and would never-ever arise?

570.   Nights are born in the morning. As they grow they need not be.

571.   The sun is momentarily in the sky. Where is it going to be in one hundred billion years from now? A being is momentarily here. Where is it going to be one thousand years later? The shorter the impermanence, the more impure the vision. White feathered birds flying through early snows.

572.   The chance made you human. Your corpse talking to you: nobody's to blame! At your burial people are saying: "He was…" The past tense makes you laugh.

573.   In retrospect my ashes belongs to my body. Mind, neither touched by fire nor scattered by the wind… Reading the ashes to trace a lifetime hindrance…

574.   The interim is endless…

575.   Defending the unity of the whole universe as "One" against the everyday experience that shows it as being made out of

multiples. A taste test will help you argue for or against it. The universe is a gigantic mimesis. Mind is its mimetic device.

576.   All things are or are not. When things are they arise from being designated as things. When things are not they're not designated as things. Such a distinction is impossible in Zen. For Zen is thinking through, seeing through, and emptying the mind of content...

577.   A clasping hand calls another clasping hand. It calls again...

578.   Morning is neither hollow, nor stuffed. As it reverberates towards high noon the ten bells of the shadow-moon vanishes into thin air.

579.   Words: even those crowned with a full moon are banned from Zen books.

580.   Dusting the old snow of fresh flakes. Far from the city's life for a week already: hearing incantations with every breeze.

581.   Clad in a flower shape the emptiness invokes your mind for a visitation. Use the same ticket as you pass away...

582.   Things move by virtue of their absolute manifestation. That is, things are always what they are and so they always manifest their true nature. By using so many intermediary devices – feelings, emotions, language, intellect – man manifests a nature-less nature. A man can find his true nature by shunning the work of those intermediary devices. This asks for a tremendous will, (discipline, and continue efforts - doubts and frustrations set aside - and life depravation). As you get awakened you realize that things move by virtue of their absolute manifestation. To point at the absolute-North is to point at North.

583.   Row nuts are better when they're eaten row. Fried nuts are better when they're eaten fried.

584.   The grass in the morning doesn't know about the sheep coming to graze at noon. The sheep at noon leaves a footprint for wolf hunting at night. Are you escorting your life or your life escorts you?

585.   The river stream knows the name of the rocks on its path. You could hear the calls as the water mounts the stony hill…

586.   The lead feet of those trying to flee a moment of immortality…

587.   Zen is a life time project. When you're done with it the absolute comes into existence in front of your eyes. There could be mingled signals "to watch" all the way before you get there. When it happens the experience is ecstatic. You'll remember it for the rest of your life though the road to get there will erode and gradually become unknown.

588.   Until the snow reveals its deep.

589.   One day I felt empty. I said to myself: Keep feeling like that and you'll get there… I always thought that one should seek nothingness outside one's body and mind. By seeking nothingness there is neither good nor evil to be dealt with. Though nothingness is not the absolute truth. Neither inner, nor outer…

590.   Throwing out empty words, then getting mute: downhill you have a choice; uphill you don't…

591.   Self awareness is always present in a way or another. Anybody has it. Zen awareness has also the attribute of teaching one to become aware of his awareness.

592.   Even imagined attachments could be detrimental to awakening.

593.   The question was if "I could still feel that I am what I am when I become one with the emptiness?" and the answer was that Zen cannot answer this question. If the answer was "You could still feel that you are who you used to be when you become one with the emptiness", it would really mean that "You didn't become one with the emptiness". Same for the answer "You could not feel…"

594.   Like birds' empty bones are designed to be light in flight, so your thoughts should be. Flying high with no eyes to look at and no ears to listen to…

595.   An eye must lift the sun upward to understand the sunrise. As one becomes inclusive to things the knowledge becomes quieter. To understand what a tree is one has to become a tree. Just tasting the honey you know what honey is, though if you really want to know what it is you'd have to merge with it, like a bee does. Go back to words, look at all those captive things that struggle to get free. If not uttered, truth gets through a mind untainted, untouched, unnoticed, and ungraspable - like a green locust flying through the tall grass.

596.   You can drop your attachments as you understand what they are. They're usually hidden in your senses. In desire one finds suffering. Even those born yesterday…

597.   Nose is a perfect instrument for smell. As the smell gets it Buddha can't refrain from smiling. No contribution – no retribution…

598.   Desires can't be wiped off one's flesh. A carcass can't be rinsed out of Karma.

599.   The absolute doesn't need a definition. If anything has to be said about it is that when one looks at it there is no "I" there, no living bodies and no developing phenomena. Energy, particles and equations… As you see it nothing could be rationalized or determined. As you explain it using a mental process, this very process makes of the absolute an incomplete advent.

600.   Walking in one direction try to be last to follow. Walking in the opposite direction try to be last to follow. Arriving later you'd live longer…

601.   Use what you got to do what you can, and nothing else. Well tuned water pipes sound like a bamboo cluster. Scarecrows adorn fields to guard the wheat. Potentials are as numerous as the sun drenched summer rains. Rare occurrences mean rare opportunities: this is Zen…

602.   Without a doubt, seating still, living with each breath the universe in manifestation.

603.   Logic depends sensibly on abstractions and operations with abstractions. Zen depends on leftovers: abstractions that could never be chewed, operations that are willfully discarded…

604.   Satori can be attained even by men born with goat feet. It's not the dance that arouses the awakening but the thoughts that know no dance.

605.   Koan: The more it lifts you up from the ground, the dipper you'd lay under the sod.

606.   The birth is not, the growth is not, the death is not… A blanket covers a hollow every night. Though horses are neighing and birds swallow dew drops, what gets in never gets out and what gets out never gets in. As it comes no more – it goes no more. Present, present, present! Watch…

607.   A Buddha ate here…

608.   Spontaneity and honesty make a wrong preaching rest with the angels. Forethought and dishonesty makes a good preaching rest with the devil.

609.   There are so many stories one could recount about absolute… And only a few of them adequately describe what the absolute has to do with the world we're living in. The road to suchness has a right of entry into it: it is called relative…

610.   Why good words are more desirable when bad words are trailing the same perfect path?

611.   The bamboo sound is emitted from a secret chamber built in the stem's marrow. On shallow water the chamber slides down. In higher waters it moves up. Sometimes in its movement up the chamber exits the stem. There is no sound left then, no lips to exclaim "awe"…

612.   Quiet your inner mind then quiet your outer mind. What happens? Are you still alive?

613.   Are there any words worth uttering, beside those teaching us not to utter?

614.   What have you done with your life? God ceased to be around. With every breeze the bony boat is screeching. Water had silenced the old path but not the new…

615.   A meal in one's mind, another meal in one's heart. No meal should be served twice...

616.   Cutting down a form makes myriads of newly born forms raise their head out of emptiness.

617.   When with a compassionate mind you hurt somebody the angry response comes back to you as a compassionate arrow. The more compassionate you are the deeper the arrow hurts. When it does, stay firm on your way, don't err.

618.   To halt concepts entering your mind you'd have to draw a firewall circle around your senses...

619.   A sutra is as tangible as a saw: it cuts attachments by cutting your mental handcuffs. Echoes of pleasure, pain and fear getting suddenly carried away. You ascertain: Emptiness is larger than the universe since it is a precursor to it. And if emptiness is the ultimate essence it means that the absolute grasped through a relative experience "of any kind" is an illusion.

620.   Tasting nothingness: touching and then spitting the knowledge with a tip of one's tongue.

621.   Nirvana: As white as a lotus flower, many times more white than a snowflake... Then the surrounding light with its blue hue, many times more blue than the sky. And then, the ground, many times shinier than a lotus leaf, many times vaster than the moonlight. Everything - so perfect, many times more perfect than what words could ever disclose.

622.   Sun climbs, flowers lift up their head to see the summit. A teaspoon of eternity stock...

623.   The elder Buddha that lives on the mountain peak can see without eyes and talk without words. No sound could penetrate his ears; no smell goes up his nostrils. His tongue has lost its taste of thirst and hunger. (The toothless wind stirred by a smile…)

624.   Step in and you're in danger. Step out and you're in danger. Buddhas, knowing no pity…

625.   The riddle of the universe: where voices are silenced…

626.   Instead of saying no to "yes" and no to "no" to avoid discrimination you'd better say neither "yes" nor "no" and take the vow of mental silence.

627.   They say that mirrors don't have memory. Neither has the image being mirrored…

628.   If you really believe in immortality wait until it happens. Do not rush. Though there is a nuisance here: if you rush you may get it too soon, if you don't you may get it too late…

629.   The authentication of the enlightenment makes you a pro: not a degree but a pedigree. The next patriarch is roaming the Highland…

630.   The question about the possibility that any of you may attain realization would pop up before each meditation. For years to go, the exhaustion from Zen work and renewed doubts will purify your brain of your ego (I) and your attachments. One day you'd let go. At such a moment all the work you have done will glow into your inner-self beyond limitations…

631.   One sunset but one thousand years of sunrise. It lets the whole living pass through (and through). Ships go down, stars get extinct; no footmarks on the neighboring wasteland.

632.   When you get older the life you let pass by is lost. The life left to be lived is not lost yet. Keep losing it, steadily…

633.   The boundless mind returning homeward: the moon seems lit up again, tossing flakes in the gentle breeze. Mind is in agreement with *thus:* empty sparrows come to swell on the windy branch.

634.   The intellect is the part of one's brain where the knowledge calls the shots. Though the world one is staring at is as-is the intellect and the intuition take different paths. The intuition spawns in the same waters but when it comes to "knowing" it flies miles away. By not knowing what it hatches a cuckoo-bird gives life to the unknown.

635.   The age of understanding lives in you. The age of spirituality lives around. If you could penetrate, there is no more understanding, no more spirituality. The universe, hanging from a hair.

636.   An untainted mind has no traces to follow. If it eats it learns with the food what Dharma is. If it acts it isn't the mind that would make the causation come into place. As far as Buddha goes, Buddha goes so far. Spring flowers fade and fall; the journey of a cloud makes a shadow express without words what light is.

637.   This is heavy: At a conjunction point between a viewer and a picture a picture asserts what it represents. To make a picture stop representing the viewer stops the assertion to reach the conjunction point.

638.   Flamingo: Plunging from the sky into the ocean. Deep and deeper… Pearls of water, a fish struggling between two long legs. The emptiness mirror reflecting (on) a catch…

639.   One fold! Never mind the mind…

640.   All living things follow the path towards liberation. If not with their tongue (as a rooster does) then with their mind (as an ox does). Being a liberated human is an effect of a higher cause: no-tongue, no-mind!

641.   Each flake, an universe. No crows overhead. The typewriter sounds: "crow, crow…"

642.   Trying to materialize and solidify your life as if you could coat a ball of air. Let it be and watch every step. Each moment is foreverness. Life is utter love…

643.   The rendering of "I" and "non-I" ends when both seem remote. Seen from a significant distance they look alike.

644.   To be close to the truth and not knowing it. Or to be far from the truth and knowing it. Though when the awakening happens the truth knows better than us about what we know or not know.

645.   Surprised by the speed with which the day vanished and trying to slow down the night's flow. On the surface the past day is still around.

646.   Cleaning the beach sand of water lilies…

647.   The eyeballs could picture the whole infinite emptiness: piles of landscapes, frozen in a photographic indifference.

648.   If the ultimate reality is none other but the relative reality it is almost certain that you can awake one day in one and the next day in the other. Zen teaches that the relative reality is a false reality while the absolute reality is the true one. After awakening though, both realities are evenly true and nevertheless one cannot exist without the other.

649.   Emptiness, when capitalized, becomes centered in phenomena. Like everything else, emptiness is no-thing of a special thing…

650.   A word steals an identity. Leaves already fallen fall one more time. The taste of dust is left to the wind to know. In sleep the sun marks are gone. No one can see this but the one who doesn't resemble a face…

651.   The sudden opening of the third eye… Empty sight in plain view…

652.   As far as the living goes, nature's greatest invention is the pain. That's how one could be certain that life is a real thing. Practicing Zen makes the pain look like a perfect opportunity to get rid of your attachment.

653.   The primal leaves sprouting from a seed still unknown to the tree…

654.   Before trying to know yourself eat something, drink as you please, do your toilet needs as if today was the last day in your life. In fact, yesterday was the last day in your life that you're honoring now by living in the present.

655.   The essence of the world is prior and also beyond all utterances.

656.   The mind is another _universal dimension,_ like time and space are.

657.   Not being with yourself is for some a lifetime feeling. The secret to keep yourself around is letting the self do the walking and talking. You just watch…

658.   Every buzz of an albatross stands for a miracle buzz. The buzz word keeps the miracle hidden.

659.   While you sleep let the door of awareness ajar. While you're awake open it wide…

660.   While cleaning the oven the fumes overwhelmed my nose. This happened on the wake of my awakening.

661.   Nobody knows what is in the fish's mind while getting trapped in a fishnet. Though we may know what is in a man's mind getting trapped in a manhole…

662.   Surrender your mind to emptiness: snow flakes falling on a fire. Flakes don't melt, the fire isn't put out.

663.   The indefinable act of blossoming…

664.   The truth that can never be proved is true. The false that can never be proved is true. To agree or not is not the point: God's hands are clothed in all phenomena that there could be conceived.

665.   Don't let a prescribed path to enlightenment to act as a substitute to the secret path of your own mind.

666.   There is no within without "without". To put God in a Zen context is like walking with bare feet on hot coals. But then, how would you explain Satori? If emptiness is a given it is neither imperative acknowledging it or rejecting it. The nearer you draw to it the faster it escapes between the fingers of your mind. You cannot say that Satori confirms or refutes the emptiness existence while the moon is still hanging above your head and the boat that you tried on its maiden ride to the sea returned to the shore unscathed. If that is what you need, a messenger to step in and create all the manifestations, why not choosing God? Nothingness

and God is like your two ears. (Dualism?) You can turn one of them to the direction of a sound but hear with both. God rallies all the Birds of the Emptiness to hatch phenomena.

667.   A talking tongue asks for consent. A quiet tongue is inscrutable…

668.   Affinities smell of attachments. Revelations smell of detachments. Though to see the essence of one thing is like picking cotton: roll the white ball, take it out of its captivity. Did the thorns make your finger bleed? Then the essence you are looking for was tainted. Try to reach it with your lips with no tongue coming to your aid. Two things at once: one done, the other undone. (Dualism?). Then there in such a thing as "the essence of one thing only".

669.   Often the mind is like a sword. You could cut onions and fish with it, though it was meant to use it on Buddha's head.

670.   In the circle where all Buddhas live the sun has become a vain thing though the moon wouldn't be able to shine without it. That is because lies are mounting with the raising sun. Soft whispers about the Way should be heard only when the moon arrives.

671.   The river talking to the fallen leaves: It sounds like an _embrace_, limitless though, in its _absence_…

672.   A layman should be concerned with the way he/she serves himself/herself and his/her family, group, society. There is a moral base of this world that he/she must be aware of and respect: it's called compassion…Only after the prior utterances make sense, Zen makes sense. If the above statements sounded too dry listen to this: When thoughts collide a light flashes and a sound is emitted. Who's seeing the light? Who is hearing the

sound? You let the thoughts go – compassion follows them until they exit…

673.   Waves unfold the sea. Glows unfold the moon. Words unfold phenomena. Phenomena unfold the mind.

674.   Life – a trail of illusions, one illusion hiding the next one. If one asked what illusion had most influenced my life I'd invariably say that God was… Zen wasn't! Zen didn't even possess enough authority to make me stop whispering my morning prayer. But Zen helped me find the secret road where things are unequivocal and the essence a matter at hand…

675.   Life is for Zen converts what death is for drug addicts…

676.   The very emptiness is an eternal living. Since it is eternal, it is beyond birth and death. Mind is its resplendent eye. Phenomena are like shuttles sent by emptiness everywhere. Homeward returning may take, for some, eons. Ghostly forests burnt to ashes, roaring oceans emptied of water, the moonlight on the vanished surface still shining.

677.   Absolute and relative are one. This utterance is a thought. But thoughts and thinking are not valid instruments to see the ultimate truth. That's why koans (like Mu) are used to help the awakening, to push away any thinking process and let a sound of insignificance ("Mu") to reveal through intuition the absolute truth (beyond the mind-world). But again, the last utterance is a thought. That's why koans (like Mu) are used in Zen practice…

678.   In order to refine the ashes you'd have to burn them one more time.

679.   Killing your thinking you kill your life. (Not to think, not to make waves, not to move on). It's like being on a board of a raft with no compass to follow and no hope to see dry land again.

That's the risk to go beyond time - facing noisy day thieves and silent night pirates.

680.   To Zen, *doubt is always skeptical but unbounded* while certainty is, most of the time, unquestionable and a hindrance.

681.   In the South the would-be wind blows hard. In the North the would-be wind blows hard. This is what is happening in a mind's deceitfulness. In front of my window the ageless tree reminds me of how many Buddhas used to eat their bowl of rice over there. Those times are still making the grass sprout around; firebugs are still making it glow, the chicken stand to attention listening to the rooster's song of the day. What else you could hope for? From their beyond birth and death situations no Buddhas are going to descend and listen to your grievances. Invoke a white elephant and you'll see the elephant rushing to meet up with you. Invoke a black elephant and you'll see the elephant rushing to meet up with you. Invoke Buddha and you'll get laughter. Hit him with a broom; throw a crow egg to his face (crows are crowing!). Fearful to say that Buddha was God? Than you better stay away from Satori!

682.   Mind traveling in silence, like smell travels…

683.   Fable: One day while walking a Zen master met half-man-half-fox Zen creatures. They could understand the words of man and the howls of foxes. To respect their Zen vows they wouldn't talk but they'd howl at ease.

684.   Three phases of Zen: I know *that*, I don't know *that-or-the-I*, I know that…

685.   The nest on the hilltop was blown by the wind. No more eggs to hatch and the mother bird is nowhere to be found. Need not be alive if in flight…

686.   If mind should have any dimension this would be "height!" That is, a dimension not dependent on anything but the clouds. When clouds disperse, Buddha appears.

687.   A rule to those who give presents: "Give only what you think may be of use…" One day I decided to clean up my house of unnecessary items. Each item I wanted to throw out – all of a sudden – became a warm presence. You can't make justice even to emptiness…

688.   Duality gets chastised; the oneness gets a warm welcome.

689.   Before time and space ever existed there was no path to choose although the Way shined everywhere.

690.   Lassa: Turning outward: Rivers of phenomena, enough to feed innumerable tongues. Why even an atom can't be part of a talk. Is it that Zen idea that - though the name claims to be the real thing - a name never succeeds to call the real object. Who are you? And you say a name. If you knock on a door the question sounds identical: Who are you? At night names of flowers are carried by their fragrance. When it snows here, it snows everywhere. Buds turn into flowers and what "blossoming" means anyway? If you keep it still, it is foreverness. Why foreverness? Words are not a relief here. Lost trails covered by the late snow. Buying bread, buying wood: trades are simple when the local customs are known. Who are you, again? A couple of more years to share smiles. The wilderness listens to the wind with indifference. From a flake-of-snow's point of view you feel like you could hold the whole universe in your palm. One small universe wrapped in a flake. Turning inward, where words move thoughts without ending…

691.   I do not know how tomorrow is going to look like. Though I would tell you with almost utter certainty and clarity

how yesterday looked like. First call of life – voluntary suffering… Go no further…

692.   You part your lips; the breath comes out as an unspoken word.

693.   A gentle passion (though with no attachments) could sense the Buddha nature in a body at the moment when the evanescent sperm is free to go. Same Zen question though pops up: If the sperm head passes thorough the window is its tail still going to be left out in cold?

694.   The pledge of poverty: Sign this and you'll sense it! Don't sign it and you'll be lost forever.

695.   Zazen could become a source of delusion and an obstacle to awakening if zeal to continue it comes from the ego's need to get reinforced. Rather than building an altruistic heart Zen practitioners compete on building Zen muscles. When this happens you'd have to ask yourself this question: "Am I sincere in my pursuit of liberation or do I use Zen in order to put myself in a position of superiority to others?" If the latter is true, the strange combination of ego grooming combined with absolute-intake will fail you.

696.   After you get enlightened life is not as lovely as it used to be. Part of the illusion is now ashes. Things that couldn't be wiped off your body cry for attention. Hunger, thirst, lust don't make sense anymore. Searching for the feathers of the departed birds? The wide mirrors around the water look like shields hiding dead frogs. The tea pot lid rattles like a lost song of life found dead. Be careful: you may get what you asked for…

697.   Dalai Lama: I would welcome him to talk if he wouldn't say a thing…

698.   Heavy stuff, not for a light reading: The absolute transcends the absolute, that is, it can neither be affirmed by one's mind (in a positive or negative way) nor negated by one's intuition. The idea is that the intuition is used to confirm what it reveals to itself; that makes the intuition's subject a fetish to be sanctioned by one's mind anyway. So, if absolute exists it is as defective as the device used to look at it: intuition. On the other hand if intuition – with its defective insight – "knows" what "it" missed in its revelation it therefore already "knows it". The absolute, if it exists becomes part of the intuition carrier, which is "us". If we think of ourselves as being part of a relative world, this world implicitly makes the absolute a relative matter, though it transcends our relative world and also the absolute revealed by us. What awareness shows is exactly that the absolute lives within us (the relative world) though it transcends not only the relative world but the absolute itself - once the absolute averts from being known.

699.   Rain falls upon rains upon rains… And then what? It calls the roots to take some action for what is worthy of phenomena…

700.   If you say that the sun is detached I'd say that the moon is attached. It would be marvelous to see a moon not following its path, though Zen would not allow that. What depends on causes is attached to its effect. While chasing liberation there is only one way out of it: returning to the clear face of the emptiness when the first phenomena began to unfold. Could you afford that? To lose a life in order to be part of what is not… Live fully, get attached! What a marvel!? Die slowly, get detached! What a marvel!?

701.   Canned Buddha-nature in wine…

702.   An unorthodox ox: Liberation from Self: Impossible! Liberation from ego: Impossible! Liberation from mind: Impossible! Realizing illusion: Possible! To seek separation from It is to merge with It. To seek the true nature is to depart from true nature. Drop now your body and mind! Did you? Don't let them

fool around for long, for you might need both of them when you go back to the office...

703.   In the context of awareness (seeing It - as) what can be expressed about it is what is missed as "It": the odor, the taste, the touch, the hearing, the view and the mind. If all these senses would be all visible they'd become invisible to the awakened, and so on and so forth. Since the senses are channels to reasoning they're shut off. And if what is missed in realization defines my reality could I say that the absolute reality is the same as the relative one? If awakening is what the world is after - the "great death" – wouldn't be wise to think of our life the way it is - an "It" now and then, here and there – as the greatest miracle of the universe in transformation. A moment of living might - in fact - dwarf an awakening to the absolute truth by three to five inches.

704.   The trees are yellow and the sky is black. Same Zen paraphernalia. Seeing the grass green and the sky blue doesn't automatically qualify you for a Zen degree.

705.   The right hand talks to the left hand: "I'm your right hand!" it says. Like armless men wrestling…

706.   The awakened state of mind is oblivious of mind.

707.   I was watching a swarm of wasps flying up and down at unison and I thought of a series of numbers following some internal rules that keep them appearing always ordered though each time in a different order. All of a sudden a gust of wind moved the whole swarm away. Then I saw the swarm dispersing. Life is similar to that story: gathering knowledge and ordering it using some rules… What Zen does is letting them go free. Free from rules thoughts are living in their absoluteness: "One" as part of "It", and "It" as part of "One".

708.   Daily duties done, the rest of the time given to prayers. No time to live kind of life during this reincarnation. I wish Karma would have brought me back as a frog that during the day invokes the unseen moon while at night it croaks obscenities at the seen moon: oak, oaf, oik, gawk, hick, yokel, bumpkin... If the wind is made-up Zen, my wind is the true one.

709.   Breath is the only thing that belongs to you and you only. Everything else is very much like yours but belongs to the rest of the world.

710.   Crows are quarrelling: No snow in sight...

711.   Awakening: Nobody can help you here until you let go. To do that you let thoughts pass by, trying not to chain an antecedent thought to a subsequent thought.

712.   Shut off your sensations, perceptions, judgments, and cognition so that you can experience the "great awakening" and so reach the eternal way of Zen sages. As you come back use your sensations, perceptions, and judgment again to live the Way. The suffering may still be there, though different...

713.   One harvests when the floods are getting shallow...

714.   To prove that attainment is speakable I'd like to speak about attainment using the English idiom: First a word about economics: If your life is worth a penny your awakening is worth ½ penny. Now, to see the ultimate truth for ½ penny is an "unthinkable" bargain.

715.   What's the secret of life? The eyes see the road, the ears secure the ride. A mind and a body bearing love! Duality everywhere though birth and death – not abiding together – are equal.

716.   Emptiness, phenomena: At the right moment they could harmoniously mix.

717.   The irreverence of the objective view…

718.   Modern science: seedless fruits, chirpless birds… Well known phenomena minus one: $(\prod-1)$ where $\prod$ = phenomena. The wind peers at one with empty eyes.

719.   Koan: A sword would rust if left idling in an old kill.

720.   You can compare your Zen practice with an absolute darkness of a road on which you walk incessantly hopping to see a light. As you finally see it you feel amused: so much work just to see the universe getting packed in an endless flash photo. You would still vaguely remember what you couldn't describe.

721.   In the shade of the hut a sudden blaze: "Extinguish your thoughts so that you could feel cooler…"

722.   Changeable thoughts are like poison to meditation. Though, if you scare away a thought it would surface - later on - stronger. Imagine always that your thoughts are dead earthworms. No need to take care of them, they can take care of themselves.

723.   The caveman walks out: outpouring light!

724.   The sky is not designed to house libraries… One can find the whole information about the whole universe in every grain of sand.

725.   Whatever is on the outside generates phenomena. Whatever is within generates discrimination. When one transcends both, the inner and the outer world, the One comes into view. Even if the view is clear, it is not yet "thus". If you project "this"

you leave a trace of your mind on it. If – while having no mental aim - "thus" appears, run for your life.

726.   The roots of delusion are channeling beams of truth: This axiom asks for a Sutra reading.

727.   Clouds in the water don't obscure its bottom. The valley's fog doesn't obscure the mountain peak.

728.   The more you distil the less substance you find.

729.   Fresh blossoms scattered by whirlwinds. Why a scattering is faceless? Upon what branches the scattered flowers hang? Cleansing spring of phenomena while shielding a flower from whirlwind.

730.   The impermanence is permanent. And vice versa…

731.   Year round, peeling white flakes off the moonrise. Not knowing "I", yet bringing it in, as a guest. A new suit to fit world's ways...

732.   With each word you cut out - the more of a saying comes true…

733.   Talking about correct posturing, correct bodily and mentally foundations of Zen practice and forgetting to say that the awakening doesn't have a subject matter per se. When there is no distinction between knower and known what would be a subject matter per se anyway.

734.   Clinging but letting go is the process of attaining a selfless "self".

735.   A circle has multiple meanings in Zen. Among others it could mean perfection (enlightenment). It is fair to say then that Zen developed a symbolic language to create meanings. The

meaning of a Zen gesture is sometimes what it images: raising a finger for instance means attention. Though an image or a gesture could have multiple meanings. The images were used to avoid talking in concepts. It may suggest that symbolic images are less discriminatory and by the extent of freedom they leave for interpretation they are more "Zen like devices". The Zen master holds his staff (hossu) up to signify, his fly whisk to threaten, a stick to underscore, etc. Some answers to tough Zen questions are either signs penciled in sand or in air, or sudden (sometimes brusque or brutal) gestures. Most of them are repetitively used and become a stamp of simplicity of what an answer might look like to an intellectual question: drawing a line or a circle, kicking a water bucket, and what is important – not using words to give a spoken reply.

736.   If Zen would be available in the animal world a leopard would try to get rid of his fur spots. Even in such a natural world Zen would function as an anti-dote to fashion.

737.   Non-Zen fair joke: Clawed people can skin a peach easier than un-clawed people. Though un-clawed people make better prostitutes.

738.   Saying with keys: Either roiling in a stormy water (of thoughts) or shining on a clear water surface (of thinking) the moon is a moon, while Buddha's mind is a mind carrying white bones under a pink flesh.

739.   Awakening: Seeing "thus" that cannot be known…

740.   Life in its ordinary aspects: every bite – a pain, every sip – a pain.

741.   Again Karma: I threw by mistake a bag of vegetables into the freezer. The next day the oranges had a frozen orange hue while the blueberries had a frozen blue hue.

742.   Words against facts: Hunting for meaningful Zen poetry like "reeds in frost bloom" or "birds, nesting marble eggs" and finding instead a Biblical no-say utterance: guilt is not what a tongue says but what a tongue does…

743.   When a potter dies the clay takes a break. When a body dies the mind takes a break. When a pot breaks the water takes a break. Potter, body, pot: just vessels. Everything else – a world either fashionable or fathomless…

744.   The oncness of the great IT: Mind cannot explore the absolute. What mind was taught to do was to explain the world as it is seen: a chain of successive things and facts located in space and time and having a beginning and an ending. But the intuition knows that the otherness essence (the essence of the outer world) and the innerness essence (the essence of the inner world – true nature) are ONE. Also, the intuition knows that the "nature" of oneness is beyond what thought and non-thought could reveal. That's why koan is so important - to break one's intuitive gate open. To attain awakening by practicing Zen through reading and comprehension is like using a mouse trap to catch God.

745.   Zen gorgeous joke: Two Satori seeking monkeys were climbing up a tree, suspended like a bridge above a gorge. As they reached the crown of the tree, the tree got uprooted. One of the monkey thought that she'd be better off is she'd *let go*, the other one thought that she'd be better off if she'd *hold fast.* Guess: Which one died and which one did otherwise.

746.   Self and the other mean duality. No self and no other mean NOT. Knowing one's Self means knowing one side of duality.

747.   Maturity is not a windowless motel room where life proceeds unchecked. The illusion of a lost childhood looms around, fragments of passions that are now surfacing as pure poetry. How sad that enlightenment gives one such a relief from what past would have meant if not forgotten. Dipped in what a few know about and still crying for the silenced past. For a wise man a lost life could sometimes look like a chilling thing. Unfortunately, this is the only real puzzle: life is too short to let you choose your way. Walk along your mistakes! Take them as what is given and have no regrets. Thousand eons from now you'll have another chance to fail.

748.   Buddha's arms outstretched in the emptiness draws blazing thoughts in a Zen mind. (The eternal fuel that burns without appetite or sustenance).

749.   For a Zen mind what is external is not welcome. What is internal is welcome only when it is in union with the external. That is, it should either be the very beginning of the universe or the very end of it.

750.   The unearthed finger of Master Gutei is doing even now Zen work: still arresting, still teaching suddenness. His finger in the air stops the waves of the vast cosmic ocean to a still.

751.   The difference between austerity and begging is "one full sutra length".

752.   Every moment is the result of previous moments. Every thing is the result of neighboring another thing. The earlier sentence is called "timely context", the later is called "spatial context". There are an infinite number of contexts. Emptiness stands for all as an empty bowl fitting an even bigger empty bowl,

ad infinitum. (In other words: "Emptiness stands for all as an empty bowl that can feed billions of Buddhas begging for food").

753.   Zen is concerned with dissolving your ego into an infinite number of fragments of nothingness. An infinite number follows...

754.   Satori occurs when there are no more relations with reality to be awakened, in the sense of what's right or wrong, what's this or that. If unborn creatures are definitely in a state of Satori by not knowing, those born could get it by letting the knowing go.

755.   Things will return into nothingness until there'll be nothing left or rather "nothing will be". All noises, thinking, dancing will go when the bones go. Rivers, mountains, stars – going with the bones also. The olive tree had a good teacher: use the spring to ensue making flowers. Use the summer to ensue making fruits. Rebirth is in the books: it is delivered with a pit.

756.   Every smile creates a new idea of a smile. That says that each smile is independent of another smile. Without a smile there is still the idea of a smile. When you can see clear through things and thoughts everything will still be there though nothing would be perceived.

757.   A question cannot be heard, an answer cannot be told! The battle plan to conquer the universe is held secret behind everyone's skull.

758.   Emptiness is less than dust and also more... Tracing the dust to Buddha; and then tracing Buddha to what things are when they're not named and what they're not when they're named.

759.   When you see Buddha it is essential to understand what you're seeing and ask for guidance. Such a happening is not to be found in a canned Zen.

760.   All day long I waited for awakening to happen. I could feel it like a breeze in my bones. There were other signs that it would happen: the water stopped flowing, the air turned translucent blue and the gate's shadow that I overlooked before faded to almost nothing. It didn't happen though. Standing lonely there I understood that patience, when looked at is like a dead horse under a whip. The warmth of the sun rising is still coming from the East. What a miracle: not to be enlightened so that I could understand what is It.

761.   Reaching the surface of the lake a rain drop still thinks of itself as being just a rain drop.

762.   You surely remember from the physics lesson on light spectrum that a rotating disk creates white light out of a rainbow of colors. Zen is like the white invisible and unifying light. The relative is its counterpart of infinite number of "matching colors".

763.   At any moment Buddha could rise from the muddy waters. Mudhead! One thought to wash it and you'll plunge back into darkness.

764.   One may surely inquire if there are words which could magically help one to know the ultimate truth, and how one could do that, as if the ultimate truth needed a special way to be harvested. One of those words is Mu. Use a permanent black marker and paint with it a thick black line over the present paragraph so that you'll not be able to see what was written under it ever again. This is like planting a seed in the soil and then forgetting about it. In a couple of weeks listen to the snowy wind with a wolf's ears. The spring is coming; Mu is going to get new leaves.

765.   If it is finite it is utterly infinite. If it is infinite it is utterly finite. Small before it grows, it goes unchangeable.

766.   Waiting for the unexpected to happen I fell asleep during Zazen. Then I had this dream that my mind had melted within my sight. The sitting pillow, stained with tears was the only proof that I slept well.

767.   Talking is not an option; a muted reflection is not an option either. Understanding is extraneous. Remember though: (This is It! Just It! This is just It! Just this is it!)

768.   The universe's hair-splitting decision between being born to die or being born and live beyond death.

769.   Is the mirror obscured by dust or just the image?

770.   To sever your attachments you'd have to accept to be misled by events and mistreated by facts. They're all part of your Karma, though you'd diminish their effect if you stopped debating them.

771.   Illusion riddled awakening: present interrupted.

772.   What is unheard is also unknown? What is unknown in the enlightenment domain? What is unheard of?...

773.   The living path goes in the opposite direction to the awakening path. What would you choose? Weeds grow inside the six walls of what's contained. Knowing what time is you know when you're going to die. As far as space goes not even a canned fish longing for the ocean could tell you where it is going to happen. The roots that grew around Buddha's bones may echo his words in the situation. Can it be so simple that what life is – is "this" – and that nothing else would follow? So simple, you might say, so magnificent! Faded leaves as beautiful as spring leaves! God's design was to limit the life span of those who suffer:

donkey that carry heavy loads - for instance - die young. I learned lately that a cloud could fly you over the fields of sorrow and that a clear sky with its cloudless claws could devour you. My choice though cannot be whispered in a living ear.

774.   Weeds grow faster at night while blossoming is asleep.

775.   One hundred years ago this stem was in bloom. The breeze is still wafting its petals. Roosters that used to perpetually call the sun are gone too. Mind can start now playing with what it thinks it is true in what there-is-not.

776.   In a world of realization a Zen frog talks to a Zen Mule: "Every wave", the frog says, "is alike any other wave!" The Zen Mule responds: "Every path to the mountain is alike any other path!" The Zen Master intervenes: "The wave of paths is the same as the path of waves". Obviously they all laugh at Zen. (It's easy to laugh after you get there).

777.   To cut an infinite cat in two pieces is beyond comprehension. You'll get two cats, all right, with everything they need, heads, tails, plastic white mice to play with… That's how duality was born out of Oneness, though…

778.   Once all knowledge is taken from you, you could hear the vertigo created by emptiness. The cat cut in two is still a one-piece-cat. A mouth sworn to silence announces heaven's great opening.

779.   The source meets the river in the woods. The moon is also there, six feet of waving wax. An owl cries aloud at all these…

780.   Self-manifesting and self-I are practically equivalent. The no-self and no-I are poles apart from both of them. True-self is the self revealed after the attachment to the self is cut off.

781.   Phenomena are offerings that cannot be refused. It's magic without a magician. Show me an illusion and I'll take it for the real thing. That's how phenomena appear to a mental siege: now, cut the mental off so that you could deal with phenomena directly, above conditioning. As you inhale air the phenomena are there, as you exhale air the phenomena vanish. Inhale is like filling it in, exhale is like emptying it out. A Zen law says that though you can penetrate a melon with your finger the "melon reality" remains impenetrable, even when it is emptied out. Did the emptiness that created the melon also created birds, animals, stars and all? Every grain of sand reminds us of mankind. Every moment reminds us of eternity. Would all phenomena be taken out of their captivity you'd see all as ashes moving inward and outward and the whole world vanishing into a point of everlasting return.

782.   The eaves are dripping: listening to each drop of water hitting the windowpane my senses became so sharp that dropping seemed impossible. Listening is surely a natural aspect of the universe; hearing is not.

783.   Emptiness has so many vacancies that it will take billion years for one to fill them up. Although, if you don't fill them up now the eternity might draw closer. Now, try to see what happens, clearly, not just by interpreting the metaphor.

784.   Mixing Zen clay to make Zen bricks.

785.   Leaves are scattering, the tall grass is moving in concert; same wind – both ways. Flying, back and forth, a stray crow…

786.   To be thrown in a world where are neither you nor I and still be able to look at the unattainable path with a living eye.

787.   It's easy to ask what your original face was before any of your ancestors had being conceived. What about your face now? Blind man – seer dog! Seer man – blind dog.

788.   A cow that breastfeed a calf makes the milk price go up. A cow that is butchered makes the price of the veal meat go down. (Dodging critics saying that economics are not among the orthodox Zen disciplines). Is there any difference between a Buddha statue made out of gold and the one made out of clay?

789.   The worlds are equivalent. The words are not.

790.   Whispering is worse than saying things aloud: not having enough water to swim but imitating a ship noise entering the Great Way…

791.   Pausing for a meaning you lose the track of the anonymous trip. You "know" the thing and the thing "knows" you. It's like identifying a coast that a boat could see while you're walking the grounds.

792.   The sound of one hand clapping or the sound of one universe moving past. What was the moon before turning into a polished penny? What was Christ? An infinite number of universes but one supper! One hand clapping, the other hand listening to the sound…

793.   While things are permanently clanging the mind does the same. Between a sunrise and a sunset there is no aftermath. Substance nowhere to be found, gaps nowhere…

794.   In an absolute world what one knows one cannot remember. It's like being dead and trying to react to people's crying and laughing around your death bed.

795.   When a child says "no" the sky is getting sealed. When a child says "yes" the mountains voice the world in the making. To guide a child tightly one has to understand his world: is it yes? Even at the beginning of the world moons went on shining, clouds dragged a boat to the nearest shore. The adult life, what a fading illusion… Moons go asleep in clouds, boats miss the shore…

796.   The rule that rules out every other rule is that a brick made out of emptiness is the manifestation of the all included beginnings. Though the same brick could be its vanishing point…

797.   A Zen pupil asks the Zen Master: "What is the difference between hot and cold?" The master answers: "One is hot the other is cold". "Then what is the difference between hot and lukewarm?" asks the pupil. "One is hot the other is cold", answers the Master. (This is called Zen knowledge by eliminating the intermediary degrees). If one asked what the difference between hot and hot is, the answer still holds.

798.   In the midstream the water evaporates under the scorching sun. Flying around fish seems unshaken. The relative eye of the swirl is swallowing the mist…

799.   Certainly, those who know can't talk. Then, there is nothing else to know, until they talk again.

800.   The mind invents the world: what could happen is already happening. The veil is up on the wooden mast. There is no debate where it sails; mistakenly one thinks that there is no land to reach beyond the invariable hindsight.

801.   The emptiness is like a cattle roaming free on an infinite pasture. The cattle owner conceals himself under Buddha's mask. Remember, an absolute moo and a relative moo sound similar.

802.   Thousand Buddhas marching, carrying wood! When fire is needed few wooden boats adventure to reach a cold shore…

803.   The absolute is mirrored in the world of physics: water is an example – as it flows, it gets transformed from ice into vapor, but remains fundamentally what it is. Self behaves in identical ways. So does life.

804.   The sky was already darkening when the big bird arrived. The barking dogs made its wings flap. This story is only half true, since at no time the sky darkened and the bird never arrived.

805.   Where "I" is, there is suffering. One says "I" even when "I" points elsewhere. And the "I" has an ego, a name (sometimes proper), impassable boundaries and learning-laden needs and desires. Dogs don't have ego. They bark and bite out of fear. "I" also can use this reasoning. Watch!

806.   A singer who is awakened can still sing, though nobody can hear his song. The hill to hill bridge can't be seen until one tries to walk on it. Like a fog that vanishes at once when water starts flowing.

807.   There is nothing more than what all sages are saying and nothing less than what ordinary beings could think of…

808.   Weighing Suchness (*The way it is*) for one second, for one minute or for one hundred years. One sees the world the way it is for a shorter time than the other. The lake surface is clear but the weeping willows lining the shore are plunged in fog.

809.   The moon that left yesterday the firmament returned today as snow. Fifteen feet north, nothing to be seen. Fifteen feet south, walking on a thin ice crust… In the bakery door, a white

hand holding bread: not a single choice to make. Neither using one's tongue to inquire, nor using one's eyes to eat...

810.   One label said: "Not seeing any mirror - for as long as time lasts". Second label said: "Everything is mirroring, no matter what". It just happened that one mirror opens its wings; the other covers with fur its tail. What about the mirror that drowns in the icy stream? Third label said: "Mirroring or not mirroring?" A sneeze is enough to change one into the other.

811.   Light on everything; under sealed wraps – the reason.

812.   Having not desire to travel while being carried by thought around the universe in a leash!

813.   While my mind is here, your mind is there. This shows two possibilities of the relative reality to exist. The one-mind world is different though identical with any other mind-world. This is true if mind itself is Buddha. If this is not the case one-mind world is identical with any one-mind world, even if different.

814.   Full moon: An unremitting light held prisoner in unremitting water.

815.   This is it: neither the illusion of a future life, nor the one tenth of a glimpse in a past one: translucent and indestructible. Though full of daily rituals...

816.   In doubts the truth hangs by a hair. To the silent possibility a fly is born to be caught in a spider web. Then, if this is not a spoken catch the fly is free to fly, though the truth cannot stay around longer.

817.   My eyes hurt: Blind folded I try to find my way to the kitchen. Hearing the cry of my cat, my mind passes through her tail.

818.   Written teachings are like clustered clouds: the sun, not a bit of it… Bathed in ideas – and looking for certainty – I smashed the universal mirror. Pure light – pure darkness.

819.   Seeing and acting! Not seeing and not acting! Seeing and not acting. Not seeing and acting! As one gets awakened the four rules become two: seeing and not seeing! Acting and not acting.

820.   My mind is the manifestation of your mind; therefore it could produce contrary results only if it was otherwise. The point is that if the Universe is one it is one for everybody. For an amoeba this "one" meaning is disguised under a one cell story. For a monkey in the watching of its mutation into becoming man.

821.   Hail: New comings are clones of last goings. Ice balls as big as a hen egg and yet nothing is hit! Water goes into the tunnel and comes out on the other side. On all sides ice amassed in stockpiles the height of one finger?

822.   Zen joke: Finish drinking your tea and bow! The leaf tea still adheres to your palate. On the way home the white-green horizon shifts the leaf position in your mouth and passes it to the tongue for an after-taste tea-party.

823.   The cessation of the conceptual thinking makes raspberries picking a pure joy. Getting the thorns out of one's skin is another pure joy. Though, choosing to eat the ripen ones and throw out the green ones spoils the game.

824.   A case to be judged: "Nature resembles one's mind": it is dual when a mind reflects it and non-dual when it reflects one's mind. Since there is no mind to do the reflection and no nature to be reflected upon nature-versus-mind is fundamentally an empty case.

825.   We could define - in Zen terms - a pigsty as being a motel in which pigs live without knowing what a pigsty is.

826.   Remember that during meditation fishes are still swimming, crows keep crowing…The whole world of discrimination and phenomena is bursting with joy or sorrow, with peaceful or fierce ardor. Don't you regret not witnessing it, not getting involved in its frenetic dance?

827.   Neither "nor", nor "nor". Seeing in the descending flights the long migratory trips: when the time ends…

828.   Exercises in Zen paradoxes: Every mind is also a no-mind; It is no-mind when it is not contained; If no-mind is not contained in the mind, it cannot be mind; If no-mind is no mind it is no-mind; If Buddha's mind is the mind of not-knowing then no-mind is Buddha's mind; Buddha's mind is also Buddha's no-mind.

829.   Zen regression: It is like well thought but undisclosed. It is like well known but concealed. It is like revealed but not known. It is neither known nor unknown.

830.   A stone sings its own song… The water it falls in is deaf…

831.   The reality doesn't flow out of one's mind. It doesn't overflow one's mind either. The experience of seeing and hearing knows more about reality than one's mind does.

832.   There is some continuity of life after death. That is, people may remember you now and then for a while. The difference of being sumptuously remembered – as a king is – or not remembered at all, equals zero.

833.   Enlightenment is just a state of mind. So is love…

834.   An alternative to meditation is to identify yourself with nothingness. The universe is as transparent and clear as mind is. A few thoughts with no words involved could teach you that.

835.   The enlightenment travels within my hara: long time being alone the house seems empty when I am there... The rope in front of the house hangs an empty cage. In this infinite loneliness to have fresh bread on the table is a non-Zen luxury. Nothing I miss more but a human voice using a "concept" to call a "thing".

836.   As you sit in Zazen try to stand up in Enlightenment.

837.   Concentrating on an object only, like a lion watching a pray, is not going to give you a sudden enlightenment. Thinking instead that you are that prey is even worse. What about two cocks in a fight, facing each other? It's like two teachers from two different Zen schools, trying to make a point, their legs fitted with metal spurs.

838.   Words-renouncing, sound of ox horns knocking at the window...

839.   Body and mind are suchness. So are mind and matter, life and death, relative and absolute.

840.   Once there was a universe in which beings watched the raising sun. Something could be said about it. Like a stork standing on one leg. Absolute posture... Forever standing. Changing legs to let the other rest...

841.   Trying to walk through the whole universe in a cross-legged position.

842.   A mind's eye continues to see the "conceptual thing". Knowing what it sees you'll have to close that eye too.

843.   Discovering in the ocean of words the three pound flaxen mast of Buddha's eternal vessel; the dark water is silent and the sharks wouldn't bite.

844.   Drawing water out of a hollow fountain I had a vision of an endless gate on which a skilful scribbler wrote: neither a passage, nor an obstruction!

845.   Cling neither to relative nor to absolute, neither to I nor to non-I.

846.   The shadow of a mountain on the sea surface is as guilty as the mountain itself of my relative thinking. Though, as the sun moves West the shadow looks less and les guilty. Eventually there is only the mountain and I. Pushing the-I away the shadow comes back. Now there is only the shadow-me, no longer reflecting, no longer mirroring.

847.   You read Sutras though you slam doors as if you didn't.

848.   The realm outside the words is neither near nor far… The realm of the inner peace is both within and without…

849.   The seven head openings – mouth, two nostrils, two eyes and two ears teach us what the manifestation of the outside world is. To see the inside world think that your tongue doesn't point to language in a manner of "not" speaking. Flavor, smell, sight, resonance, touch become then unknown senses. Like a laser beam the mind merges with its clear and coherent nature.

850.   While I was rhythmically breathing I heard the strident rooster's song. I suddenly understood that if I wanted to hear a different song I'd have to wait for a different bird to come by. The shade of steel of my window melted away. I heard my teacher

saying: "A true bird never sings". With my mouth open gasping to inhale the fetid air.

851.   Zazen joke: A journey to nowhere: people assemble for a communion of sorts. In a rush to get there you forgot to save your old life in a group photo. Now that the chant is over how come you couldn't find a single flaw in the floor after two hours of contemplation.

852.   What is Buddha? Remember the "three pound of flax?" What it means is that Buddha is not just a pile of flax, an indefinite quantity of flax. Though flax could be replaced by marshmallow, the weight has to be the same. In the world of the absolute a substance is phenomena while a measurement is a universally sound and an irrefutable dimension. The proof: "At the beginning of the universe three pound of emptiness was precisely equal to three pound of flax".

853.   Three pound of flax washed in three pound of water: no dust remaining, the weightless smile of Buddha printed on every atom.

854.   Awe and astonishment: Who's observing and who's being observed? The "I" left me for a-NO-other-I when I married the whole universe…

855.   Throughout the universe there is no speck to mirror your sight and no hole to resonate your hearing.

856.   What an irony: to take leave from life so as to lift from the ground the dead universe. In the name of the ultimate truth I buried memories, feelings, knowledge and even the sword I was taught to fear: Karma. If life is a dream, why did I kill it for the illusion of a great journey? Out of the window the bleached face of the snow man laughs awkwardly.

857.   Self-building is non-Zen. Self-destruction is not Zen. Self building a no-self is Zen.

858.   No more footsteps on the beach sand. Yesterday there were traces of fox paws. Even the bird I thought dead left the shores.

859.   The smells issued from your nose makes a rose blush.

860.   The color you paint, the song you sing, the fragrance you wear, the flavor you cook, the thing you touch: all those sound very much as being attachments. To find what do they mean beyond attachments resign from life for a moment. The teary eyes of your dying horse could tell you what you loose. To fulfill a desire you have to consent to it. That's why I'm saying to you: keep the desires to yourself but let the emptiness know about it by whispering into your own ear: "To mourn a horse that has twenty more years to live", that's attachment.

861.   When I was young I used to sweat poorly. Now, my sweat can drown easily an ant. The day is too short for a rat to make enough milk or for my body to sweat much – enough to make a pond in which a frog could swim.

862.   In contemplation of your own mind: no things to be seen there...

863.   One day a window washer reached the one hundredth floor of a building. Seeing an open window giving into an office meeting he dared to ask: "Is this the 100th floor?" One of the occupants said "yes" and then closed the window, shutting off the communication. Zen works in a similar way: Don't question your progress by using a marathon stick! As one approaches the Zen finish line a confirmation could be a set back. Even a Zen Master, as he tracks the progress of a pupil, would wait for the moment of realization to occur before confirming its onset.

864.   The only reason to play drums is to exhaust your hearing…

865.   The primal moment of the creation looks like a speck of dirt on the universal mirror. (It is considered impure and sufficient to it-self; then why, for eons, it starved so much for a human holy company?)

866.   Doing group Zazen: the source outside the words is shared. Some people drink a lot others hang about thirsty.

867.   Where consent exists the known is not the answer. Flowers in bloom don't have enough time to be named before they fade.

868.   Blackened snow covering black waves… The eternal boat shall be decked. You're still roaming, being pleased by the water sound… The emptiness is annulled! Ready to accept the cheap jewel of those who are born to die? Inquiring the gate: "The moon is rising - though there is no absolute meaning attached to it!" "Rising or descending, shining or engulfed by shadows… They all are the same! Unknown mysteries shall unfold…"

869.   Because one is contained within the other an unborn baby is one with his mother. The universe contains us all.

870.   Satori: The world slowed down to a halt for a moment and then it flew back into reality. It looked like dreaming of being trapped inside a transparent iceberg and not knowing its top from its bottom as you awoke. "There are worlds in relation with other worlds; there are truths in relation with other truths".

871.   The boat: name it and it is there. Consciousness is like a mast. You take down the sails and bring the outmost reality into

existence. What is this boat? You can't name it for there is no boat there.

872.   In dreams one's bones are still attached to one's flesh. When they manifest themselves they're frcc of attachments.

873.   Understanding oneness is like riding onto two opposite light beams trying to reach the departing point. Roughly speaking, oneness has nothing to do with understanding.

874.   You cannot put into words what's Satori. Try to use your body language. Mounds of words that are inexpressible live in one's body.

875.   Truth is the technique, morals are the principle. And within the morals is I, you and the rest of the world. The practical usage of Zen comes from following those morals. Enlightened Zen is everything else…

876.   I looked with much sadness at the maple tree loosing its leaves. But then, the spring came and I felt so much joy when the tree got its leaves back. Then I heard my puppy saying his first word: "Raff!" I answered: "Raff!" Suddenly I understood that the whole world lives into my mind. No more leaves falling, no more leaves coming back, no more "Raffs!" How could I give that lost knowledge as a present to somebody that doesn't know it yet? Why the nature deceives us by apparently changing what will never change? Like a baker blowing flour into one's eyes…

877.   No thinker - no thought! Thinker? Mind cannot reflect itself. To reflect the world it needs words and logic. Full moon – high tide. Actually causal forms (moon) could be sited far away from the effectual forms (waves). If you let go that - the wheels that move the universe could be heard nearer. Like the stork that builds a nest on the roof of my house: I never went up to see it, but I know it is there.

878.   Even a little insight got through an incomplete Satori, gives one, more knowledge than a book of all thoughts ever expressed. When a full Satori occurs love overwhelms a book of all the thoughts ever felt.

879.   Going to sleep after abandoning all hopes to see another day alive. The sparkles in the fireplace, the scar on my arm, the dogs barking outside, the pain in my feet… All seem so prefect. How can I be objective when paradise is outlived only by subjective minds? Nothing seems more important than to live one more day. Think of this when you have plenty of days left and don't err…

880.   When you're saying something be aware of what are you saying! When you are doing something, be aware of what you are doing! Awareness! Zen follows from it.

881.   Enlightenment lies in a no-mind approach to seeing.

882.   As you see things moving and changing try to hold your mind still. In the same way as, out of your thinking, things could slow down their moving and changing - from this holding - your new mind emerges.

883.   A fresh thought is like a fish in a net. Straggling until a hand throws it on top of the pile of fishes.

884.   Zen Monastery: only a minuscule window.

885.   The bird-man could fly. The man-bird could reason the flight. Though, there is no flight to be reasoned about for no one ever took to the air.

886.   My mind is lodged under my skull. No other place to shelter it! If awakened, with all my previous and future lives

annulled, I may let it levitate. As it levitates my mind is going, for sure, to look for a no-skull shelter.

887.   Quarreling over a logical cat, some holding its head, other holding its tail and pulling it apart. The stagnant summer heat shaken by a breeze...

888.   Mind! You are like a clear nothing. Nothing to be felt: thoughts coming and going, caged in a body of air. Dwelling nowhere, abiding nowhere, and adorning one's body like a crown made out of transparent dust. A breeze to wash it, same breeze to wipe it clean. Transparent and clear like a new window. Knowing that the glass window is there... Though, you can't see it.

889.   Zen life and Zen realization should not be confused with one another. While Zen life is mindfulness, Zen realization is mindless. Mind and no-mind bid for worlds of no semblance. Getting out of Zen life and into Zen realization is like swimming in a lake until the lake swims with you.

890.   Fog is transient, life is transient, and cosmos is transient. The metaphysics are not transient because they are empty.

891.   There are a few Zen schools but an infinite variety of Zen and an infinite approach to awakening. This eccentric statement should warn you not to follow Zen as if it was another dogma...

892.   A general sense of reality is a general sense of absolute. General but not particular.

893.   Donkey Zen: To have bitter pine needles for lunch and reason about while carrying loads.

894.   Zen dilemma: A trapped rabbit starves between to piles of fresh carrots. This is a Zen quandary: you have Buddhism on

one side and Tao on the other, while you decide to sit in Zazen instead.

895.   Learning how to survive as a fog while seeing the clouds leaving the scenery.

896.   Spring blossoms: an elephant is dragging a raft, its mast crowded with halcyons: this is the scenery that Buddha saw before going into his last long meditation. I look at it and it was as if someone standing behind Buddha was whispering numberless words so fragile, so ephemeral... The scenery became Buddha himself. From each shore a boat was sailing off towards unknown destinations: there was neither a guiding coach, nor a breeze to listen to.

897.   Imitating good Zen: When the wind doesn't blow the sparrows don't chirp. You could see the mountains with their white peaks unfurled. On the road that connects the villages two fellows met again and began chatting: "The time when the wind blows is not known", one said. "The time when the wind stops is not known", the other responded. Then they hit each other on the head and walked in the opposite directions.

898.   The wisdom of birth precedes the wisdom of death. In-between just enough time for some innocent play...

899.   Past winter you couldn't say that snow wasn't transitory. Canned snow is still a good trade for those who can't afford Zen.

900.   In the heart of Zen there is emptiness. Obviously, one cannot expect love to emerge from there. Then what is this fuss about getting awakened? Just to have a taste of universal frost in your mid-summer life and contemplate the no-wind icy peaks? Or to listen to the cocks and crows crowing? Or to gather scattered leaves to fan a bonfire made out of bones and dead tongues? One

would have to accept that the intelligence could be used to measure stupidity and that stupidity is no measure to intelligence. Why then would you expect love to come out of emptiness? On the other hand if emptiness thinks of itself of being so much of everything - the absolute primus movens and the absolute end of all - why it didn't keep the phenomena chained and hidden into its non-manifested essence? One would have to conclude that, among other truisms, if love is the manifestation of emptiness, emptiness is also love.

901.   The overseeing irrelativeness is the source of the under seeing absoluteness.

902.   Satori is always described as an accidental happening. And it is always happening when one is the least aware. When you're on a cliff, in a split second of unawareness you could lose your life in a free fall. With Zen you'll encounter the same danger even if you were sitting onto the bottom of the ocean.

903.   Obviously, to kill an absolute bird one would have to shot blanks.

904.   Zazen: The fall of objects in disgrace! Mirrors don't reflect anymore a reality. Faces, flowers, snow flakes – all vanish in a stream of phenomena. All the while one is pulled in - the other is pushed out. That's our life, what we are able to draw about. The claws of my cat scratching the door remains the only proof that doors and cats interact as complex phenomena.

905.   Sudden rain: empty drops, wet intervals. How could you distinguish the drops from the space between them? Then, as the rain stops one would question the pond – its glimmering…

906.   Try it first, live its consequences later. This uncertain advice works also for Zen.

907.   The million skies in a handful of dust. Chased by mind all clouds are gone. Only one blade of grass on this mountain peak and the snow wandering in the slow breeze. The delighted mind freezes to death. (A casserole of white beans would be an appreciated contribution from emptiness at this time. The shrieking condor floats above in circles waiting for me to die. I'll throw myself in the village frenzy tonight. Though grief stricken by the cow that they're going to butcher, lots of people would forget for a moment what emptiness is while eating her entrails). Thousand ants around a grain of rice that fell from my dinner bag. Strange, at this altitude where only Buddha could live the ants have their own cow to devour.

908.   Mind, so fragile: a breeze would throw it in distress. Also so strong to make a mountain fall to pieces as it whispers!

909.   Giving up desire and pleasure, picking up indifference and pain.

910.   Immerse your mind into emptiness as if you would let a drum sink into the water. Drums under water sound muted.

911.   Knowing and knowing again while the truth is still hidden. The face of eternity puts on view its eye: copper reeds cut by the wind in the middle of nowhere…

912.   Let thought after thought pass by. Then catch the afterthought by its tail, hold it, don't let it go through the gate. Listen: a drop of water renders a timely eternity in its fall. Now, let it go…

913.   Anti-Zen letter: "So much is clear that a definite thing happens at a definite time and that's what Zen would talk so much about: that things completely dull and ordinary have a scheduled appearance. A full moon advent, cocks announcing the sunrise,

meteors vanishing in the outer-space, flowers blossoming... If a fact is a logical necessity then Zen ordinary things are not only possibilities but certainties sealed under physical laws. To ignore this is agnostic, simplistic, purposeless, causeless, effect less".

914.   The mysterious "no-thing": to reflect on it you'd have to drop the thinking. The abysmal "no-mind" thing. Emptiness itself, faintly echoing... Dead words are passing by. They can't say anything anymore. Is killing an utterance a crime? Think of so many languages out of use, like Latin or Sanskrit: myriads of forgotten words. Far back they drowned minds in near to the ground ecstasies. In Zen view when the language was alive those who used it ran downhill. What a victory for Zen now that the languages are dead and those who knew them can be found nowhere! Life knows neither love nor hate in a language that is out of use. Though, what Zen is afraid of is that every sound of a dead language is in search of an utterance. What does it mean that for thousand years Zen tried to kill words and utterances? There are so many shadows behind words: people embracing, loving, tearing, dying... A dead eye can't see this; a dead ear can't hear it. Zen ignores the fact that without words even the emptiness would be utterly lost and forgotten.

915.   There is this wild bird in the sky and the wild fish in the lake below. The bird didn't start flying yet and the fish is too small to be seen under the cloudy water. You can activate the Zen vehicle without changing the story. Though, if you let the bird fly the fish emerges from the water. If fish stays unnoticed under the water the bird is unable to move its wings.

916.   Enlightenment may never come. Though, be sure, if it came, to let it go...

917.   Karma is a thinkable concept. Its effects yield what Karma asserts. Zazen is a way to suspend what is thinkable and so its effects. Realizing the truth clears the way to redemption.

918.   Ponds are flooding, fires are swelling the air. For Zen, those are aspects of how emptiness expands its manifestation to make it visible to the blind.

919.   You wouldn't find anything Zen-like not being ethic-like. Though nobody could express clearly why it is so. For a monk everything seems to turn on monastery work, abstinence and poise. Awakening is what a monk does for a living. For ordinary Zen subjects Karma and its enforcing ethics come first. "Ordinary Zen subjects are like extras in a musical where the leading characters are all monks. They all play their role and act in conformity to their roles".

920.   "The anxiety doesn't enter the mind" is different then "The anxiety exited the mind". Not accepting (letting in) is different then discarding (letting out).

921.   I cannot reconcile this perpetual dilemma: 1) the universe created the mind, 2) the mind created the universe. A dog chasing its tail is not the same as a tail chasing its dog. This shows that mind is just an attachment to reality. The knowledge is like a thorn under one's nail: as long as it is there it hurts "the mind". As you pull it out it relieves the pain of the mind.

922.   Poetry makes easier to anyone To Whom It May Concern that there are things unattainable in life. If enlightenment is one of them it is though the last one you should be concerned about.

923.   An un-hammered drum (mind) makes neither a pleasant nor an unpleasant sound.

924.   On a hyperbolic horse even a mouse can win a race. Be realistic: life is not a trophy you can carry around as if for granted. Do your homework first: you'd notice that empty rooms have

character and that silence is neither a handcuffed sound nor an overflowing void. Want some evidence? Light is there even when the lamp is not lighted.

925.   The never noticed failure: that we're not yet there...

926.   Being aware of the oneness precedes the awakening to a noness of the emptiness. Although after the awakening to a noness of the emptiness, being aware of the oneness, follows.

927.   Emptiness: endless body beyond birth and death. Unknowable, inexpressible, unperceivable... Being here and trying to express it. Going there and becoming inexpressible oneness.

928.   To shelter liberation one has to let fall attachment, duality and evil doing...

929.   Trying to understand and at the same time letting it go I found myself laughing about almost everything. On the contrary, my wife was always like crying. The point is: don't think of your Zazen practice as being a recognizable weakness of sorts. Let the emptiness sort it out for you.

930.   Emptiness breeds phenomena. Beer malt breeds flies. That's what chance can do when conditions are met. Emptiness giving a free rein to arrows...

931.   The Ether is translucent; though present ubiquitously it is invisible to the naked eye. One way to see it is by getting enlightened. The other way is to keep your mind unaffected by things and events so that you could notice how reality slowly changes its aspects while you're on your way to be awakened. To become translucent the Ether has to move from the in-and-in awareness onto the out-and-out emptiness.

932.   The self is like a mirror that reflects nothing. One calls it "self" in an attempt to give shelter to one's ego. And what ego is?

A history of one's life made of insoluble needs, tendencies and fixed ideas built around them. Another empty thing?

933.   Every Zen saying is a brainwash. Every brainwash is not like forgetting. What do I still have knowledge of? I'll let this question to be wiped away along with others.

934.   Words entangle your mind as nets entangle fish. Take a step back from seeing: the bull lost his horns. Take two steps back: the bull lost his forehead. The moonlight irrigates the desert…

935.   To find the path in polyphony you'd have to replace every string with a wind folder: a sound is for the ear what a halo is for the eye. Bringing forth sound, trying to break the sealed tight space…

936.   You cannot climb up a tree if your mind is centered on watching the moon. Though, your true nature can…

937.   Cause and effect are like two half-sisters. The common parent is emptiness and that's how they resemble each other. The other step parents are manifestation and reasoning.

938.   Not to live in duality one would have to deprogram his/her brain, that is, to erase sixteen billion years of phenomenal manifestation of emptiness.

939.   You stare at "I" and "I" stares at you. "I" is the passage in, you're the passage out. How your portrait would look like after you remove the "I"? A white man on a black horse would feel the same as a black man on a white horse. If "I" was the one that would chose the path you'd follow, who's going to chose it now? Be sure to bury the "I" in a shallow grave just in case you may need it as you break free from your Zen pledge. Meanwhile,

another "I", more compassionate, more humble takes over the breathing in and breathing out though knowing no life.

940.   The day when I woke up emptied of knowledge I felt still in love with that world that I kept secretly locked into my heart. Call this an incomplete awakening and I'll show you then my broken nose.

941.   Every living moment dissipates. After one dies and rots what is left are ashes. Learn to give compassion before it is too late.

942.   Watching how details unfold: the caged lion is growing white hair… His howl is free of significance. Not able even to catch a fly on his tongue he knows finally that he is not God…

943.   Getting knowledge through a feeding tube one word at a time, one sentence at a time, without seeing what is out there. Or knowing what is out there and for the sake of awakening throwing up through a feeding tube one word at a time, one sentence at a time. One of the sentences to be erased: "When I was a child I knew that my parents were not children" since what I understood lately was that they were.

944.   Commuting by ferry my thoughts get lost in the waves. As the boat decks at the pier my thoughts are still parting the waves. So many days I have been ferried from shore to shore that I can recognize every wave by its shape and sound. During the foggy days I neither can see them well nor can I hear well their muffled sound. When this happens my mind stops parting the waves and rests. I'm then the boat reaching the other shore.

945.   A moon comes into your sight as you rest. Speechless, but still able to throw a glance… To avert its light is pointless. To get up from your bed to see it clearly, what a wonderful dream, what a wonderful marvel.

946.   Getting rid of attachments: An "I" living in opulence is a better "I" then an "I" living in misery. Though there is room for equal compassion when one thinks that death is going to carry both with equal indifference.

947.   Unsatisfied by what you see? Unsatisfied by what you hear? But still, confident that beyond all that – if your tongue doesn't rattle – the seeing and the hearing are the embodiment of satisfaction.

948.   Two birds, approaching, and flying as one in a musical duet. The coordination and the harmony shows "what" is beyond mind though who would dare to explain "what"?

949.   The vaulted rooms of one's brain can accommodate so much knowledge. Cleansing them through Zazen feels like withdrawing from the living world. The face you're washing every morning is not your face. It is the face you owe to Zazen, part of it being here, part of it being there. Glancing at the emptiness behind your eyes…

950.   I was doing unorthodox Zazen on my lawn trying to let go when something unexpected happened: from a stem above my head a bird let go droppings on my head. The weight of droppings was so enormous that it brought tears into my eyes. As I emptied my mind I didn't feel a thing. Though slowly the word "stinks" and then "wash" came into my mind and I saw with my mind's eyes a picture that I set eyes on while reading an old farm almanac showing a dead bird on a lawn. All thoughts during Zazen are like bird droppings. You can't see them though you know and feel that they are there.

951.   A God lost in reveries is not God. A being without reveries is not a being. Reveries give way to meditation; meditation gives way to emptiness. Then what? A God lost in reveries is still a

God. A being without reveries is still a being. Do you understand? To qualify the absolute is like shooting arrows in dark... To put a stamp on a relative is like seeing a target with no arrows at handy...

952.   When mind and matter are not separated, this is called non-dualistic reality. Reality vanishes completely and "knowledge" is reduced to nothing. Without boundary the emptiness shows its one thousand eons of untainted bounty.

953.   A being is a manifested form in the infinite world of forms: a human form has three attributes: individuality, ego and self. Getting rid of one of the attributes illuminates many...

954.   At sundown the moon shows her pure face then at dawn it turns her face away. Reason, justice, Heaven – follow the same trend. Wearing light if light was given and dark otherwise. Mirrors, numerous as words.

955.   To raise a question and leave in a hurry before the answer hits you. Going to climb the mountains you could still hear the echo...

956.   Those who got awakened had difficulties to put their hat down. Those who didn't get awakened have difficulties to put their hat up. Carry it for a while and then let it go...

957.   You know that nothing goes: keep going...

958.   Black humor, Zen style: burning coffins to survive the cold; getting shelter in the morgue's coolers to survive the heat.

959.   A cock crows and billion of miles of Buddhas wake up. They have slept there where the night found them, facing the wall. Then the roll call starts: you'd call one Buddha and before getting the whole name out they'll all be gone...

960.   Doing good to others with no rewards given, upholds your purity of mind. Inner morals don't show any reflection in the mirror. Rewards do…

961.   Loosing your eyes and whatever comes with them: eyelids, eyebrows, etc. Same with the mouth, though the tongue remains a poisoning arrow. What about ears? Should you wait until they hear a bamboo stick falling or should you cut them off too? Touch them out of cowardice! They're still there…

962.   Zen: Crash an apricot pit, eat the almond, and throw out the broken shell.

963.   To look for a lamp in pitch darkness is like waiting on a night with clear skies to see a lightening. Illusions are "the darkness"; "a night of clear skies" is the channel of consciousness. The "lamp" is your mind. "Lightening" is awakening that occurs without logical preconditions.

964.   The feathers of a pheasant won't cover a carcass of a duck… Fortunately, pillows don't look into feathery issues…

965.   "After life" has a religious color. "Before life" has a Zen one. Both are empty, but only one cannot be undone.

966.   When a number is irreducible it is called prime number. Just a thought: how in hell the emptiness came up with such a bright idea? Obstructed or unobstructed the nature of the prime numbers stays the same. What about if emptiness is nothing else but a huge prime number, irreducible, inexhaustible, ungraspable and permanent? A number whose traces could be found in every wave, petal, eyelid, horse or horseshoe… They may have called it already the cosmic constant which sounds to me like a bark in darkness…

967.   Working to resolve the conflict between what Mu says when I think Mu as opposed to what Mu says when I'm one with Mu.

968.   A barefoot cat trying the fresh snow: one, two, three steps, one paw in the air till a snowball falls from the cherry tree. Three wide leaps back to the house. A bird chirping wholeheartedly tells the story…

969.   A nursing fox thinking of what awakening means to others: fish wearing that mask of innocence when they're needed for lunch.

970.   When a flower in blossom claps its petals the golden Buddha draws on moonlight to warm his feet.

971.   Bad and good are neither similar nor different. Think of a line between good and bad. The lower "bad" gets, the more it resembles good. The lower "good" gets, the more it resembles bad. Let's say that you observe a foreign culture in which you see an event as being treated as good while in your own culture it is considered bad. It is correct to say that, by knowing that, you'd be able to ignore the event as being bad though you'll not be able to accept it as being good. That's a method you could use to weaken your discrimination. Take any event as foreign so that your opposite judgment - even if it looks inadequate - could prevail. For instance take friendship as foreign to get rid of attachments and enmity as inadequate to detach (de-attach) yourself from it.

972.   A bamboo stick is not aware that it could be the source of one's enlightenment, despite the fact that, witnesses say, when the awakening happens, the stick shows a Buddha face…

973.   One owns a bowl the other owns a mountain. Both eat rice though.

974.   A just awakened monk witnesses the next moment the arrival of a police force. He points towards his teacher and says: "he made me do it!" After a moment of confusion the police leave: "Wrong address". The teacher says: "Would they have found out that you stole my teachings you'd be sitting now in prison". "I wonder who was going to sit in the prison if there was no-I?" said the monk.

975.   The ice is slippery. So is the excrement. What's the point? All of a sudden you have a reason to meditate while you walk.

976.   A cock is famous for its eloquence. By not obeying a Zen law the cock speaks out. "Why "It" when pronounced is different than cock-a-doodle-do? Did the cock pass already the awakening test? Of course! That's why its song awakens!

977.   Realizing the truth is a hard task. Making it manifest in your life is even harder.

978.   In the house of the awakened the show cases are empty. The door left slightly ajar is silent. The skunk is the only ignorant thing moving around as if nothing happened. Its smell: awaken-less.

979.   "I" is a house to shelter the emptiness and the emptiness is a house to shelter "I". When the emptiness comes to pay a visit to "I" there is no "I". When "I" visits the emptiness there is no "I" either.

980.   Self found: No longer an arrow pointing outward.

981.   As you sit you listen to Buddha Dharma. As you talk you listen to Buddha Dharma. The incantations of the dead –

accompanied by drums made out of emptied pork skin… Same sound – as it used to reverberate six thousand years ago.

982.   Every moment fishes in the ocean of eternity. Every single moment there is a catch.

983.   A sparrow leads the choir: birds singing Zen songs. Swiftly - like a black web - they fly to the sky, wing to wing, and come back the next moment like a black throw. The drizzle is also there, so thin as if reminiscent of what used to live around here forever. With a broom a monk is cleaning the old chimney.

984.   Emptiness: What mind could see without eyes and ears.

985.   The countless snow flakes come hurrying, then, as they reach the window, they dance. Tailless oxen pass through.

986.   Devil sees his reflection as being God's.

987.   The word "tree" is surely ignorant that it is a sign used to point one's mind to a thing, which for the sake of this example, is a tree. The tree also doesn't recognize the word "tree" as its name. If you want to be enlightened don't think "tree: when you see one - accept its handshake with a smile.

988.   You can borrow everything else but life.

989.   Never to listen again to this beat, never to smell again the incense. At least I know how a moon is choosing its path through the fog: moving from the blossoming hilltops to the icy peaks in a whisper.

990.   Self is vertical, mind is horizontal and vertical, ego is a wooden structure that could be located behind one's heart.

991.   In the mirror that the emptiness builds around you phenomena are like a locust storm. Held captive in a cloud, freed

as rain. As you light a candle you see too many. As you light your mind you see none.

992.   The path to transcendence is within your birth and death span. If there is more than one path to choose – choose one. Each egg in hatched to fulfill its promise. Somebody mentioned flight. If the chick does-not-break-its-way-through-the-shell where the flight goes?

993.   Snow flakes - flickering horizon.

994.   When I was a bison I used to like to chew up lavender flowers. Right now I like to chew up lavender flowers.

995.   Biology: Animals are not allowed anymore to grow into humans.

996.   When "I" and self are shunned, nature appears as God's resemblance.

997.   Keep watch about what you're not going to say?

998.   When you're living in the absolute there are no words you could use – for there is nothing to be understood or to be explained. It's like the absolute defrauds us by arresting our tongues.

999.   A marathon runner recognizes a good road from a bad one from the taste of the dust accumulated on his tongue. A fisherman does the same while tasting the ocean water. A baby could find all these in its mother's milk. At the beginning of time the memory of all tastes were already posted on the blue prints of the firmament.

1000.   You cannot achieve more than Karma allows you to. Though there are means in life to lessen Karma effects by getting rid of bad clinging. Is there any good clinging? As far as Karma goes there are. As far as enlightenment goes there are not.

1001.   If perception is not adequate to awareness then surely it has to be circumvented. How do you keep clear of perception? Remember: to be true a reality doesn't need to be perceived.

1002.   If it is sacred it is not Zen; but realization through knowledge is impossible. Therefore, realization should be set apart; Accordingly, Zen is sacred.

1003.   A residual mind could make a mountain of pure crystal give way to dust.

1004.   When the awakened one walks around, his shadow follows him faithfully until a fox comes on his way. The shadow departs then and ducks. One could hear the stillness moving about: the iced pond cracks, the nocturnal eyes glitter.

1005.   Listen to the wolves that couldn't reach the peak: howling wildly!

1006.   Mountains reflect the light of the moon. All places are safe except the insatiable river with its rapids. Though the stream going uphill is flawless.

1007.   An old tree: "The flowers of my youth are gone. Every day I lose leaves. Would my trunk stand the test of time for one more season I should dedicate my life to Zen?"

1008.   Honesty within the spoken and reverence within the unspoken: one praises innocence, the other praises One.

1009.   Awakened ones are those who never worked for their awakening. Though, in all cases awakening smells alike.

1010.   Sitting still in Zazen and letting your mind moan is not an option: wouldn't you better get involved in daily activities and keep your mind still?

1011.   Similar objects trail their differences. Identical objects call the entire emptiness to look at: walking on different paths, both seeing the dweller of the emptiness that they're merging with.

1012.   It is also ruled that riders that turn back from the Way should get reborn before coming back for another ride.

1013.   Mountains shattered by light: emptiness unraveling. Light shattered by rising mountains: emptiness unraveling.

1014.   "Absolute cows grazing absolute grass" sounds philosophically similar to "Relative cows grazing relative grass". When one is absolute all are absolute; as one is relative all are relative. You'd never see an absolute cow grazing a relative grass! Why?

1015.   Zen twist: "Songs of grief for new born, songs of joy for the departed one".

1016.   Getting awakened in New York: cars are honking, trains are screeching, copters are buzzing. In such an opulent noise the emptiness is blossoming. Peace and silence could still be seen in the bulging eyes of the unexpected.

1017.   How to measure the depth of shallow waters if not with a stick.

1018.   Empty your mind and keep it at ready. The universe was stolen from you at birth. To get it back you'd have to catch it under your feet. Keep your ears low to the ground; listen to the birds hurriedly parting their bush. The universe is crawling with mountain high legs. Catch it when it reaches the road of anticipation, keep it locked under your feet. Wait then for the Great River to wash the mind-forming-dust away.

1019.   You'll not catch a Zen fly by opening your mouth.

1020.   The emptiness and the universe are conversing with one voice. I wonder if the emptiness would one day empty the universe so that it could to get rid of phenomena and Zen!?

1021.   Bones that fly and bones that float... The only lesson to be listening to is what the intimation means for the living...

1022.   If found nowhere things can't be defined. In the realm of "nothing-to-be-found-into" mind still thinks that something must have been overlooked. From logic we know that what-is is-not and the what-is-not – is! It means that there is no such thing "that can't be found nowhere". In the realm of "nothing-to-be-found-into" there is indeed something to be found. The no-thing!

1023.   Was the emptiness already there when the universe began? If so the universe doesn't necessarily exist. What if the universe is the one that generates emptiness or the one that calls out the emptiness to fill out whatever is left vacant? This wouldn't be so bad for what we call knowledge, would it?

1024.   Words are absorbed and then they lie apart: tongue is the traveler, teeth are the bridges...

1025.   Your stomach can teach you Zen better than a teacher. When it is hungry it makes you know what hunger is. When it is full it is like knowing what full is though you're in the no-knowing. If you have a chance to look into this matter think of knowledge as food entering your brains. As it enters there cut off your thinking and let your brain feel like a full stomach, not saying yes and not saying no.

1026.   The crows are back, all crowing...

1027.   Moon's gentle light! Like the washing-water, pulverized by the wind. Soap emptiness! What would you call eternal and what relative? Half light is always left out...

1028.   If you <u>don't</u> live in pain, to think of pleasure smells like attachment to me.

1029.   If the rain teaches you what water is then surely you missed the lesson about water? Though, if the sand teaches you about sandstone look out: you may hear a saga from it.

1030.   It is very difficult to learn how to forget.

1031.   Keeping a mind away from thinking is like keeping a mirror clear of imaging. So is the iron not willing to rust or a cat barking?

1032.   A donkey's talk: "You're not talking about a donkey's suffering being hit by a whip while climbing a hill... You're not talking about time that humans lose while reflecting on subjects like "what life is?" Truly speaking, I think that, chewing grass and carrying loads makes me a fair Zen master..."

1033.   Zen paradox: In the spring trees are getting clothed in the expectation of a hot summer. In the fall trees are letting their cloth go in the expectation of a cold winter.

1034.   The best place to do Zazen is on a tip of a reed. Your both eyes and both ears – throw them to the wolves...

1035.   Consciousness is not emptiness, perceptions are not outside phenomena. To equate them is like saying that a device set to measure is not the measurement but whatever is measured. When duality ceases there is nothing that is not equal.

1036.   "Who am I?" is sufficient to solve the no-mind quandary. The white clouds sink into the ocean waves with a roar, but the mountain peaks are still afar. The road seems unobstructed but the Way to get there is forever new.

1037.   A lion will never chase an imaginary gazelle...

1038.   Knowing is a hell-of-a-bore. Zen is a hell-of-a-bore. What's left? Take a look: the autumn bush gently disposes of her leaves while the rain starts muttering. After a potent Zen summer you'd have to cleanse your "three pound" mind of confinement.

1039.   The endless river that runs through darkness...

1040.   You can repeat your mantra until you see gulls picking your carcass. Bowing and reading Sutras wouldn't help either. Imagine a lone tree dying in a forest. Why wouldn't it complain? There is no tree born for one forest only. All of us are lumber... Don't say you didn't know! Nameless parents, nameless teachers, nameless lives, nameless priests, nameless grave diggers.

1041.   My nostrils are issuing statements about scents; my ears do the same for sounds. To have my ears process the scents, stop beating the drums.

1042.   *Natura naturans* is by its "very nature" – timeless.

1043.   Action flows, result follows: it sounds like cause and effect though - when one acts – the cause runs away. When result follows, the effect draws near.

1044.   If man wouldn't have eyes he wouldn't see. What kind of world than would be the world of the seen? Or the world of the hearing with no ears and no sounds?

1045.   You try to hold back a speech and feel ashamed having it anyway: detaining a reality in words deprives you of a step ahead to awakening. Simply put it: the more you talk the further back from the target you travel. Though, a very skilful archer…

1046.   Trapping a word in the web of a sentence…

1047.   Sisyphus was a Zen master no doubt: carrying a stone to the top of a hill and letting it go down and carrying it again to the top of the hill and letting it go… The moral: every act is a new act even if it looks one and the same. Where the beginning is, there is the end; where the end is there is the beginning. Life is like a fine lace that disintegrates with each breath. When lights go by, darkness follow. Though, if each step is a beginning, as lights go by, more lights follow. Without being seen the moon cannot be predicted.

1048.   In the hands of the ultimate cause the effect is not predictable.

1049.   In emptiness there is no self and no other. Late snows seize the plum flowers. No spring to paint, no painter's palette to be seen. Towers of white bones with no sound, nor smell. Seeking further, seeking deeper: the original ox under whip pulls the plow of phenomena that pierces the emptiness. Thousand eons of glow and beauty…

1050.   Every morning, in the silence fenced by the bathroom's walls, I could hear my bowels saying Buddha and then again, Buddha.

1051.   In the universal furnace a life values more than a newly born galaxy. Gazing into emptiness, weighing a living word with a handful of dust. Don't you see? A thought is a crowned manifestation of "This"! You wipe out a thought you make a dent into reality. The thought is the igniting fire. What's real is the smoke coming out of it.

1052.   You'll not see it, you'll not hear it. What is absolute is buried in no-thing.

1053.   The racing nose to a hound is like the invisible made visible to a cat. Very far away the moon knows of no one.

1054.   To be transient while worshiping… This is fully understood and clear. But not until you succeed to see it in front of your eyes. The huge round shiny belly of a Buddha moving with every breath, up and down. A poor offering would never empty it out. A rich offering will never fill it up. The floating island of reeds, in full blossom…

1055.   The haphazard past yields to the haphazard future.

1056.   The amazement of awakening: a contemplating bliss of dissolute forms and movements that freeze in a moment of revealed eternity. If you think this sounds too common think of a cat with diamond eyes that would not hesitate to let a mouse eat her whole furry wardrobe; or of a fox falling in love with a hen; or of yourself, trying to roast a chicken in a chimney spark…

1057.   Awakening: the suffering of a thorn penetrating a skin.

1058.   Forms, shapes and colors are silenced by an eye asleep. Only the clap of the bones a sleepwalker makes and the crowing of the cormorant lost in fog.

1059.   The silence could be silenced by seeing love in one's fault.

1060.   After awakening the mind is like a broken fence. Nothingness comes in through the hole, knowledge gets out. The fence could never be patched-up again. It shall perish broken when you shall perish.

1061.   When you do Zazen remember: the failure to get enlightened has a wonderful, wonderful alternative: even in the case you got it…

1062.   When awakening is happening there is no room for consent. The taste of Hell is the same as the taste of Heaven.

1063.   Living in by the rules of Zen? You mustn't use your mind to follow them. If you wanted to get to the roots of truth you'd have to follow Zen lies and never long for living a good life again.

1064.   Journeying the Earth for a life time: if you don't enjoy the ride go back to your childhood. In the wake of each day, opening the eyes to see the indivisible: thinking that the world is a boundless entity hiding a treasure. Knowing "not-knowing" and not knowing "knowing": what a treat!

1065.   To measure what future could bring to you cut first with an invisible hatchet the invisible greenery before you walk.

1066.   Doggy Zen: summertime heat, sunny rains evaporate while a pigeon's shadow crosses the road, voices fade in the muted resonance, and waves get lazy trying to reach the shore. What an ideal time to curl your tongue out of your mouth and not bark even at a hostile visitation. (Splashing icy water on Buddha's marble bust).

1067.   Doing Zazen is like flying in an airplane and not wanting to know if it will ever land.

1068.   A moon without shine is like a scavenger looking for gold in a sewer.

1069.   What is born not to last looks like a temple in tremors? The body erodes; the mind gathers more erroneous facts. Why don't you just enjoy the sweet smell of flowers and the clarity of a hand scooping out water? A proverb to be invented: a winged thing is meant to fall… It falls yes, but its flight stays intact.

1070.   The mystic moon meets the mystic river. Leaves that I knew nothing of if not scattered…

1071.   When reality comes through your body life goes all-out. When reality comes through your mind life stagnates. When reality comes through your pure awareness life awakens; then, the emptiness unfurls.

1072.   When a gate opens watch which one is closing! There is no way out once you cross the infinite threshold…

1073.   How happy a flower must be when it blossoms! And then when it closes its petals to make seeds; and then when its seeds are scattered around by a gusty wind; and then when it sleeps under the warm layer of snow; and then when it wakes up at spring time; Awakening is like that flower that lives through all stages only once in a life time.

1074.   Two roads: one called "ephemeral life" the other called "everlasting life". Walking straight one road you meet the other.

1075.   Squeaking like a pig getting into muddy waters: too tempting not to go for a dip. The decision belongs to one's will. And the will is less Zen-like than the desire is. Making mistakes is trendy, more so, than wearing a Zen straight jacket.

1076.   Until you take the words out of your understanding you can't see it. (The universe is known to flee from those that talk). You're then living within the power of discrimination. A pause in speech and you're there again – the border where wind stops…

1077.   In baseball when a pitcher throws a perfect ball the batter gets enlightened. When the batter hits a home run the pitcher gets enlightened.

1078.   The clear sky floats faster than the fastest cloud.

1079.   Reading about awakening you become more knowledgeable about what awakening is not.

1080.   Drifting along unknown shores… Isn't it strange that the added "unknowns" deepens your feelings of eternity? Eternity = the fear of unknown!

1081.   Wrapped in fog, the mountain peak. Even to those who can pierce through.

1082.   Men who have the ambition to get awakened would be better off if they enlisted in the military or in the history ranks of famous ghosts. Ambitions could help one become general or even be proclaimed Napoleon Anew Emperor. To get awakened is to aspire to achieve nothing and to live with your doubts beyond getting fully awakened.

1083.   What is awakening? For thirty years the answer is still lingering on my tongue.

1084.   Every day paints a Heaven.

1085.   The truth hidden in a cry is bitter than the one hidden in a laugh. Above both of them the same ceiling: nothingness.

1086.   After awakening you keep looking back at what had happened. And you can't get anything factual about it. Often, as you get back to it you find that it is no longer there. I always thought that "awakening" knows more about the awakened than vice versa. Emptiness greets you on a cosmic ground with a great shout when it backs away and becomes silent. You ask: "Tell me, what does this mean?" And you get no answer: like a quicksand swallowing a full cherry tree in blossom… Vanished! Neither here, nor there…

1087.   Political Zen: The truth can be found in a broken pledge.

1088.   "When you meet a man of the Way on the Way, don't greet him with words, don't greet him with silence". Run away from him, as far as you can. Don't ever look back. Danger!

1089.   I got enlightened when I saw the emptiness with my own eyes. Seeing is teaching you to see. Who's teaching the seeing?

1090.   Journal, May 16, 1982 entry: "Almost ten day since I got awakened. Silence is made out of noises, white hues pour out of colors. Nothing new then, I think. The cat's purrs sound like a pyre of fragrant woods sets afire. My eyes are hollow; my guts are aching of so much emptiness. Then there is always this strange taste the bread has, as if made out of dust. The mosquito bites on my legs make me laugh. Showers of ashes; the sky is low and high. In the empty hours of the last night's insomnia I counted only two words that left my tongue: "How" and "Why". I think something great is going to happen soon. My mind is in a stupor. No more things to hold on, no more things to let go".

1091.   A rose in a Zen posture: wearing weeds all around to hide its thorns.

1092.   No bloom without gloom: one grasshopper is hopping, the other one is dying. Life goes on as if both were hopping. It is that just that one passed on its hops to the other.

1093.   You make an unknown step and by chance you meet the original face. When emptiness is not active the mind rests…

1094.   Seeking eternity, finding emptiness instead.

1095.   Suddenly "present" became so important that I completely forgot that I used to live a normal life before getting into Zen: lots of memories, still green, forgotten! The past is not anymore an interpreter of the present. Then, who am I?

1096.   Out of the darkness the rain appeared: tirelessly falling. Where are you, childhood? Faith brought me here on a breath. What is going to happen now? My life is insolvent, my death is meaningless.

1097.   A lost snowflake doesn't need guidance to hit the ground.

1098.   Journal, June 11, 1982 entry: "All at once…The road under my feet, the sky getting nearer and the muted sound of the void: I ask, I get no answer. Several weeks passed from my awakening and I'm still in search of what I have possibly missed? My mind won't tell me a thing. I don't want to get inside the house though searching the rain for a Heaven's message would just strengthen my sneeze. Dashing out of the thistle, the magpie soars".

1099.   The immeasurable look of a stone head.

1100.   A tree is not driven by consciousness. It doesn't have an ego. That's why when it sleeps it has a deep dreamless sleep. When it is awakened it is fully awakened.

1101.   A strange case: The hut is opened. You could see traces of straws and the dust coated sandals. But the awakened is not there. Nobody knows where he went. Wise people live in spite of awakening; not inspired people die for it.

1102.   Is a non-human a different kind of human or just an animal? I'm talking about angels, ghosts of warriors, deities, regular spirits, peace loving apparitions, shadows of the unenlightened, karma-auditors, Mu-enraged reincarnated-Zazen-punks.

1103.   Zazen: Mu, hurrying towards you from anywhere, resplendent, with mountainous feet and oceanic wings ready to swallow the ashes of your mind. "Do I have Buddha nature?" you ask. You can't ask such a question. "Yes, you do!" You can't get such an answer either. "No, you don't!" is the answer that challenges you to get there. Throw your body into fire, jump off a cliff to annihilate your mental involvement: the mind road has a dead end, an impasse that you'd have to break into pieces. Mu helps you accomplish that. But even Mu vanishes as the clear void comes near.

1104.   Is the water ascending when you stand on your head? Nature is indifferent to what knowledge path one is seeking. Though on the hut window the wooden Buddha head looks completely covered with snow. When it rains Buddha is wet, when the sun shines Buddha is dry. That's how an enlightened one is mirroring the seasons.

1105.   Empty, empty, empty! Pouring tea in a broken cup…

1106.   From the empty void IT made all the worlds. It brought forth image, sound, smell, touch, feelings, understanding and consciousness. Deaf to calls, blind to revelations. In a clear spot of water IT shines when the moon shines. IT is of assistance to the winged to fly and to the clawed to climb. If you go in the mountains you could see IT in the clear sky: a blue eye that is not aspect of a comprehension. Though one could use a Zen prophecy to look into IT: present here and now, IT can't be found anywhere. Having eyes but no face, having mind but no head; IT's identity is nameless, and IT's whereabouts traceless. You seek IT afar, IT is near. You seek IT near, IT is afar. What is it? Is it thus?

1107.   Nature is just a living messenger: not using words as it looks into your eyes…

1108.   Staring with a fox's eyes at a rooster: that's when well tuned instincts hatch desires for the conditional world. Shall we put a blanket over fox's eyes? In the moonlight, both, the fox and the rooster go dancing with their own shadows. Then, the five senses retire for a night of sleep.

1109.   The seeker tries to find his true self. The cat is chasing her tail.

1110.   Searching for the lake's bottom you see your face reflected: no awakening though… How could you search for the original face without guidance? Your tongue should know no life. Under the morning sun the lights are climbing firmly; under the evening moon the lights cry aloud. Lost on a loneliest path and finding a guide you trust most: yourself. Searching your inner being you set your eyes upon the universe… The universe sets its eyes upon you. The great silence of the Greater Self. Bees above flowers, but the buzz is gone…

1111.   The music is a living ear and the flavor is a living tongue. A dead ear can still hear the wind; a dead tongue can still taste the air. As mind interprets, the no-mind knows.

1112.   Saying Zen buzzwords is like tasting a snow ball mixed with grains of sand.

1113.   There can be no truth without limitations. It's part of what ephemeral means in terms of logic.

1114.   "One" returns to "one" and "all" returns to "one" and "one" returns to "all" and so on and so forth. The undiscovered principle of one-in-all-in-one is shy on saying that when a cow makes a cowweb flying lions know no long life. The universe was not born as a "one" child of a "one" mother. There was some penetration involved when it happened, all right. That's why discrimination and duality are not as bad as advertised by Zen. Discriminate as you need. If you don't need, don't discriminate. That is, why would you stuff your mind with debris when you can learn faster what emptiness is from a scare-crow? The eyeless guardians on the path of the unknown flights…

1115.   Awakened after death and still able to clean the dishes without the help of a maid.

1116.   Mythological joke: If man would have only one eye his hair would be equally parted to allow it to open. A mom would say: it's time to open your eye baby! Eye for an eye would be truthful to what it says. Or: it's an opportunity for you to see. If such an eye releases its vision mountains of Dharma would rise as far as an eye could see.

1117.   An arrow in flight is truthful when it hits the intended target. When an arrow misses, God forbids seeing it hitting what emptiness makes us call "the unexpected"…

1118.   Speaking about wood becoming ashes and about bodies becoming ashes and then attending a all-night un-utterable Zazen where trees are trees but not in your mind and the smell of the cloth you just washed has to be fragrantless like rain water. If you can't avoid feelings, throw your feelings in a fire… Ashes within=ashes without or even better inner ashes=outer ashes.

1119.   Zen: A prayer in which vainly God awaits to be invoked…

1120.   Fear is vain. And as a result the courage is vain also. Crying or laughing is not going to stop the rivers from overflowing at spring time. As far as courage goes, I, personally, want to be a soldier only during peaceful times.

1121.   If the sea if filled up with silence then darkness is like how the moon would sound under two feet of seawater.

1122.   In silence pain becomes truthful. Crying is like refusing to acknowledge that where is rotten cabbage there has to be smell. In other words a heavy perfumed body wouldn't make a hyena enjoy better her lunch. Things surrounding the truth are marginal. Innocent men are innocent even when proven guilty. One laugh at a bare body mirrors the Heaven's intent. Even a truth that was born yesterday will live forever. There is no sanctuary for what people could utter. Take the green color out of a leaf, leaf stays. Take a leaf out of the green color, green stays. Things that are complex make "truth" look like a mix of oil and water, "shining" like a gush of wind, "smelling" like a deaf howl.

1123.   To attain enlightenment and get back to your senses: you don't have a choice…

1124.   The universe of the awakened is like an intersection of transparent curtains inhabited by Gods. As you go through one you miss the other. As you step back you lose all. The right path is that overwhelming question that everybody has to answer on his own.

1125.   Inhaling and exhaling: you don't have a choice. As you call it, it vanishes. Not even a Buddha would escape this stillness.

1126.   When I wasn't born the time wasn't born. If I'll not die the time would not die. My dilemma: while the universal container survives both principles, in the case exposed here, it does not...

1127.   How does your life respond to your Zazen practice? Whispering...

1128.   Silently, come to the conclusion that oneself is a loving center of all that exists. If you take hold of this meaning you could be full of tears when the moon is rising and full of laugh when the moon descends.

1129.   Attainment: It is as if one were to put the whole universe in a sack and go away with it.

1130.   Water is bound to erode. Mind is bound to think. At the very beginning when there was no water and no mind, what they were bound to? Mind yields to the water what water yields to the mind.

1131.   When no thought arises the innocence takes charge. All the universal things – in their stillness – stare.

1132.   To understand yourself you must light your lamp at night and blow it out in the morning. Properly done it will help you see what keeps you going. Lighting a lamp is like home-coming. Blowing its light out is like ever departing. The light is put out, the wind starts to blow. Though there is an echo here: the light is put out, the wind starts to blow,

1133.   Most of the stars are dark. A bareheaded moon reflects the sun's rays. All things are embalmed with emptiness. The incessant light of a dark universe – the only phenomena that lasts.

1134.   A Zazen room: As a window, it can give you lesson how to see through. As a door, it can give you lesson how to open yourself. The walls are just obstacles that obstruct your becoming… If the floor is your bare mind and the ceiling what you have it covered with, they'll all help you see this room crumbling…

1135.   Late winds from the north smell like snow. Clear flakes on an empty nest.

1136.   When stainless clouds gather above the mountain peak the moon seems utterly lost. Living this very moment is always waiting for its return. If you see moon no more, so be it. If you live, the clouds would disperse. If you don't, they'll flood your body and mind. You'd then see the place where moon rests.

1137.   A throat is meant to be used to breathe, eat and sing. The tongue is just an in-and-out messenger for all.

1138.   Virtue enslaves a man to Heaven, while sin enslaved him to Hell. A naked body is not enslaved to anybody and anything. Born free and free to act. Then what about mind, the enslaver? The foul waters of the thinking mind or of the true self lost in feelings and affections… I'm running now on the neglected road called The Way. I reached the untainted plateau of Mount Summeru. The whole universe is scintillating about, except the living.

1139.   There is no alternative to waves when wind blows.

1140.   Life is like a place where one lives. The small moments are like precious presents, each arriving and offering the light and buzz of the universal drum beat… And then departing…That's all!

1141.   When your mind grasps a thing it looses the infinite. Such an occurrence never surfaces in logic.

1142.   Buddha's wooden statue: A mirror is a hindrance to what the world look like. Thought to look into it one has to hold a mirror by its handle. Examine it closely: eyes are blinking, nostrils are taking air, lips are staying together in a tight smile, and ears are traveling on opposite directions. Although, so much in contention, they're attached to the same wooden head. No matter how long you're going to look at it, you're not going to comprehend what is this until the wooden head is used as fire wood.

1143.   The mountain ascended in front of my eyes and then vanished from sight like a floating landscape drawn on thin paper. At that instant somehow I "knew"…

1144.   Knowing that one day you'd go why don't you accept things as they are? Not trying to change events in your favor is sign of acceptance. Life is unceremonious. Today you see it ugly. One day after tomorrow it may look beautiful. Don't presume that with every snow flake a crow is coming. The frogs are heard croaking at the pond though it is a damn cold day.

1145.   Teacher to student: To scissor cloth is not easy; it is even harder to fashion it if not handled by a good tailor.

1146.   Between a seed and a plant there is this infinite and empty space of possibilities. Seeds that know no life are nameless plants. Emptiness hides myriads of opportunities. You might discover one day that life rules above emptiness and that all that froth of enlightenment is what Champaign bubbles are for: they don't add nothing to the taste, but increase the awareness about what tasting is.

1147.   On your race uphill tiny flies may gather around your head. They're part of your mind. You'd have to take them in with you while awakening.

1148.   Listening to the silverware sound and getting full.

1149.   This butterfly might have traveled long way to get in the middle of the town. All windows which it passes by on its way to nowhere take notice of its shadow. Be never in doubt that what keeps it aloft is your mind.

1150.   In the true way of Zen when a sword is drawn a head leaves a body. Leaves-falling is another Zen situation, not as grim though…

1151.   It is well know that a word or a sound can induce the attainment. One may ask, how come that a *perception* (hearing, understanding) can induce the attainment while the whole practice of Zazen is meant to turn one away from *it*? The answer is that when you're listening without hearing there is no dualism in the sound. "In the silence of a non-dual world a sound could awaken to life the whole universe".

1152.   When one opens his mouth rivers stop in the midstream, birds fall from the sky, fires get extinguished. But the fog and the smoke keep rising. At the city's gate, outside bulls can't get in, inside bulls can't get out. You could think about speech as devil's device. (Though, if you let it go, they get back to moving…)

1153.   In Zen the inner life begins and ends with the cock's crowing. In ordinary life it is the outer path that calls the shots…

1154.   Alternate story: In his afternoon customary walk through the garden a satori seeker saw a frog sitting in Zazen on a lotus leaf. He wanted to ask the frog for advice but wouldn't dare to interrupt her Zazen so he sat down on a patch of grass and waited for her to end her sitting. As the frog ended her Zazen she leaped and disappeared under the water before the Satori seeker could ask her any question. Though in the split second that the frog hit the water the plop sound made him attain full Satori. The moral is that people who are finishing their Zazen could make sounds that help others awaken their long awaited enlightenment.

1155.   A long breath intake binds one to life. As one exhales – the emptiness travels in…

1156.   That the absolute and the relative share the same reality seems at least comforting. As long as one lets mind go without striving for the short lived enlightenment the universe will answer in a true manner to one's inquiries.

1157.   The wail of the autumn heron in the midst of - soon to be covered with snow - lake. Hold it still! Don't speak…

1158.   Listening to the rain through the window like an oyster inside the shell… As I open the window the rain sound is flawless… As I close it I still hear the whole sound by reading my memory. My mind rains…

1159.   You don't need to use torchlight on the way of seeing your true nature. Ancient Buddhas are gone. Today's Buddhas are involved in daily chores.

1160.   A bull can say "I am a bull" to a cow. Whilst a bull will never be aware of being a bull when carrying loads. Furthermore, if for a bull a load doesn't have a name - it still has weight.

1161.   If you know what a pen writes before writing or the song of a bird before she sings or the purpose of a trip when you see a boat resting upside down on the beach sand you're on the way for a true learning. Your spine carries your head with bare hands.

1162.   God! What a wonderful face among the heads of the spring flowers.

1163.   In its outer shell, the universe appears as being made out of bits of known things and facts. Though, well trained Zen eyes could see how the known aspects of the world interpenetrate those aspects beyond understanding.   This mix, though not perfect hangs onto awareness. While the discrimination of the eyes gives adequate answers to matters of practicality, Zen eyes scrutinize the absolute.

1164.   The wind whistles, God appears. They're now one on one, staring. The woods jammed with pine trees are at a loss.

1165.   Living happily a normal life and dying at peace with oneself makes a sublime moment of awakening seem irrelevant. Shut off your sensations, perceptions, judgments, cognition so that you can experience the "great awakening" and so reach the eternal way of Zen sages. As you come back use again your sensations, perceptions, and judgment to live the Way. The suffering may still be there, though different…

1166.   Autumn: God takes a ride on every wave and every cry…

1167.   Beaten or caressed by the wind the wheat looks like a bliss. And the reeds in their marches… Listen, they all converse, though, letting no sound to emerge unaccounted for…

1168.   Now that you "know" what emptiness is, pretend that reality is what is and not just a mind chasing its own tail…

1169.   God designed things that are white. So – white is known. What if, just if – the white was unknown. The cherry tree would then be heard croaking like a crow on a hot day.

1170.   A flower loosens up in the morning and squeezes down at night. Her blossom though is timeless.

1171.   Rapid eyes see in slow motion. The deepness of space carries history. And truth is everywhere. If you look right or left the truth emerges. Discrimination or indiscrimination. The clearing is wearing a dew lace on each grass blade. Early morning and yet, the sun announces a hot day. Flies like green leaves conceal their flight. As reality shows up the truth go in exile. One says: fears of knowing are claiming all those names in the graveyard.

1172.   When a firefly removes its sandals before going to bed God's design of the world is suddenly revealed.

1173.   The present and the past: mind could be neither a refuge for knowledge nor an instrument to measure the immeasurable. Flying around the universe in a dew-drop.

1174.   The essence will still be unknown to those who bow their head to a stone statue of Buddha. In a ceremonial one has to take Buddha's statue for what it is: just a stone, as one sets Buddha's shape aside. But then, with no Buddha shape, has the stone an essence any longer?

1175.   The numbers on the ceiling divide what is indivisible. The letters on the floor can't say a word about it.

1176.   There are two fundamental Zen principles: one is to try to look into the incomprehensible and attain awakening; the other is to follow the normal course of life in purpose and scope. The first one teaches one how to obtain a moment of awe-enlightenment! The later one helps one master a life as if it was a

Zen life. In any way of life the sun is rising when the moon is falling and vice versa. One might say: meditating uselessly I wasted my whole life trying to listen to the emptiness' original call. Others, who lived plainly and unimpressed by the noiseless echo of the beginning of all might say: I wasted my whole life with no will to see what is beyond a bird's flight. To use life as a shield against emptiness just breathe steadily: you'll live forever.

1177.   The seal of the mind snaps: myriads of forms are sighted watching you with more insights than your own conscience…

1178.   Taking a koan for practicing is like swallowing a cherry that has an olive taste and waiting anxiously to see what is going to come out after digesting it.

1179.   Heavy clouds are carrying the moonlight towards the mountain peak.

1180.   Hidden source, hidden truth! Some stumble into it by chance. Others are like those fools searching for a buried treasure in a desert ground. To see the untainted original face some have to do steady work. Washing floors and ceilings, washing ceilings and floors, until the last stubborn spot is gone. A fly droppings still keep one hostage in the realm of the learned principles.

1181.   The tentacles of the world locked into one's mind: floating into empty waters…

1182.   An old woman was telling her doctor how she swallowed by mistake a Christmas bell. Whatever she did afterward, she could hear the bell ringing in her belly until the day when she fell that she became one with the bell. She fainted when she eventually found the bell in her stool. The koan is like the old woman's story: It gets into your body and mind until you become one with it. As you get awakened the koan goes away.

1183.   Canned words that could help you pass through the gate: (emptiness enclosed).

1184.   Gulping a glass of emptiness is like taking a direct punch under your belly. To ignore life in the name of an alternative truth is what a fox would like to call "fish wisdom".

1185.   Staring at a mirror and trying to avoid its reflection I saw the Happy Buddha smiling. His marble teeth and his tongue were all gone. Still keeping his own eyes in the view…

1186.   Emptiness is more than nothingness though they appear equal in foliage…

1187.   The Buddha's statue that I brought home has that unbearable smell of rotten cheese. As I threw it out the smell turned out to be worse. As I brought back Buddha's statue the smell miraculously got lost to sight.

1188.   Thinking aloud while talking in a whisper: "We're all Buddhas".

1189.   The pig that changes its name to horse is not going to win a race. The moral is: be what you are, discover who you are. A borrowed name doesn't come with a long tail attached to it.

1190.   The ageless time got trapped in an ephemeral mind.

1191.   Nirvana cannot be bought and cannot be sold. For somebody who wants to keep his ego intact after enlightenment the only trouble is that there is no diploma or medal to confirm it. Nirvana graduate is yet another idea that will fit like a glove one's business oriented fingers.

1192.   Incense – nonsense. Ocean bound fragrances…

1193.   Seeing a wrong thing as truth is human. Most people die without knowing their neighborhood. Goat skins are not warm if not wore fur-inside-skin-outside. For a goat this may sound so unnatural…

1194.   Reality is hypothetical. The absolute is hypothetical. The enlightenment is an illusion. Buddha is the name of my dog. The enlightenment is like a bark. The absolute is its bite. Reality is painful.

1195.   A butterfly never starves between the petals of a rose. The mind does…

1196.   Chopping onions and trying not to separate myself from the experience, I cut my finger. Then to record this Zen happening I wrote this koan down on the back of my palm: "Chopping onions and trying not to separate myself from the experience, I cut my finger".

1197.   All encompassing, all compassing, all compassionate…

1198.   Through its senses the body filters phenomena before offering them to the mind for consumption. Somewhere, on the silent path, mind reveals what body never knew about: take a look…

1199.   Words give to a world an image. Images give to a world a path. Eyes starring at Buddha pointing elsewhere...

1200.   I don't understand why nature seems more alive for the one that is dying than for the one that lives. But then, I know that when the mind lets go and is ready to pass through the gate, there are moments of unobstructed contemplation…

1201.   When the emptiness is on your side the world falls silent. When it is on the other side the regulated sounds of the day start their trip: birds are shrieking, winds are whistling, pines are whispering and the boat engine is belching in the shallow waters...

1202.   Getting visions not through your eyes and knowing the seasons from examining your own ashes.

1203.   In life and also in Zazen there is one bow you make when you enter and another bow when you exit.

1204.   A koan is an indestructible wood horse. You whip it to race, it doesn't move. You climbed its saddle; it carries you to high places. Don't ever try to get rid of it, for if you do you may find dinosaur bones in your drawers.

1205.   When you light your lamp the mountains get nearer. One step ahead and they'll move back. It is known to Earth; also it is written in the moon's log.

1206.   Who stole the flowing secret of the river? Or the flying secret of the bird? Or the living secret of the beings? Found hidden in a word that said nothing...

1207.   If you want to take care of Mankind you may hear Mankind asking you to take care first of your own business. Mankind is complete and self sufficient to itself. Washing your hands before meals is what Mankind expects from you. And if you're not aware that you washed your hands wash them once more.

1208.   If the emergence of *this* occurs within discrimination it illuminates thoughts kept for eons in darkness. As far as mind goes this highlights the absolute within the relative. Think with no thoughts of the "talking", talk with no words of the "saying". What is it?

1209.   Dualism: swimming like a fish but behaving like a fox.

1210.   Amoeba! Sorry for not carrying eyes… Is amoeba the only carrier of the emptiness? Not having legs to dance, beak to crow, ears open for echoes… As one goes up on the evolution scale the clouds get milkier, the boundless universe collapses with each resonance…

1211.   To practice Zen we sit. To become Buddha we do everything else but sit. To fail being Buddha we stand.

1212.   Before my very nature shows any sign of permanence I'm not going to put a hood over my eyes. Watching the clear sky in ecstasy I hang all my cloth on a flag pole. Naked, ready for a nightly bath in the cold river. My feelings of gracelessness, the only scoundrels!

1213.   The formless and soundless emptiness manifest itself in forms and sounds. It manifest itself thus in order to be known though it doesn't have any knowledge about itself. Emptiness revealed as suchness?

1214.   The peak snow never melts. Either the ice is century old or it must have snowed incessantly for centuries on this peak. If snow comes from the same universal womb, the green pastures must be old alike. The moral is: if you like to know what century old stuff means go for a walk on the mountain pasture.

1215.   Look within to see how your inner life pays respect to the outer life. If you think you do well in this "respect" don't say a word; otherwise, squeak.

1216.   Know yourself if you can. The body is the house where mind and self live together. Mind looks for the self and cannot find a trace of it. Is it a no-mind going to find it?

1217.   Words deceive us even on matters of immortality. Seeing everything as is and yet being pushed blindfolded towards the no-knowing. The boat touched the river bottom. Birds pass overhead; mountains come and go with the floating water. No sounds though. You can't go back, you can't move forward. The hollow landscape is of no help and no man would come to the rescue.

1218.   Like the winter's moon: snow white for a dropped eyelid.

1219.   What is Buddha? An obese man carved in stone. Now tell me: Is the stone also Buddha? If so, why don't you buy the original stone used in carving? You must not say Mu!

1220.   When a body is leaving the Heaven's sound echoes alive.

1221.   One could certainly say that he/she was born. One could certainly say that he/she will die. Birth from which death follows, and so on… One could not certainly say that the Everest snow cap will ever melt. The moral is that feeling the eternity in one's life span is hard-hitting.

1222.   No time to spare? Above your head is the moon; below your head is the downer deep.

1223.   If the mystery of what this very moment is lies in the clapping of one hand it means that the boundless universe will never be known. A fruit sweetening in the sun is the only miracle one gets. "Live free", the rooster crows. "Die free" the owl echoes.

1224.   When the enlightenment is "known" to whomever it happens some contradictory aspects of the reality stop to oppose each other while other aspects get slightly disjunctive.

1225.   If one awakens during an act of courage one becomes invincible. If one awakens during a stupor one remains in that stupor for myriads of eons. If one could let go the awakening the common path would become the Grand Way: pleasant if it's pleasant, painful meanwhile... But there is nothing wrong to delight your spirit with the luxury of some spiritual discipline.

1226.   On the Way words told are like lianas. Silence is like the sharpness of a snowy landscape under moonlight.

1227.   Zazen is like the fog on a mountain peak. When the fog is thick you don't see too much and are still climbing. When the fog is thinner you understand the dangers and stop, waiting for the fog to clear before climbing again.

1228.   God counts the head of the herdsman as part of the cattle inventory.

1229.   Where "I" talks, the ego listens. If the "I" goes on a ride the ego's entrails are served as a specialty desert to monks worldwide.

1230.   Satori: The passage of time is iced up in Zen. So is the space. When Satori evaporates the heavenly gates close down: the passage of time becomes swift, the space becomes fluid again. Waken up from its dormant fabric the bear goes out to find sweet honeycombs and water. The honey is sweet, the bees' stings are painful, the water is refreshing and the ground is a good scratchier. (What a wonderful life: Live it plainly, forget the Zen folklore...)

1231.   On long legs one could see more than one could see on short legs. Though on long legs one would have difficulties while sweeping the dust or cleansing his feet of cow shit.

1232.   If you hear a tree talking be careful: wooden words can start easily forest fires.

1233.   A Zen man is a man whose eyes lost their sight and whose tongue lost its speech. So, he can tell you more of things that have no sight and no speech, like birth and death.

1234.   The melon flowers sing, the rice flowers sing: the song comes down the hill – as Buddhas gaze one at each other.

1235.   Coming and going the spring unfolds a few leaves on a branch of a dead peach tree. This year no leaves sprouted. (Those few leaves that meant more than a whole orchard in bloom...)

1236.   A mosquito Zen meets a spider Zen. They greet each other then the mosquito Zen starts talking about Buddhism, Zen Tao, etc. After a while of uninterrupted talk he asks the spider Zen: "You didn't say a thing... Are you not interested in enlightenment stuff?" "While you talked about it I knitted this three pound of flax net", said the spider Zen. "What's so great about it?" asked the mosquito Zen. "Try it!" said the spider Zen. The mosquito Zen tried the net and got caught in it. "You understand now what three pound of flax mean?" the spider asked. "You have now enough food to practice your Zazen for a while" the mosquito Zen said. "As we are at this point", the mosquito Zen continued, "Tell me what Buddha is?" After a moment of thought the spider Zen said: "Everything is Buddha". The moral is that you still keep being enlightened if you eat what you catch. Everything is Buddha means that sometimes you eat Buddha to carry on.

1237.   Satori: It's not going to last an eternity. Not enough either to see in a mirror how your original-face looked like.

1238.   What is Buddha? I'll tell you if you ask me nothing more...

1239.   An ignorant would be thrilled to know that in the mind there is "nothing". Though that will keep him not interested in awakening. A wise one would let "nothing" take over. In an empty room lots of sounds come from outside. In a room to be emptied the outside sounds are pushed away.

1240.   The universe guides us how to move from knowing to knower and then go back to not knowing to realize our truth.

1241.   What is the way? A breath! Innocent solitudes! Children on their way to the river... The sea of laughs and cries. Though the eyes help they're not part of the tale. The ears disappear with the last echoes. The finest scents fill up the empty body before it reaches the unknown. A butterfly bakes on a rock as the autumn ends.

1242.   The moon, still like a gravestone. Your mind is inside while your body is emptied. The mirroring sky is the only presence.

1243.   The truth shines better in a piece of cow shit than it does on a gold leaf. Shit wither, gold withhold. Though, the ultimate grave will see both neither true nor untrue...

1244.   Emptiness: Being born but birthless, being dead but deathless: the web of doubt got ripped by a ray from within.

1245.   Egoless is a precondition to see the True nature. Trembling like a leaf, roaring like a dying boar "I" goes into exile: Mu and "I", both becoming eternal while sniffing life with a last breath...

1246.   There are vacant seats on the front row reserved to Buddhas. Expensive seats. If you see an ox on any seat it is obvious that the ox is overstating his case. The question is if an ox is Buddha by birth why is he waiting to mature before taking a seat? The other thing is that since an ox cannot pass his tail through the gate he cannot get to the row in the first place.

1247.   Joke: In their quest to awakening Caucasian monkeys are more resourceful than Peruvian monkeys. So what's the meaning of burning incense, bowing, running inside the hut with a giggle to avoid sudden rains, spilling tea drops on wooden floors, fanning the shadow of the moon while squeezing a fart by contracting the muscles of your buttocks while doing group Zazen?

1248.   The straight line sings the Heaven's song.

1249.   Flies loving and ants loving make my Zazen unbearable. Even on a mountain peak under corrosive ice I could see them flying around once the sun is up. If Zen was an universal law wasn't it supposed to see to it that the insects would act in accord with what Zazen needed? If not, it's clear that an ant can't have a Buddha nature. If you want some privacy in the house of Buddha use bugs repellents.

1250.   If the world one sees is not real then to see a moon with five paws roaming the woods would be a sheer possibility. Don't look, and you'll see it…

1251.   No landscape in sight? Then you know that you reached the no-shore land.

1252.   The constancy of the events empties them of sense. That's why attention and awareness are needed: as you eat your mind is eating, (eating, eating – be attentive)… As you play your mind is playing (playing, playing – be attentive). Every single moment initiates another moment. If your mind is far away your life is lost. Cook as if the whole world lives on your cooking. Never let your mind depart from it for a mere second. Read in your mind the way you should cut onion, and then follow your hand path to the oven, free from other thoughts. As you set up the cooking timer remember that time is your friend watching for the food not to get burnt. As you eat biting deep into your meal you can get easily awakened.

1253.   If you arrived at your destination don't go further. If you did not, don't turn back.

1254.   All rivers are flowing. So does one's mind. Mountains irrigate the surroundings with moving shadows. The faded trees let leaves go. The rain on the roof sounds like a quickened drum beat. Be the drum!

1255.   Nature is flawless if the mind doesn't intervene.

1256.   The thoughts come from one's ears, eyes, nose and mouth. To invite thoughts to leave you'd have to constantly pock your head. Zen way to achieve same result is to get rid of attachments. When vinegar flies don't smell vinegar they leave the place. Emptying the house with no chair to sit on and no bed to sleep on… Be the attentive visitor.

1257.   Fox songs attract fish singers.

1258.   To sustain hope one must follow the compassionate road with no diversion or deceit. The question is: should one grind the synthetic koan to get awakened or make some room in his/her conscience to reflect on suffering of all beings? Some assent that life is too short to be taken seriously. Wake up, eat, play, laugh, cry and sleep. The rest shall be at God's mercy. Awakening for the sake of seeing the ultimate illusion is an egotistic and powerless game. A good word given to a sufferer can propagate like a warm day all over the universe.

1259.   On a rainy day you wear a raincoat. On a snowy day you wear a heavy coat. On a Zen day you wear Zazen.

1260.   When the lips part the thoughts line up for attention. The mind has to choose which one to pick. Some thoughts wear bells on their tails. Trapp the noisy ones as they begin to sound! A bird in flight doesn't know of the hunter's intentions. Seeing lightening they hide in thick bushes. There is a rainbow in the sky when the little birds learn *to fly*. When what flight is becomes known, the mystery of what "*to fly*" is, is lost.

1261.   Yet not – "Not yet!" At the instant you'd get wrapped up as a whole, the time and space will vanish. A single eye to open the gate! A grain of dust to close it!

1262.   Like an answer to a koan, the silent mirror brought force a baby mirror. Nonetheless, my teacher says, the wall mirror spat out her Karma.

1263.   The door slams, your thinking stops. In the silence that follows you could see through the wall… Make sure you got the whole picture before the bell rings: In the foliage a blue magpie is picking its wings…

1264.   Truths held under the absolute seal sway at the first breeze. Then, the world of the unknown crumbles with the first rooster crow…

1265.   The fraternal look of a Buddha's statue: smiling at the brief thought that equals one's whole life.

1266.   This is not "what-is" and it is not "what-is-not". A pot, though a simple object, is not a pot. It is not a duck either. But when you cook a duck in the pot, the pot becomes immediately what the pot is and the duck becomes immediately what the pot is not…

1267.   When, almost obsessively, I used to practice Zazen, I started to have strange insights. One day I had the insight that the inside of a flower pot is the same as it's outside. Though the pot in my mental image was made out of ceramic I could easily push its bottom up and get the reverse pot out of it as if it was made out of a sheet of plastic. I understood that the reality-as-is represents "some reality" and that the mind can create a totally different reality out of it. That's how I started to look at reality as being nothing but sheer phenomena.

1268.   When the modification of the mind-works occurs the first tendency is to control it. The right attitude should be instead not to ignore it (be aware!) while letting it go.

1269.   A word leaves a pattern into the air, a thought does not. Knowing without saying is like seeing what is seen without pointing at it.

1270.   The bones in the cave used to sit in Zazen. When breathing went away, they collapsed.

1271.   Certainly, nothing is permanent. This is good news for hatred, or, for the sake of the example for any other malady. That love can't last forever is a pity. Though, if you look at the transient world with the eyes of a child you should love life as no other better game in town. Worthier still, than eternity.

1272.   Using the whole mind to see each thing, one thing at one time, shining in the ocean of the infinite emptiness.

1273.   In real life innocence can get you in a lot of trouble. In Zen, it could be a one step to awakening. While awakening, one might realize that all things are innocent, regardless…

1274.   If truth exists, lie is a disease. If truth is doubtful, a lie is like a spice that lends some flavor to "nothingness".

1275.   Someone says: "This awakening sham!" which is a critique too harsh to swallow. We're all thieves while trying to get there, and there is no judgment one could apply to those that succeeded to steal it. Either Mu or no-Mu, every ride-to-achieve-it asks for some integrity of character. A cracked pot can't hold water. I learned all these while carrying one.

1276.   Those who advanced their spiritual quest beyond birth and death will never be reborn. Thos who did not go so far have still hopes that they will be reborn.

1277.   The universe is perfect: it is square round…

1278.   The billions of traces onto one's mind are like an ocean of water assaulted by weeds. Zazen uproots the weeds one by one, making the water crystal clear.

1279.   After awakening any path points towards the original and ultimate truth, which is "thus" anyway.

1280.   Awakening: confirming nothing else but that knowledge is truth and that there is no other reality but this. Frame your words; put them in agreement with facts. When grounds stand you're alive. When grounds shake your life might be questionable. You could say in both cases with poise: I'm here and now. Even when it comes to eternity you'll have the last word.

1281.   Dropping a reflection in the mirror – like dropping body and mind…

1282.   From the foothill to the mountain peak, there is only one illness that can cure a medicine: Illness-Zen, Medicine-Knowledge.

1283.   Million years ago, the same snow falling on the same mountain made no attempt to be seen. Now, it is seen though as it is restlessly moving with each puff of air its mystery deepens. The little fleets of broken ice will never touch the river's bottom.

1284.   Going down the ropes is easy. Going up the ropes is hard. This shows how using the same vehicle (the mind) one could get easily down and out of Zazen and hardly back up and into it.

1285.   A wise man keeps sitting in Zazen using his feet on the floor. In the right position there is nothing else you could do to attain peace. Zazen in levitation raises alarming questions about what ground is for. Thousand archers charging their bows with no target to hit.

1286.   A bird passed through the oak leaves like a rocket. I could see through the hollow she made the swelling ocean awakened by its cry.

1287.   Mind has, as any other box, a side that opens and closes. Then again, where is the key?

1288.   Moments that wake up in one's breath: Besides some common way of living watch the trees in their nightly shrouds, halting the wind.

1289.   A mocking bird is wired to eat fireflies. Fireflies are wired to run away from a mocking bird. Though they don't intimate each other they're dancing on the same tune.

1290.   If awakening is the end of seeking, it is just the beginning to those who want to serve. Trailing your own steps from dawn to dusk! And this painful thought, that at the end, your task to help others – even if you started it already – will never be complete.

1291.   Like a hermit setting his hand aflame to prove to himself that he's still alive and well.

1292.   Gathering fuel to make tea: a one foot log afire to taste a tea leaf.

1293.   Attachments are like little birds chirping with every breeze. They know no way to silence. (The attachments are the breeze, you're the chirping). One way to weaken and in due course to get rid of attachments is not to hold on stuff beyond simple necessities. A pretentious label would sound like: "Zen is the twilight of a copious bourgeois life". Though, once one reaches awakening one can go back and be again a bourgeois. The emptiness doesn't care.

1294.   Snow returns with every winter. It comes with each mind thinking snow. That sound of swallows that you can hear no more.

1295.   In a clay pot the flower of spring… Though, the root is the fathomless miracle to take notice of.

1296.   One doesn't know what another man lived through while being awakened. The experience is so personal that a man's sorting to get there is a completely different than another man's sorting.

1297.   Zazen: When somebody knocks at my door my neighbor answers. I hear him saying: "I didn't see this guy for weeks. I think he's gone! I hear sometimes a moan. I think it is his cat. He has a cat, you know! He named her Buddha".

1298.   The past is no more, the future is not yet. And the present keeps devouring the bitterness of having all these let go, without getting anything besides living…

1299.   When you do good things Karma departs. When you do bad things, Karma returns. Keep a safety distance from its path and you'll be okay.

1300.   Awareness could be a new way of teaching. To show, for instance, what is the difference between glass, stone and a brick, without using a concept; you could use a hammer to smash them to pieces on an iron block. You'd have the iron also explained, implicitly. In the relative mind of course the hammer would be "what smashes" and the materials "what is being smashed". An enlightened mind wouldn't be able to make such a distinction.

1301.   Every teaching ends up with touching the ultimate question: is the immediacy of life worth of being subject to meditation? What about the immediacy of the lifeless world?

1302.   Want a different life? Live first this one till the end. On the bedroom walls hungry mosquitoes wait to see your body become a delectable sleeping bag of flesh. Your body serves always a purpose when you live. Your mind is its voice… As you feel the sting your mind says "Ouch!"

1303.   Thoughts are like cut flowers. Only if Buddha holds them up you'd get their insight.

1304.   Going and not going, moving and stopping. Now, <u>there</u> is <u>here</u>. Don't ask where <u>there</u> will be tomorrow. Live this minute a minute longer.

1305.   No beginning – no end. Like a gust of wind in the desert: going through, going through! A gust of wind… Enough marvel to enrapture a myriad eons of thinking.

1306.   Each thing at its time. Each time as long as it lasts.

1307.   Form is something that is seen but is inexpressible. The same is the sound.

1308.   After being awakened you'll continue living. Though, the expectancies would prove to be poor: neither every tree is going to blossom nor hatred would change into love.

1309.   One mind can erect one Buddha. One egg can bring into being one bird. A mystery is hidden in whatever we tell. Why do we utter words? Not a thing can be thought without discrimination! Mountains of words, hills of tales, none giving an answer... When a voice fades and goes – its question still lingers. Scroll filled with question marks burned by day to keep warm, their ashes scattered by night to clear the air.

1310.   Metaphysics comes from afar: that is God, time, space, matter and the origin of everything. When emptiness manifests around we could see it. When it manifests within we get awakened.

1311.   The emptiness (wrapped in forms and shapes): I wish the path to see it wouldn't be just a paradox.

1312.   Under the blue arch of the sky a crow's angry cries put at test a principle to its core: peace of mind is a mind at peace with whatever life brings forth, including anger.

1313.   The original face – a faceless Buddha.

1314.   When reality is the host, the mind is the guest. When mind is the host, the reality is the guest. When none is the host, who's the guest? Who's the host?

1315.   Hanging like a tomato on a string beans vine? A string bean is the fruit of a string bean vine. A tomato is the fruit of a tomato vine. The individuals are born in Heaven. Now, where the intimation that all things are empty comes from? Keep your jaws closed; cover your ears with your hands. Look straight in the eyes of Buddha and see through it.

1316.   The mysterious lost childhood. From its secluded memory nothing perspires. What had happened is not important. How did it happened, why my present metaphysical form cannot see anymore what was my past? The water I used to bath in looks in my memory like a lacquered rock.   Clouds stopped floating. Was it real, this past? When a dog dies first his smell dies, then its eyes die, then eventually his ears. His body freezes. With one's childhood things proceed the same way. As I try to unlock its jaws my dog's barks sound painful. And yet, I take my childhood as it was… for granted. Maturity is what awakening is not. You own the universe and you don't know it. As you loose it you get answers, wrestling with the God's whiskers. The knowledge of deceit? Then one day the innocent thought haunts you: you go an inch further: the food starves you and the water make you thirstier. Then it is time for you to embark on a different boat. I thought that all roads eventually escort one to the same destination. I forgot that when my childhood ended the cherries were still blooming on the hillside and that I wouldn't waste a breath without being that sweet smell when passing by. Now all that Heaven ended. You greet the moon, you get a reply. You meet a fox you just stare at it, in distrust.

1317.   Remember, when you're born, you're a stranger. When you die, you go home. Please mind your steps before you get there. The universe is showing you a path that is just "It".

1318.   Zen soldiers: In the midst of a war being at peace with the whole universe…

1319.   Shake the light in a glass and you'll see after a while darkness. That's how a world you think about gets replaces by the

world of the unknown. Stacks of pots, filled with things that
cannot be undone. Mostly spit...

1320.   Fear of life is more terrible than the fear of death.

1321.   The <u>impermanence </u>of a bird in the air, flickering stars,
flooding getting back to the river bed, a log turning into ashes,
aging elephants being removed from the circus stables, one
minute earlier or one minute too late, a tongue sticking out in a
picture taken one century ago, confused by the crossing roads...,
cocoa crops burning, soap opera plots, shadows as we live, not yet
born but marching towards the one hundred birthday anniversary,
truth - utterly true though it lost its meaning, when you finally got
used to it – it is all taken away...

1322.   The cupids with bows and arrows are overlooking the
Lovers Pond. Ducks swim around, unaware...

1323.   Reality is an angle, mind is another angle. It just happens
that they meet on occasions.

1324.   To awaken to this drum beat and realize that is placidly
coming from your mind. Just yesterday you thought that this
reservoir was empty. As unpleasant as this thought may be, it is
empty indeed. Finally, you're a Zen addict.

1325.   In life there is either night or day. In Zen they are still
there, though you can't take them in vain anymore.

1326.   A dead moth in a spider web knows more about spiders
than a living moth. Though in the eyes of the spider such
knowledge doesn't mean much.

1327.   A no change world ever talks. Its manifestation never
gets witnessed.

1328.   Mind is not born so it will never die. How wonderful? Knowing that, watch the butterflies in the garden; so beautiful and so ephemeral. You must know by now that your mind will outlive them.

1329.   In a sunny day an answer given about rain fails the mark.

1330.   Taking a nap amidst weeds and bony grasshoppers: I hear in their song a saw cutting slices of nothingness. Wild birds answering. Dew glazed white poppies like huge snow flakes covering my eyes…

1331.   On the edge of the Way – thousand barriers. As you penetrate one the chilly ghost of Buddha stares at you with a lifeless eye: "What are you seeking after?" he might ask. "Go back! Live your life, cherish every moment. But remember: the compassion you give to others benefits this barrier that you just passed through". Then Buddha might blow his nose and say: "Pretty chilly in Heaven!".

1332.   A sample of Zen: Wrap empty stuff in something, like what your senses want, and make it intelligible by inventing a word for it. Then empty the word out of your mind.

1333.   The realization of the Oneness in every moment of life is called living one's oneness. A moment of oneness followed by another moment of oneness, etc. Does one need to live in a rigorous way to achieve this? Zen says: just do one thing at a time and be aware of it, as if you're one with your thought. Don't wobble! Struggling thoughts bring about contradiction. When contradiction occurs there is less awareness. (With the advent of modern computers multitasking operating systems are now common: they are non-Zen machines, of course…)

1334.   Water: to pour it or to taste it means to have a conversation with the water. Watch as it rolls its tiny drops: flickering wings drawing patterns of universality! Everywhere...

1335.   A Koan is like placebo medicine. If you don't question its power it cures you of duality.

1336.   Doing Zazen you live longer by being absent from a world of transactions. The no-lose-no-gain principle in life sounds in Zazen like no-sooner-no-later. When mind ceases to trade you could hear the wind eroding a gravestone. Is the grave stone ephemeral? Is the wind ephemeral?

1337.   Language is as uniform as emptiness is. Only its usage is broken. As one abolishes the mind the truth is still there. Dropping the body and mind, what a wonderful, wonderful deed...

1338.   If logical mind has limitations, the intuition follows it closely. If you discriminate badly you have a good chance to have a broken awakening: that is, you'd walk with a foot in the village's cesspool, and another one on the surface of the universal ocean.

1339.   Start Zazen when you have nothing more to say...

1340.   "Your philosophical background makes emptiness seem difficult to conquer. Don't despair. Stop thinking. Your knowledge will be easily forgotten".

1341.   Zazen posture resembles a religious practice: a posture that can never suggest life not even to the barking dogs roaming around. Closing the outside boundaries of articulated thoughts to an inside of undifferentiated blossoms... Dogs are asleep outside; cats are bracing to catch a koan mouse...

1342.   Zazen: Not knowing where you go and not being worried when you'd arrive...

1343.   Zen is a game in which the player is asked to play with things as if they could be equally resolved by the mind: the mountain and breeze are equal, so are a flower and a cow-shit, hatred and love, an atom and the universe. Words are teased to get out of the mind; on the other hand they're teased to do first some explaining. I like best the expression of the unspoken in a spoken world…

1344.   You can't reason out Zen things. Every day is a road to Happiness. Wearing a Zen badge could have some impending effect when the road ends in front of the Hell's gate.

1345.   Neither high, nor low – in one's thoughts. The unsung morning breath, the immeasurable horizon marching forward. Now and always, here and everywhere…

1346.   Since everything existent is empty, talking and listening point to the same outcome: emptiness is loosing ground by gaining weight. (Would emptiness gain ground by loosing weight?)

1347.   What's the meaning of the Sun coming to the West? Is someone trying to make a mock at a Zen koan? The Zen beat up drums are pierced, and the koan calves are now those big bulls showing their profile behind the gate's gap. Still craving for a Zen secret? The bulls are just visiting here and are trained to stop moving and stand still once their tail reaches the glass's broken corner. One bull is talking to another: "It you think taking something useful for the road leave home your tail!"

1348.   Zen Joke: A man fell and broke his two arms. He suddenly understood that he cannot fix a broken arm using the other broken arm. The moral is: Brake only one arm at a time and you'll be okay.

1349.   A horse takes a wave as a whip and a moon ray as a horseshoe spark. But it takes the water, shining or not, as something that'd quench its thirst. For a horse, at least, water's truth is in the drinking not in the thinking.

1350.   Coming back after penetrating the barrier: the dew on the grass blade looks like a starry firmament. The words of Zen masters are as empty as their rotten skulls.

1351.   To steal an awakening you'd have to get in its very proximity.

1352.   In one's body, a captive mind. In one's mind, a captive Buddha. Like an eagle flying above a mountain peak: looking for a pray, it docsn't see the mountain.

1353.   Oh, Buddha! Deliver me from knowing so that I could see the truth.

1354.   The limpid sky surrounded by cumulus clouds: white hair around Buddha's bald head. Under snow the dead sleep of snow-tops. Above snow, the dead sleep of snow-man.

1355.   One lives in All, All returns to One.

1356.   Anger is like a gutter. Hanging on to thoughts of hatred, that you cannot make go silent! A big rat passes through your mid damaging the brain's furniture. If you can find in darkness the blackboard (on which is written in chalk: EMPTY) and the wooden shoes of the first Buddha, you could surely save yourself.

1357.   A koan is like a cat's paw: silent when moves alone, scratchy when faced.

1358.   Light is light, dark is dark. They're both harmless. Though when you put a light off you could feel the darkness' long teeth tasting your bones.

1359.   Silence rejuvenates the unutterable words.

1360.   The difference between a bow and a rain-bow is that one is used to aim at; the other is the color and form of that aim.

1361.   The firefly is chasing its own shadow. From one grass blade darting to another grass blade: short flashes fired with all its might. Playing hide and seek with the emptiness. "Peek-a-boo!" Who's talking?

1362.   No breeze – no emptiness.

1363.   The past is like retrieving a shadow from the mind and placing it on hold. The conclusion that "you never thought that it would end up like this" applies to the future also. That's why the present has to be always the only one's concern. What is life if not presents chained together? By taking care of the present your future may become later a better past. The saying "learn from the future how you can correct your past" is just another way to say that you should live manifestly involved in the paradoxical present: a present becoming past and also a present becoming future.

1364.   Mind turned upon body to ask about matters of life and death: an illusion walking on two feet… One set out to follow the mind, the other set out to follow the body. Then, there is the self… Remember: the hunter has to put in thoughts what a falcon puts in the act… Your mind is the hunter, your self is the falcon, and your body is an ephemeral target…

1365.   Being one with your life doesn't mean that you're one with the whole universe. The illusion of the enlightenment that you're one with the universe is so ephemeral that the only way to get it back is by repeating the awakening experience. Since you can never repeat it, you're at a loss…

1366.   Knowing that the whole universe lives within and still going places to find it?

1367.   If you run, pay attention to your feet. If you sit, pay attention to your mind. Serving tea, pay attention to your hands. If you burn Buddha, he's not going to confirm your awakening.

1368.   Cut your finger before pointing at "THIS" and you'll get it in a flash.

1369.   What is beyond life and death is also beyond what is obvious. The vastness of this very moment when there is nothing to be known about, besides silence. A saw cutting firewood is heard now and then. It is raining on the other side of the road though the morning was here as bright as it was there.

1370.   Born to get clothed. Dying to get naked.

1371.   Somebody complained one day that if the present would be longer than a moment - let's say it would be one hour - he'd be able to plan better for the future. I thought of his grievance and I found out that indeed each present is exactly one hour of present.

1372.   Seating in Zazen like a vulture floating above a mountain peak…

1373.   Like the tossing of a ball: if it rolled towards South it stays as perfect as if it rolled towards North. What's not perfect is part of the imaginary surroundings.

1374.   My mind starves for words that could look straight in the eye: like a color does…

1375.   Shades of wings whiter than the snow. The sky is so close, a blue mist all around. The girl who was gathering daisies earlier comes by: "Have you ever seen the entrance?"

1376.   If you find a relic worth having wash thoroughly its bones and throw them to the dog. If you find Buddha's bones do the same. What school of Zen is this? It is the school where one awakens his Buddhahood before seeing Buddha's bones displayed in a case. And the moral is that a dog should have more regard for a Buddha's bones than a Buddha seeker.

1377.   Turn your face to see the ancient lamp carried by a shadow. Turn again to hear the bamboo talk. The ego that kept only to itself consents to go. With no words the thoughts follow. Not a yawning moment before it strikes: ghostly faces serenely coming into view.

1378.   Suffering will let you suffer. Whistling will let you whistle. The white snow looks like a white horse. One and the same original face for every man: scented swords...

1379.   Talking or not talking, having a speech or being speechless? It takes a lot of courage to do both. Words are malignant, so are the pauses between words. Dharma lives in the act only...

1380.   When the state of mind is foggy the river misses the ocean and the kindred Zen-spirits grow claws and fangs. The stained mirror is like a quickened spring in the midwinter: springing leaves learn what freezing is. So sad and as loud as things are said here, one can see no flowers across the clearing...

1381.   Trying to see the wind you may stumble on a tornado. Better not knowing? Let it come to you now and sweep you away.

1382.   The emptiness conquest: what koan is better for a quick and inexpensive awakening? With Zen getting a solid marketing position monks eat better rice nowadays than Buddha himself. My advise is: If an expensive awakening comes onto your way, bow deeply, let it pass.

1383.   A firefly climbing up on a ray of moonlight.

1384.   A Zen remark either fails to open one's eyes or it fails to close one's eyes if they're shut.

1385.   The emptiness fills the sky with so many stars. They sail by midnight. At down they're all gone.

1386.   Enlightened and yet coping with irrelevant knowledge – like a body that forgot what eating is: or if the howls mean that awakening strikes back!

1387.   A fisherman would understand better what holding still and letting go means. Focus on one act and you'll lose the other. (Fish set aside, the whole universe is besieged in a catch). Now, figure out a way to come clear of this mess.

1388.   Watching the mountains ascend and the valleys descend and marking off the point where no ascending is and no descending.

1389.   The nest on the mountain peak was used as late as the last millennium. Skeleton birds are still hatching…

1390.   The pain of being innocent: to sport with sharks in the presence of immortality.

1391.   The gratifying shores of a mind in which the moon shines incessantly.

1392.   The way to Heaven is the immediate state of mind: plum flowers dazzle a bee; rain – a pure throw; no hidden presence into the clear; the limpid water greets the Great Silence.

1393.   Winds from the East rinses out dust from the West.

1394.   Neither sleeping on a knowledge pillow, nor bouncing like a no-mind on a Zen-net.

1395.   Water builds clouds. Mind builds illusions. That's how the blue sky gets hidden. The clouds move freely so that the mind could see the sky. The illusions need more than a gust of wind. Beat the drums as loud as you can, whoosh them away! Till then, the *One* will linger inscrutable.

1396.   The original face taken at face value.

1397.   The darkness paints the moon shinier: a murmur of light through the woods, this whole early autumn…

1398.   Thinking: to feed a needless mind with food of its own.

1399.   A cock: awakened by its own incantation.

1400.   If monastery Zen is the only authentic Zen then the urbane Zen is like cleaning one's yard of imaginary horse-shit.

1401.   Arithmetic: If the conventional teaching of a lifetime values   one penny, a Satori values two pennies.

1402.   Mind as clear as a mountain lake in a peaceful autumn day.

1403.   With each word we learn we create an object. Of course, philosophically speaking, there is some "objectivity" left to the object itself. For each individual the created object has some unique characteristics. To see the essence of a tree for instance one would have to use a hatchet to cut off any personal traits that one has added to that tree. Then with an even bigger hatchet one would have to cut the background, as if it was a curtain, and let go. The tree is now empty clean, ready to be seen through a direct learning.

1404.   Talking about various degrees of enlightenment, that is, about various degrees of doubt.

1405.   Careless talk makes reality scatter bones around. Once the tongue moves the reality starts failing. When you say that it's an inch away, you can't see it distinctly. If it's there no thought could fill it up, no word can empty its roots. Odd talks, even silences...

1406.   Flies are singing Zazen when they fly; bees are singing Zazen when they work; mosquitoes are singing Zazen when they sting; in the company of such noble beings why do you feel afraid to jump in and sing your own song?

1407.   Zen as an intellectual pursuit: truth is beyond what anybody, including Buddha, knows. Though the delusion could be far beyond what one doesn't know. And again, seeking the truth through knowledge couldn't be worse than seeking the delusion through ignorance.

1408.   Words are traveling since the beginning of the world, sometimes echoing, most of the time brushing things, and even impinging on them, pocking at... When a word and a thing confront each other, usually the word wins. (Zen: no mind, no word, no finger used to point at, no imprint of steps on a freshly snowed ground).

1409.   Devotion to Zazen has merits. Though, being in the office – absorbed by duties – and still having Zazen poise and zealously seeking the truth within – has even more merits. Grace may come to you unexpectedly; be prepared to accept it, don't turn it back…

1410.   The wind is knocking at the window: a leaf touches the ground. In the fog, the bridge goes nowhere.

1411.   Mirrors are like rivers. If there is moonlight they reflect. If there is no moonlight they both accumulate shadows.

1412.   The mind facing itself: no mirror to reflect, no mirror to deflect. There is a moment when the seen and the seer overlap: in the swing of the scarlet stem there is no word to trail after…

1413.   Words are worse than sentences. Not to know the words usage makes the sentences worse. Not using a tongue while talking makes all talks taste like sugar plum! Taste one, taste another one… A full box of sweets and yet you complain of feeling hungry!

1414.   The koan introduces both, a story (with its characters and events) and the hidden trap. The story itself proves to be the trap where the intuition is caught wandering. Despite the fact that - neither the trap is visible, nor the reward held in reserve within - they're brought forth by the mind as such. Accepting a koan is like taking a rabid bull by its horns knowing that if you can't master the holding you'd get hurt. To say that a koan is a Zen puzzle is like saying that a hurricane is a version of a breeze. Be careful!

1415.   You leap in and see the continuum. You leap out and see the boundaries. They're just both fine where they are. Flowers are more numerous at spring time and the fox follows the old trace of a fish she already ate long time ago.

1416.   What is cold amidst "cold" things and hot amidst "hot" things? Don't sum up, don't differentiate either! What is "cold" is hot. Even deeper: "What is "hot" is cold!"

1417.   Raindrops gleaming onto the window. They slide on the glass, some in a rush, like caught in rain traffic maze… There is a code that they're using: if they leave the surface they become rain again. If they accumulate on the window pane they become what they used to be. (This is a light example showing how things return to one - original thing - though they're seen as diverse identities in transformation).

1418.   The stagnant water of Zen transcendence is producing knowable arguments such as "the universe can be completely described by the following propositions: no-ness is emptiness; suchness is its manifestation". Those two abstract propositions should not have an impact onto one's life as long as one's life is in agreement with reality.

1419.   Puddle: a lodge for raindrops.

1420.   Can a koan help you expedite your awakening? It depends… If it frustrates you, go back to basics: traditional Zazen, breathing, meditation, feeling at peace with yourself and the universe. Avoid the vastness of a koan if you don't have a sword to cut a cat in two halves, as needed…

1421.   Things are what they are until the mind touches them. Mind awakening lets them keep intact that definite odor…

1422.   Once you penetrate, you understand… As you get thrown out, you understand. Nothing seems to speak more in your favor than your own awareness…

1423.   Before-awakening mind: hanging by a thread in a last standoff with reality.

1424.   The innermost self lives unaffected by events. In Satori one could feel its presence and sense that it has nothing to do with one's body. Something feel sad about that lurking inside the only thing that remains intact as we live or die, is the part that we barely know anything about. And so is God!

1425.   If things go all right you'd find no un-hatched eggs in the cuckoo's nest. The bigger the egg the more thorny to hatch.

1426.   Mu is for Zen like an arrow pointing outside the plane of perception: when it aims you don't see the target. As the arrow hits - the target becomes one with the non-perceptual and unlimited field of your mind. Mu is the arrow and the bearer of the arrow's target. Seeking no mind but getting it awakened: what a treat!

1427.   The sudden blaze, the sudden freeze. Mountains echo the sound of a snow fall. Birds fly without moving their wings. The peak is bare. If there was self you couldn't see it. A harmless thought tells a fleeting story about the mist. As if no life was left hanging on behind. All things sing: Love, love. Nobody though listens. Just the echo.

1428.   Holding blossoms in one's view to dog them from falling...

1429.   Function and essence are like a sign of life on an icy peak. Is the moon penetrating the clouds a sign of life? The wind is ringing on top of a frozen grass blade.

1430.   (If you search for it, you'll not find it. If you talk about it you'll lose it). What's this madness, to be enchanted by a thing which – if attained – is not going to make you rich or famous? That is, to want to die hundred times your life just to live an instant of eternity? This is the inherited will of humans to be equal to God.

1431.   The frosty reality in a short glimpse: a (all-knowing) cognizant reality listening to the universal silence.

1432.   If the footsteps are seen the thoughts trail phenomena. They could be feet of dead Buddhas. If there are no footsteps, the thoughts can't strike. Emptiness has no name to be called upon and therefore there is no logic that could extend it beyond what we call reality.

1433.   The awakening is untimely, so death is.

1434.   The white swans in dark are dark. The black crows in dark are dark. Dark seems better fit to help out (close) the mind (door) not to seize and set apart. That's why Zazen…

1435.   A creative dialog about attainment is a deaf-mute situation.

1436.   Flowers are water-loving. Fish are water-swimming. Ice is water-freezing. Three different kinds of phenomena linked to water through an empty dash.

1437.   The laugh at Zen is like throwing smoke into the fire. In an open space a doubt doesn't find a shadow to chase. In a closed mind a grain of doubt can start a sand storm. Finger pointing can stir a tide.

1438.   You attach yourself to a thing (or a being) and begin to miss it: the infinite original totality disguised as a parrot!

1439.   To get clearly awakened and then to be called to separate mist from a cloud; hard to do it, but don't call it impossible. Getting rid of mist and picking up the cloud (what's left of it) keeps your mind still awakened. After all, mind's residue is just a substitute used to sweeten a Zen tea.

1440.   The fundamental question comes from a mind – otherwise, without an origin, it wouldn't become a question when asked. Then, where the answer comes from? If it comes from a discriminating mind it is not a fundamental answer. But then, could any question be called "fundamental"? The wind is raising and the leaves are falling, the snow is melting and the spring flowers are erecting their head. Why, for eons already, Buddhas get together to listen to silence? Because in silence, question and answer sleep together, like a tongue in a mouth-kept-closed. Not even a one hand clapping can wake up this story from snoring.

1441.   Life is a pilgrimage to nowhere. Death is a pilgrimage to nowhere.

1442.   On the way to awakening your life looks like an interim day-dream. If you understand clearly that one illusion leads into another the awakening is the only sustainable pursuit. Though, you'd have to understand that there are myriads of other pursuits as good as awakening or even better like for instance counting the frog leaps of the stones you throw on the water surface, wow! Or playing hide-and-seek with another Buddha.

1443.   Awakening is not a fairyland. That's why it should be regulated.

1444.   To affirm that knowledge is the cause of man's departure from Heaven is like saying that in the history of civilization, generation after generation inherited more and more mistakes. Zen poetry exemplifies the very contrary: reason has enough subtlety to put the unutterable available for reading.

1445.   One word to grasp and the universe is no longer one.

1446.   The emptiness is the source and the destination of all phenomena including one's thoughts. They arrive like leaves carried by the autumn wind, like flakes of snow blanketing a field or like tidal waves that obliterate a continent. And they go away the same way.

1447.   Bow down: in the sand the – almost undistinguishable – foot of differentiation gathered a few dew drops. The mind intervenes: not enough for a boat to sail. As the thought gets in, the sun initiates its scorching eventful work.

1448.   The spoken world is a hindrance to the truth. The unspoken world is unattainable.

1449.   "Now" is "always". If you take a gentle approach to life you could feel it. The Iron Gate softens when the breeze blows and hardens when left in solitude and neglect.

1450.   The mind holds the keys to the gates of Heaven and Hell. Before opening any door there is this mountain it has to climb: sweeping the snow on the peak and seeing no gates to open… One must make good use of those keys though…

1451.   The spring prompts a mind to blossom. The cherry flowers in no need of an interpreter.

1452.   In the monastery you could hear the wind blowing ashes. You know who is or what is. To no avail. Ashes don't breed flies. Memories don't put flesh back on bare bones. Though monks say that on full moon nights one could hear Buddha taking to the oxen, sometimes so loud, that one could barely sleep.

1453.   The awakening walks on silent paws.

1454.   Mourning the eternity: the celestial drought sank a forever bloom. Missing the spring arriving; missing the winter departing. No more first coming, no more next coming, no more last coming.

1455.   Unable to get rid of distinctions one may love the hatred and hate the loving. In a word of differentiation stench is rising from the sand imprints.

1456.   If Buddha never existed, whoever wrote the Sutras was Buddha.

1457.   Zen Teacher and Zen Student: The clawed cat caught a clawed rat. After such a long comradeship! The rat was overheard saying: "I'm innocent!" "Though you're already awakened", the cat said. To a cat, awakening is a hefty reason, to lunch on innocent rats.

1458.   Old fox, more repugnant habits: looking for a dead fish in the hot stream…

1459.   Don't think of it, just meditate on the line between sifting in and sifting out: not even the most experienced shepherd would then be able to help you separate the sheep from the goats…

1460.   The agony of an ego: to bury the "I" or the eye…

1461.   On a road of stone a metallic bell… On a metallic road a stone bell. When one sounds deep the other breaks into ashes. Which is the bell sound the mind would turn to? Sweeping ashes, not fearing life…

1462.   Mind game: Clinging to events that are friendly and opposing them to events that are hostile. No-mind game: welcome both equally, let them be carried by a gust of wind…

1463.   You call every tree a name… At the roll call time no tree is answering. Things avoid the glance of the uninvited…

1464.   Words should pass unanswered. Stories should live in an un-reasoning world. Coloring for relevance, letting it be transparent for revelation…

1465.   My shadow, your shadow…

1466.   The silver moonlight and the owl with its anguished crow: when we were there we felt at ease. We feel at ease on the mountain peak also, though we lack a heart to feel so. Suchness is stillness. Even the herds in the valley stopped moving. The cowshit tainted breeze, so rich at the foot of the mountain – nowhere to be felt around here.

1467.   Concealing God under the ordinary human face is what an infinite compassion is.

1468.   The millstone sounds like a recited sutra. Hard when words make sense, light on the icy grains. Buddha shields his ears from hearing. As the millstone stops, the silence reconciles with the outside breeze, dripping mist…

1469.   Things awaken in emptiness from their unfathomable sleep.

1470.   Buddha statues are born in stone. Grass pierces the dirt running from their shadow elsewhere. If you see what this is you know the way. If you don't see through you know no way. Only when you'll be ashes what other eyes could see might look like emptiness to you.

1471.   My newly born baby is awakened by definition and, of course, can't say a word about the experience.

1472.   When emptiness doesn't manifest itself how could it be known? Neither phenomena to be perceived nor essence to be revealed (directly grasped!). Icy winds blow over the cosmic ocean…

1473.   After awakening, how the relative reality rises back from the ashes of one's mind? By listening at dawn to the rooster's call before getting up, and at dusk, to the rooster's call before retiring.

1474.   Zen affirms that what we call ordinary truth can be viewed as an ultimate truth when we're awakened. The two worlds are sharing the same grounds. Zen is just narrowing the gap.

1475.   In this world, at a given time, we're all Gods. In the same world, at another time, we'll all be nothing but scattered Zen bones.

1476.   The stream, wave after wave. One wave and then the next. The solitude is colorless. Above the shattered waves, the rainbow!

1477.   When the many is reduced to one, the one is reduced to many.

1478.   To be head-shaped means to be a being: flower's head, hummer's head, mountain's head are like clouds over the river of the being.

1479.   Get close slowly so you could hear the hush as the river water gets mixed with the sea water. The wind tirelessly working on those small waves that sound like an extraneous remark: being just a swarm of air.

1480.   Words are to the truth what pollution is to the air.

1481.   Who fell from the tree last night right on the middle of the roof? A white elephant. You could see it sleeping now like a baby on a grass patch. For the ancestors such a happening meant bounty. You could see the sky through the hollowed roof; last night's white cotton clouds are gone. Shall I help the white elephant climb back up the tree or repair the roof that sheltered me for so long? I could see the stars now, the moon, like a congealed pack of arrows heading incessantly towards the luminous lake.

1482.   The white dove touching the winter harp. Milk mixed with flour...

1483.   Stepping on the ground and thinking how stable it is, while becoming aware that it is moving in all directions...

1484.   Many minds live in silence most part of their lives. Sometimes bringing new things in one's mind means less than throwing old things away. This would say that knowing two words is already too much, so one would have to be thrown out. Heads that stand up tall are nearer to the clouds...

1485.   Flip-flop your hands, experience a bird's flight.

1486.   A faded awakening: I still could remember the blue bird flying on the clear sky. Always above the peak, never seen in the pine forest. Who was the archer? Under the sun she was like a blue bow. Under the moonlight she was like a blue arrow. Her body has now the smell of foul water; her flight has the smell of stale air. The bird paused in the air for an infinite break...

1487.   The common sense is a delight if it suggests a higher mental ground.

1488.   A cold pillow is like a solved problem: you can't sleep on it.

1489.   No need to clean the mirror, its reflection is long gone. Paint it black; protect it from being looked at! The road is on the outside… The journey is on the inside… Mirroring as non-mirroring is like seeing by not-seeing a seen that is non-seen. Penetrating the emptiness like an arrow that points to itself…

1490.   Things abandoned on a beach are recognizable examples of emptiness. The scavenger, at dusk: picking up empty things, throwing them on a pile of nothingness…

1491.   A bird that wears wings can fly unnoticed if it is part of a flock.

1492.   Skipping a winter to see how the next one looks like: crows circle the granary following the exact flying pattern of the last year's winter, storms scurry without warning, the warmth of fresh bread lasts too short if removed from the oven.

1493.   Saying that Zen embodies the absolute truth (and using "body" to express it) is like saying that the manifestation of the absolute is captured in a relative (embodied) idea-of-the-absolute. It's like describing a wine to a taster. Though, to taste the wine - this is a different story.

1494.   A contemporary legend says that I was born from a star and that I was going to live forever and that I was going to have ten children, all Buddhas, with a lone woman named Karma.

1495.   Stories about people walking on water as though it was solid ground are all metaphors. What do they try to say? If what we see and hear are empty states of mind - like an image mirroring or a sound echoing – then, by extension, all-human states are illusions that could be liberated, so that their logical outcome could be vacated: the effect of gravity is reversed (walking on water), the matter is taken as being void or empty (and lacking attributes such as weight, consistency), particulars are equated with generals, relative equals absolute, finite equals infinite, etc. In reality the feeling of awe and delight during satori is limited to a peculiar state of mind that experiences total awareness. There are no miracles in it and no miracles to follow. Common para-psychic occurrences such as foreseeing, telepathy, hypnosis are as real as one's perception. Though, if perception is empty even those a few occurrences are empty as well.

1496.   Following sound and chasing form I got to see the waterfall: a formless reality reviled in a conditional fall of matter?

1497.   The boundless virtue of an unutterable thought.

1498.   Eat your rice, take care of your broom and sleep with an eye open: the invisible vinegar flies are getting ready for their maiden flight.

1499.   Zen joke: A Chinese emperor, very skilled in Zen, had two twin daughters whom he named Karma and Dharma. Every day they used to quarrel, get into fights, hurting each other, equally. The moral of this story is that when you name things you expose them equally to the aim of principles.

1500.   The spring flowers covered up with ice. Sun ceased to be, moon ceased to be...

1501.   A monk asked another monk: "What is the point in time when the sentient beings will be all Buddhas?" A teacher that were passing by, and overheard this, said: "Now!" As he walked away, the other monk said: "When Hell and Heaven will shake friendly hands". Another teacher that happened to hear this said: "Now!" There was nobody carrying a stick around and the whole scene ended without a harsh treatment.

1502.   The swan was still flapping her wings when the fox ran by. "The swan is not a hen", the fox reasoned. The swan stopped flapping her wings. Seeing a fox and not flapping, hearing a saying without moving your ears…

1503.   Inhaling is like grasping life. Exhaling is like letting it go. Death appears in-between as a subject of a brief interest to the mind.

1504.   To wait for the iron rooster's crow and to open the door giving nowhere. When the mind flickers the truth hides in pitch darkness.

1505.   What a whole life of meditation is worth of? "Three pound of flax".

1506.   Plastic flowers have the same effect on a meal fragrance as thinking has on a Zen koan.

1507.   If the truth is clear – if not uttered – how is it getting recognized? The silence is in the water but not in the water flow. The gravestone still reminds of a boisterous life that passed away. The wordless pine tree watches the heavens moving along with the seasons. The teapot is whistling with ostentation…Only the stillness could take the lid off it.

1508.   Blinded by clouds… Waiting for the blue patch of sky to break my solitude…

1509.   Dry leaves in a clay pot: the yellow sprouts appear first; as they turn black they're effortlessly disintegrating.

1510.   Snow covering the pigsty while the pig howls loudly.

1511.   The mind is in equal measure reality and thought. Empty phenomena empty the thought as well. What about the essence? Beneath a few half faulty takings the rows of mirroring images are plain like a nose on one's face. Though, when a crow is unfolding her wings on the Southern lawn the Northern lawn reflects the change. In the essence there is neither a nose to run one's fingers over nor a mouth to moan about it.

1512.   Ultimately the momentary is eternal and vice versa.

1513.   Counting Buddhas: as many as the dew pearls in a green grassy savannah. More or less a few. The sun at the high point makes such a comparison baffling.

1514.   To grasp the truth and have nothing to say about is like thinking and have nothing to know about.

1515.   The endless flow of phenomena: if they all return into one could "this" be called endless? Maybe, if you're not shy on seeing into another reality. Hollow skies gather hollow clouds. Are they going to rain or that's how one would look at a breeze in another world. Clear clouds sprinkled with ashes. This morning it returned to one, next morning it moved into brand new tidings. When all return to one there is no path to chose. When one returns to many there no path to avoid. Though, mind howls like a wolf at the bright moon. What is to be taken as truth when the mind wrongfully looks for understanding? Fallen leaves, formless wind. Mind – unable to choose between starving while eating real stuff or feeling full of emptiness…

1516.   When the sun stops moving, the pigeon hides away. The rooster still has a crown on its head winding the time in its throat.

1517.   Entering the realm of a "time without intervals" and a "space with no measure".

1518.   A scarecrow never takes a break when crows fly by.

1519.   A stick in a conversation with another stick: "How do you control your anger?"

1520.   What a tongue tasted the eyes ate utterly.

1521.   If you wear worldly objects people are going to respect you as a worldly being. A worldly breeze makes a worldly sound.

1522.   Wind carries the imperfect word of windy, though as "windy" becomes principle waves go up and down on the lake surface.

1523.   With every birth the origin shows its face. With every death the origin hides its face.

1524.   Time is ultimately "decay"! Space is ultimately rebirth.

1525.   Some may not be used to God: it's like saying that blooming is meaningless.

1526.   Silence and light on the mountain peak. Too chilly for a scent to fly by.

1527.   By erecting a mountain you can keep the dung in the valley. Burnt by the sun it looses its smell, drenched by rain it looses its shape. The elements spawn nothingness.

1528.   To a stuffed nose a cherry bloom smells like cowshit. But then, to a blind eye a tree has feathers and a featherless chicken is a feeding breast. The moral is: If you feel it you miss it. If you don't feel it you miss it.

1529.   The moon damped with snow... Frosty leaves... The essence lies where consent does not...

1530.   Nowhere to enter and (seen from an inner afar) nowhere to exit.

1531.   The timeless yesterday is gone. The morning shelters the daze though it knows that the timeless today is one and the same with the timeless yesterday.

1532.   The snow has no fragrance. The water has no taste. The glass has no color. The shadow has no sound. A peacock moves its tail and the reality starts chasing ghosts: what-is-not hides what it is. The snow smells like fresh cloth, the water tastes like a miracle...

1533.   One awakening for everyone and for any other one also...

1534.   A thought stopped by a setup is still alive and well inside the trap. Keeping thoughts as hostages? Mistake...

1535.   Neither spoken nor kept unexpressed! Just a little blow of a breeze for a boat to sail with the speed of light to the other shore. The mind is still listening to its poisonous drum: like the sound of a broken icicle.

1536.   The passage of life: getting fed while in the womb, belching while getting out.

1537.   Behind closed windows listening to the wind's whisper: I can't understand a word though I can see its intentions watching the floating leaves.

1538.   According to the facts under the ice the stone looks dry.

1539.   When a moment repeats itself, what one did right the other does wrong: how can there be a repeat when a moment never arises? And if aroused look intently for some sign of a repeat... Like a tiger smelling old blood...

1540.   The Way: like a tune that sounds but has no immediate meaning. It knows no timing either...

1541.   There is no remedy for death. And also there is no remedy for its message. Meet your days as if you were that immortal diamond that always talks to God by reflecting its light.

1542.   The universe lives inside one's eyes. Especially if one has doubts...

1543.   Unseen objects are non-utterances. Seen objects are non-realities. Hens are nevertheless attached to the eggs they hatch. A Zen egg has to pass through a Zen colander to be chosen. Only after that the dull period of hatching begins.

1544.   The thousand eyes of a dipper handle... And the life of the wide spoon: dizzy to hang on; dizzy to be left to go... The tormented tongue...

1545.   The moon drowns in the pool: turbid waters fleeing the swirl...

1546.   You can hear not only what you're listening to: Even a faint sound of a shadow dashing across the water.

1547.   Conquering the life without a sword, and making death a lone happening...

1548.   From a manual of Zen for gardening: "The good way to water the plants aligned on the windowpane is to hold the watering pot at a certain distance from the leaves so that you'd not hurt the plant and then, while sprinkling, to hold your hand under the sprinkler so that you could catch the drops that would otherwise damage the wooden pane. If the plant gets damaged this is not what one calls Zen. If drops of water damage the wooden pane this is still Zen but not enough to help one get awakened".

1549.   The dead peach tree sprout a tiny flower, like a song that would suddenly yield the Way to the long quietude: (a pink-pale blouse holding heavy white breasts)...

1550.   The universe loitering phenomena in subtle corners of one's mind...

1551.   Samadhi: Like a flower in a warm winter day. It came too early to outlive things that are meant to happen.

1552.   The blue ocean that I know for fifty years: a body of water of immutable indifference. I cried so hard when I discovered that in essence what I thought wasn't true.

1553.   A bleached moon shining on the sea of birth and death.

1554.   <u>Affinities and accord</u> create stronger attachments than <u>differences and dissent</u>.

1555.   Boasting about Earth and Heaven but missing the point while changing your own diapers.

1556.   Adding a prayer to a curse is like applying the same justice to good and bad. Listen then: frozen waters are rich in canned fish...

1557.   The wetness evolves in dryness: hold your thoughts! Both dissolve...

1558.   A bitter taste belongs to a bitter tongue. The stench of the bleached bones comes with the morning breath. No presence, no greetings... The tongue that knows how to approach the "awakening hollow" could still say "This is it!" without leaving a trace of it throughout Heaven.

1559.   The flagpole is more important to crows than granaries. Crowing on high grounds is better than eating on low grounds. For a Zen follower: the weight of what you achieve is equal to the height you reach while climbing.

1560.   The pine-lined street in the village is the wind's horsewhip: clouds float above, clouds float below…

1561.   A dog barks at an eclipse: like refusing something new to be named…

1562.   To find the Way you'd have to let the Way find you…

1563.   The moon rising in a full-length dress: empty shadows encircled by empty lights; empty lights encircled by empty shadows. As if it happens during the day light…

1564.   The sky is an open gate. Around the granary the crows resemble one's thoughts. When the wind blows they get restless. The straws-lined alleys are built so that crows wouldn't get lost…

1565.   Bare hypotheses, bare conclusions…

1566.   On one side, the shore. On the other side, the shore. That makes the river resemble one's sea of thoughts channeled by limitations.

1567.   Neither obstruction, nor a free pass. Go straight-ahead and you'll tumble down. Take alternate ways and you'd never get there.

1568.   An exit may lead to a new entrance, though an entrance may never have an exit. Be aware!

1569.   An isle having a number on a map is not going to help you enjoy your trip. Numbers are as unreal as names are. Bees are busy, grasshoppers are hopping. That's not because we say so, but because the abundance of facts cannot be lived through a mere abs-traction.

1570.   What is that for which there is no next to it and no precedent to it either?

1571.   If no time is "past" to it and no time is "future" to it, the thing is not yet born. If no time is past to it and no time is future to it, the thing is timeless.

1572.   A sticking out tongue might try to answer the question: if you think that something is arising in this picture look for the missing part. If you think that everything is there you can't neither get in nor leap out.

1573.   Thanks to the winter freeze I can't tear apart the pile of leaves. Finally, another word – "pile" – got integrated in my mind landscape.

1574.   What's this? "I don't have a name for it yet".

1575.   The beginner's mind is the moonlight dipped into the water. The expert's mind is like a cloud blocking the moonlight.

1576.   The universe is the embodiment of emptiness.

1577.   A Zen straight-path to the Zen end-road is rare. Oxen work their way through mounds of clay, unabated. Crows fly a straight line between heaven and earth with no labor. On a straight path the progress is hindered. Though, if you change the path you may have to change the horseshoe on a dead horse.

1578.   On an indirect path to Zen fogs would be forming, mountain hums would draw near, and mirrors would arch over -

making the path uncertain - an illusion that would dim the expectations. One could glimpse at the way through if one has enough resolve to carry on. The horses lodge downstairs, the owners lodge upstairs. The questions one should not ask: "Is the end-road near?" or "Is the end-road afar?"

1579.   Taught by a breath about Zen: nothing less than the air intake…

1580.   Let the balloon go, glance its way up. The heaven gates are wide open. For a while it may wobble listening to the wind. What is translated as windy on earth is lost further up in translation. A ball of gold catching the sun; sparks where only a few adventure to go.

1581.   After carving - a stone is not a stone anymore. Though the natural elements don't know that. For water or fire a stone continue to be a stone until smashed to smithereens it becomes dust.

1582.   Vacant inns invite guests. Busy inns turn them down. Failing to get to a place forces one to travel more. Hence remember: Shaded from view there is a lodge waiting only for you. A lodge that you didn't chose and yet a lodge that didn't chose you either.

1583.   Understanding at last not to listen to my discriminating thinking…

1584.   The older one gets the older his/her Zen gets. To the extreme, when one departs this life, Zen departs this life also.

1585.   What is forever possible is what the present is.

1586.   (_Iro-futo_) – Unreachable by the path of thought. That's enlightenment in other words. Simply put, no question has an appropriate answer and no answer could be taken as given. Emptiness works in its mysterious ways: when a thing is empty it can't be filled up. When a thing is full it can't be emptied. If the impasse appears one easy way to go through is by kicking over objects standing on your way of going through. Things that are standing on your path of awakening have to be emptied by all means. With the same kick you could empty an empty thing or you could empty a full thing.

1587.   When the deception ceases the words expire. One exit opens at the sound of one thousand knocked down gates. Perfection of the stillness: a wooden moon with shining cheeks. Even a dog shit spreads glitter miles and miles around.

1588.   As far as Zen goes a cloth flower has the same chance to get enlightened as a plastic flower has. Even so, by following the mirage of the true thing a crow may take the rooster's song as being useless.

1589.   Death is poorer than a feeling since it can't be improved.

1590.   Goby desert: A dust storm is a storm using dust. Roofless bunkers are hosting its winds; the sweet fruits get their skin dusted. A proverb here says: a Buddha caught still breathing values twice as much as a Buddha statue and thrice as much as a framed picture.

1591.   Where the faceless past meets the faceless future.

1592.   The beginner's mind sees everything as this, now and here. The expert's mind sees everything as that, then and there.

1593.   A tall stem with a small shadow imprint. Waiting in Zazen for another spring day, not knowing that blossoming already started. The grass blade made it through the blackened wigs of snow. (What one implies in a talk about spring? If it is ever-blooming it can't strive for emptiness. If it is transient it resembles a bottle shard polished by a gravelly river: ephemeral and so of no consequence).

1594.   Under the imminent danger I felt thought-free. Very awake, unobstructed by eye lashes, witnessing a free fall. The book explains: "As long as you are sure that you can come back from there…"

1595.   When you see an earth bound eagle think of the back side of the illustration.

1596.   When one speaks nothing is left to the mind to do but comprehend. When one doesn't speak the luster of the lotus leaves pales and the long pillar at the gate stops screeching. Silence then gives way to silence. The mist in the mirror is as unclear as the mirror in the mist.

1597.   A thought could carve a road on a mountain… A word would grow its weeds…

1598.   Clatter of passing feet, no form in sight…

1599.   Zen: When the mind hatches an empty egg.

1600.   Harsh lives go by without hope. Light lives go by without spirit.

1601.   Zen practice: The water fall is noisily becoming a jingling river. The river is jinglingly becoming a silent lake. The road from pure noise to pure silence… What's this? Death in its quiescent becoming? As you go back to sail the rapids, does the lake become a counterfeit?

1602.   The autumn leaves burn in the brick oven. Flocks of birds fly away from the acrid smoke. It is so cold that the particularity of the fire seems to be just a borrowed contrast that explains what the particularity of the cold is.

1603.   When water comes ashore you could hear the frogs squealing aloud overnight…

1604.   Controlling an emotion by replacing it with a murmured mantra! At night it will surface in your dream as a tiger crouched in a hazardous pose.

1605.   Ice dripping from wooden statues. Whenever the breeze blows a pink nose protrudes through the thin blue layer. Turn off the breeze so you can see it.

1606.   A rain knows everything about each of its drops.

1607.   Taking up the task of doing nothing.

1608.   Seated among Buddhas a dragon: silenced by its howl a bird looses her feathers. (Read: wondering at the strange presence of the dragon among Buddhas the bird disposes of the image of herself).

1609.   If you meet Buddha say "Hello Buddha!" from me. If Buddha meets you, watch out!

1610.   Experiencing a Zen leap: you'd have to lift up you foot, bend forward, lengthen your front foot while bending the back one, use the back leg as a charged spring, cry aloud and jump over the hill. The hill is domed like an archway and the forward foot meets a slippery patch of ancestral moss. It's slippery, isn't it? In Zen they say that the success is noiseless while the failure is noisy.

1611.   "The enlightenment is not worth bargaining for!" "Who ever told you to bargain to begin with?"

1612.   As far as seeing go the eye is self-supporting.

1613.   Attachments during a storm are stronger than attachments during a breezy day. Who dares to clasp hands during a storm? Fish are quiet since they live under water; birds are noisy since they live above. What for birds is attachment, for fish is detachment. Until a bird spots a fish…

1614.   Reversing the snow: flakes rising with the wind…

1615.   Every fraction of a second the universe renews itself. How come that every time it gets renewed it ends up as a deception? Isn't it true then that emptiness renews itself also? (Of course the question sounds intellectual and so the answer is empty).

1616.   A planted word-seed is followed by a tree-thought.

1617.   If you ask what life is under the heavy blows of your fate the answer will – obviously - be negative. But think of all your untaken days from the future… They're not encased in memory. They are free of rejection and consent, very much like things growing out of nothing. A miracle gulf of phenomena waiting for you – that's life.

1618.   Dragons with horns are a milder species than snakes. Though, snakes transcend easily their appearance…

1619.   A fox in a mad pursuit: searching for the moon buried deep under the water. They say that the light doesn't ring a bell if the water doesn't ring a stone.

1620.   Matches are ephemeral flames. Humans are ephemeral Gods.

1621.   If you think that your life is infinite you can accomplish more in less time and still have an infinite time ahead to accomplish more. Meditation on finitude is as unwise as trying to speak to the dead.

1622.   Being deaf to what you are saying…

1623.   What lives inside has to let the outside burst forth alive. What lives outside has to die to let the inside burst forth alive.

1624.   The path back can't avoid the same mistake from being repeated.

1625.   Thoughts cannot be wiped off one's brain if senses are not wiped off one's body. Did I try to say too much? If you say yes you could still hear the thoughts whispering. (To see, not to think, to get the truth without yielding an inch to understanding).

1626.   When the snow melts it looses the color. I wonder if crows have anything to say about it…

1627.   When an answer is given, the question departs. Then the answer gets indexed into the brain and becomes material! This is the process one has to make over: the mind should be like the white beach around a sandy deserted island. In the moonlight it should look like an incinerated universe, clear and vacant. The wind, not carrying even a grain of salt…

1628.   And after many an understanding, suddenly comes the enlightenment: the mysterious clarity which appears beyond seeing…

1629.   Words are rusting once written. And if they don't rust right away could you stop their sudden death? The word "torrid" if thrown in a stove gets frozen. That ultimate truth that shows up after the words are all incinerated…

1630.   Phenomena and emptiness: The deck drowned under the swollen waters. But the boat is still floating.

1631.   The monk gardener is trimming bushes. (*It's always "this" or "the way things are" or Suchness that bothers me. Words and thoughts are then forgotten and cease to exist*). One weed is in its late bloom and the monk spears its life. Though, you could see the grisly wounds he had done to the old trunks. "The broken promise of not hurting a living thing that has no name", I remark. The monk turns back and hacks the weed… "Is that Suchness?" I bother to ask. The monk raises the hatchet…

1632.   The smoke that departed this morning from the chimney looked like a fish eating the moon.

1633.   Eat like a Buddha, drink like a Buddha, work like a Buddha and sleep like a Buddha. You can skip the activities that are not part of your schedule. But remember: with each act some awakening arises, the eyes of the unknown are moving into your beat.

1634.   Birds wrapped in ice flying above clear furrows. The wild ones go north. The bare mountain goes straight to highest spot. The moonlight spreads its golden light like a pale glaze all over heaven.

1635.   My drum is broken. You could see the emptiness floating out of its belly.

1636.   Hefty perspective in life: being covered with snow from head to feet. The cold extinguishes most of my thoughts. Should I let go?

1637.   Sooner or later to feel sun's flames scorching your body would cease to be a metaphor. The ocean would be iodine mills by then and the waves a forgotten reality. Same will be the sentient beings, the mind and the Buddhas. That time, the remaining pieces of reality will not be anymore some kind of favor granted by one's mind. What would then be? Even a sandstorm has such a grace, coming and going, visiting a waste land. What about the chirping of a baby bird? Myriads of stars and myriads of moons can't weight a fraction of it. Suchness spreads out as living beings and comes back as emptiness. But after all, where Suchness goes?

1638.   The head of a flock of crows is tied to the path to follow.

1639.   Pay attention, be one with your act: when you aim you are the target, they say. When you throw a ball you're the basket. It may sound unreasonable to ask you to do the same exercise when you're in pain. If pain starts you're the pain. To relief your pain smell a stone, become a fragrance.

1640.   When a thing is measureless is enough to think of a yardstick to make it shrink.

1641.   If the relative world would be replaced by an absolute world all illusions would be certitudes, bridges – though still connecting shores together – would become invisible and the ever-moving storms would freeze like a flock of flamingoes trapped in a glacier. Perhaps, we'd be able to realize if it happened that we live in the best relative world possible – the world as is. At the river edge the arched clouds rise in the morning and fall down at night. The absolute time is buried nearby… You speed to get there, the time stops. You stop; the time shudders though it wouldn't move…

1642.   Countless flakes though one can see that there is only "one" snowfall…

1643.   A monk tells to another monk: "I heard that Westerners sit in a Western Zazen while the Southerners sit in a Southern Zazen". The other monk replies: "Northerners are exposed to Southerners' weather. Same Zazen, just different".

1644.   Fireflies: particle of fluorescent wood with wings…

1645.   You pass through what you see: thin and thick, firm and soft, light or dark. Quite a forever journey: too early to retreat, too late to change directions. Feeling perfect in any circumstance you intuit your life as a mist filling a cloud with water. Every moment vanishes without leaving a trace. The glares of the roots on the old dirt road are like the aging fingers of the emptiness sprouting in all phenomena – old or just aging…

1646.   When footprints are meaningless the understanding is irrelevant: damped with fresh snow, too small to see…

1647.   The ocean is in recess. No rivers can get in, no rivers can turn away. After so much work no roars to be heard, no breeze to breathe. The comfortable universe reviewed but not told about. If one loses the desire to see it moving one can't stop a mule follow a horse race. The gate to the race is wide open and the water hardens. Devoid of movement a horse race still spears to be a horse race.

1648.   A chimney without smoke is like a lizard without tail.

1649.   This living thing doesn't have body or mind. Though it has a self. To see the truth hidden in this utterance you'd have to drop body and mind. Don't think twice! Don't think once either! Rings spreading around a bird plunging into the black water. From wave to wave the airborne message gets dimmer and dimmer. Silence got in, truth got out! It holds a fish in her beak. If you see it you'd start laughing and this laughing will never stop.

1650.   There is never too late when one dies…

1651.   As you previously requested, I'd talk to the crow if the crow agrees to talk to me. Flapping is not saying: falling feathers gathering around my ears is not talking either…

1652.   Sealed in simple knots, within the reach of the thousand senses…

1653.   An empty eye gets filled with emptiness in its manifestation: light, shapes, forms, colors, texture. It drops all of them onto the infinite field of one's mind. It is there where they get stuck or, in an innocent way "look at and discard…"

1654.   The beginning of beginnings is the ending of endings…

1655.   Emptiness ready to proclaim its power: on a translucent throne a Crystal Buddha laughing… If you say this is the mirror of the beginning you're mistaken… The universe swallowed up by a mere reflection? To foil your own understanding go and milk a tiger, drink some hot lava in one gulp… One flake of snow can make you the home of one billion germs on sleds…

1656.   To be blind like a body but not dead, to be deaf like a stone but not stony. Even the grace to see the truth has to be empty…

1657.   If you think of it you get punished. If you don't think of it you get equally punished. Break this seal and you'd know how all things that are there began and ended. This gravestone lived through so many thunderous celebrations. The name carved on it is gone, cavernous like a shadow… When the wind blows the moon is shining on. When the wind stops the moonlight widens to the end of the universe.

1658.   The ego should live in the valley while the mind reaches high altitudes…

1659.   Body lies under ground, only a few stones on a heap reminds of it. A cricket made its home in a hole-way. A lucrative mind is finally put to rest while listening to the cricket's song.

1660.   Movement is to time what arriving is to space…

1661.   Not knowing the intentions of your mind when it gives so much freedom to your tongue…

1662.   Hopping from a top of a hill to a top of another hill: the grasshopper's hiss never changes.

1663.   The universal meaning of a cry…

1664.   The sun: burning past its red color and beyond the loneliness of a solitary fire.

1665.   Snow as remembered while seeking within…

1666.   Kept under the wraps of one's concepts a thing seems reoccurring! For a beginner's mind its return is again and again a story still untold.

1667.   To obey the laws of phenomena but refuse the words that helped you learn what they are…

1668.   Trees convulsed: the wind robs the mental landscape of a moment of serenity.

1669.   Your concern should not be to get out of your thinking but instead to live utterly within. Nonexistent should be as important to your thinking as the existent is.

1670.   Fish could not be seen, ducks could not be heard... The mind still makes the mountain wear green clothing and the river flow...

1671.   A word can stir a wave. Waves and waves as words pass by...

1672.   Hoping to release the arrow before it gets dark.

1673.   Peeling of a oven-hot apple to unleash its essence: the season king has a smelling acquiescence while hiding the truth about it. Smell it, fall for it, while it is still too hot to handle...

1674.   Zen is taking "up" as up and "down" as down.

1675.   As time becomes history old motions are hardening, the space becomes depthless and the ocean mirror un-sailable. A Zen koan still moves around, like an uninvited ghost...

1676.   The beginner's mind is like a bridge that let one pass through. The expert's mind is like a tunnel cluttered by falling stones and debris.

1677.   When wood burns, bugs get fried. When wood freezes bugs get frozen.

1678.   Things conceal what senses reveal. That's how one can understand phenomena. As soon as one sees an object, what the object conceals is what the view reveals. Reality is though more complex than what one can reveal. Could we say that the science is that extra sense that reveals more than what an object conceals to senses? The atoms floating in void space are still phenomena. The deeper the knowledge goes the more this idea of universe-creator-of-illusions makes sense. Physics and Math would prove one day that emptiness is a matter of fact not just a zany Zen idea.

1679.   The awakening guides one's mind back to what it was before it became mind.

1680.   When you contemplate the emptiness, the eye of the unknown sees you.

1681.   To emptiness, the five senses are like the five fingers of one's hand; they're used to apprehend or let go phenomena. Emptiness brings forth phenomena to manifest itself. It developed the five senses to help them control fully its manifestation. As things stand in front of one's mind they're empty as long as the mind doesn't reflect them. But for what the mind was made for they're as real as they come. In other words, emptiness wasn't blind when it created the sight, the smell, the hearing, and so forth. To want to go back to that origin before emptiness began to manifest itself is a bright idea, though the emptiness would clap with one hand to applaud it.

1682.   The falling water is heavier than the mounting water.

1683.   Zen poetry is a blend of what a nose cannot smell with one nostril turned inside out while listening to a one hand clapping: in other words, a fragrant bird dropping on a lotus leaf is still dropping while the hand is still clapping…

1684.   What is within reach is discarded. What is unattainable is treasured.

1685.   Hanging over a cliff with the thought of liberation at handy. Once it happens it can't be undone…

1686.   To misinterpret means to interpret in a wrong way. To penetrate the essence is different: no barriers to remove, no tongue to move its bone in and out. Between the eye and the target not a single point of discord.

1687.   Seeking liberation or using it as an excuse to understand what bondage is…

1688.   An inward bow doesn't know what an outward arrow is. In other words, an inner bow doesn't know anything about an outer target.

1689.   Water recedes, the riverbed dries up: No mind can explain how the lone swan lived for more than a decade on a patch of grass. Like a Zen monk, looking at the sky, waiting for rain…

1690.   Awareness is like the permanent icing on a mountain peak. Revelation is like a temporary icing of a prolonged winter. Understanding is like an ice-made-of dipper holding hot soup. Misunderstanding is the hot soup itself.

1691.   Days are ever departing. Nights are ever arriving. Luckily we all know the schedule by heart…

1692.   The beginner's mind is like a primal morning with no eye imprints on its luster. The expert's mind is like thick bushes that never blossom.

1693.   I began to understand why objectivity is such a flawed concept…

1694.   There is no such a thing as essence: though, if you could see through this you could become free…

1695.   Staring at Buddha's statue I saw his right hand moving slightly. Convinced that it was an illusion I called my neighbor to have a look. He confirmed that indeed Buddha is moving his right hand after a lengthy stare. Other ten witnesses saw it happening. One day a child passed by, stared at the statue for a while and then serenely said: "Emptiness… The fact that Buddha is moving proves that he isn't moving at all".

1696.   When the dusk falls the moon rises. When the moon falls the tide rises. When the tides falls the tide rises.

1697.   Mind versus no-mind: the way a boar yields to a lion…

1698.   Circling Buddha's statue with a hidden game plan is not going to convince Buddha to start a conversation. You may know a trick or two like that, that may have worked in the past. First lesson: a stone is indifferent to enlightenment. Second lesson: guiding cattle to the right grass for grazing might enlighten you more than a myriad of Buddha's statues.

1699.   The beginner's mind is like a wonderful story that doesn't have yet a narrative. The expert's mind is like the precarious thinning of a spinning rope that one tries to climb up…

1700.   An angry letter from an anti-Zen fellow: "How come that a human universe survived with a false understanding of what truth is and brought to fruition such enormous undertakings like explaining DNA - God's code- or landing on the moon? The emptiness is a convenient way to undo passions that are flawed or correct the events of chance (like redrawing karma). What about things that carry with them the base of our belief? Should we treat them as sheer phenomena? You'd never feel at home with Zen if those questions arrive. The amnesiac Zen has no straight question to ask and no straight answer to get. A relative reality is worth its phenomena. With each moment these phenomena are mushrooming to a mountainous level which can reach with its peak God's feet without bowing. Even if one genuinely bows one can't get there faster…" You are right! By using Zen one can get there slower…

1701.   The beginner's mind is the innocent witnessing. The expert's mind is like a shanty town with no room for happiness.

1702.   The beginner's mind is a snow bound flake. The expert's mind is an ocean bound moldy boat.

1703.   The beginner's mind is like a spring fountain. The expert's mind is like an ornate grave.

1704.   The beginner's mind is like a breeze-whispered flight. The expert's mind is like a beak crying in a noose.

1705.   The beginner's mind is the silent road headed for the horizon. The expert's mind is like a long-fenced junk yard.

1706.   The beginner's mind is a circle-shaped emptiness. The expert's mind is a blurred stream.

1707.   Echoing the unheard of…

1708.   When the moon sinks into the pond water you could scoop gold from pure mud.

1709.   If you are not afraid of this flashing essence, that you may call "the unseen as" aspect of *It*, you might be able to sense its presence during a deep meditation: cleared of relative influences, every aspect of *It* gets accompanied by a sudden, spontaneous and subtle manifestation of something that you can't point at. Some say that in this intuit process the subtle mind-substance experiences a merge with the universal mental-substance. Is this a vital illusion? Just having it, is not enough…

1710.   The deeper one goes into the knowledge of what existence is the holier life becomes.

1711.   An arrow striking a hanging sack full of trash is less valuable than an arrow striking a live target.

1712.   Shipping old news to a dead fellow.

1713.   Colors erupting from a peacock tail: yesterday's tomb is already forgotten, another tomb is open for parties...

1714.   A bird got trapped in an out-of-order music box: listen...

1715.   The storm came with the night. In the morning only a few things were left untouched. At my arm length a wolf cub licks dew drops from a maple leaf. When disaster strikes, Zen takes over...

1716.   If you ever loose your sense of humor remember this: oxen never laugh, goats never smile, sheep never cry, horses never talk.

1717.   Hesitation, doubts, fear before awakening means that you're not ready yet to jump over the cliff. That you're vigilant about the state of your mind is okay. Though, the preoccupation with your doubts should be left alone. If you let it go you'll feel like an arrow that stopped in the air before continuing its way to the target. Remember, an arrow could travel for years before reaching its destination.

1718.   A bubble blowing toy bear meets a bubble blowing toy kitten. They stare at each other.

1719.   Science versus Zen: A whale spits water back into the ocean. An ocean spits water back into the atmosphere. As it rains, distance appears between rain drops. It is as if the atmospheric phenomena recycle the biosphere phenomena. What really concerns me is the exact distance in inches between the raindrops…

1720.   There is always a way to arrange the fruits on a table using their natural order…

1721.   As long as they were married they fought about the meaning of a Sutra line: "That one shall not have doubts when turning into the universal form…" Then one day he fell from a cliff and died. As he was brought home and placed in the middle of the living room, his wife opened the casket and began reading the sutra. When she finished the line "That one shall not have doubts when turning into the universal form…" she asked the dead: "Do you understand? The sutra is talking about what you do now… Say something if you can… No more doubts! What a lie!"

1722.   At nightfall stores are closing, flowers are closing, eyes are closing. The owl is calling back her ego: "OWL! OWL!"

1723.   The assumption that an object and its reflection are identical is false. Also, the assumption that an object and its reflection are not identical is false.

1724.   To see beauty or ugliness and not discriminate; to feel love or hate and not feel attached; to know the good from the evil and accept them equally; what else is left to the living? The "great death" takes them all…

1725.   There is something uncertain about what takes place when a rabbit raises his voice against a wolf…

1726.   If you ever got enlightened did you ever plan how you could save your life from becoming a grain of emptiness? To lead your mind out of Satori and back into your life you'd have to plan your rebirth.

1727.   A peacock may conceal the obscure beauty of a cacophony…

1728.   To bring fresh knowledge to an old subject you'll have to forget most of it. To be awakened you'd have to forget your whole life.

1729.   Be tactful when you ask and spontaneous when you answer.

1730.   Crowds watching in silence the funeral proceedings: all of a sudden a child voice is heard laughing, loudly laughing and laughing. Everybody laughed afterwards. Ceremonies are always mediocre improvisations of shows, made to enchant the children.

1731.   A flower is analogous to an eye seeing it: that is, the cosmic body for what-the-flower-is is identical to the cosmic body of what it is seen.

1732.   If the reality is not real we'll call it the unreal world: did you feel your thoughts hardening?

1733.   The bird kept flying after being hit by the arrow. Sometimes targets travel longer than their hunters…

1734.   A peacock wide-opening its feathery tail: an unobstructed manifestation of light. Snowplows working on each flake, thoroughly…

1735.   An infinitesimal green fly cruising a moss…

1736.   On the highest peak the silence is hopeless: like a sound that your instinct says is not within reach. The ice is hard and clear like quartz is. A wrong step and you're easily on your way to be remembered…

1737.   Stars don't talk. Winds are blind. Mountains don't listen. To whom then this universe was given to enjoy? So much coloring, so much chanting… Mind embodies the universe…

1738.   A fly embodies a flight akin to a falcon. They just mirror their flight differently.

1739.   Cynical philosophy: The divisibility of the reality in what is known and what is not known gives to one the impression that the unknown may continuously modify what is known and vice versa: God may not be such a good idea; devil may not be such a bad idea.

1740.   Satori is in limited supply.

1741.   An infinitely large point is still a point. That is, it is circular, black, finite in size and used at the end of every sentence.

1742.   In a particular sense stars are similar to our sun. In Satori stars remain being stars. Nothing would make them hold any other characteristics. Stars therefore don't have any connection to Satori. Weeds for instance don't know that stars exist. Do they? Even a fox seeing a starry sky knows that stars are neither good nor evil.

1743.   Thousand of green grasshoppers hopping in the green grass. Change green to yellow when the autumn comes…

1744.   The pine forest on the stony hill: gutted by fire…

1745.   Living! What a crap… Drinking coffee in the morning, working, having an afternoon siesta, drinking some wine and then hunting for afterthoughts. The only good thing is that I do this for forty years waiting for something to happen. If this is Zen I could continue doing it for another forty years. If this is not Zen but life I'd better pack my casket and go…

1746.   The red fox follows the trail of the red hen…

1747.   Zen is the invocation of emptiness. A response from it is like seeing migratory birds coming back to their origin. A lack of response is like riding a wooden horse that never turns his head no matter how hard you whip him.

1748.   Intake the azure…

1749.   For Zen the smell of a rose and the smell of horseshit are one and the same.

1750.   The incense is still burning but its fragrance is not.

1751.   In Zen, apart from how many things you'd have to sort out to get awakened you'd always find a more "few" before it happens.

1752.   The moon would still shed light after the universe will be extinguished. That's because entities that reflect the attributes of another object survive the object's demise; naturally, this explains why a thought, at its turn, survives one's loss.

1753.   Sometimes a pot holds stuff that is different than what the potter had in "mind".

1754.   At the bottom of the pond a piece of shard shines, small triangles of light, like a broken moon… You can measure its luminous strength by comparing it with the shining of your spit...

1755.   It snows without flakes.

1756.   Life calls for action. Death calls for the six flavored senses to rest. All tuned senses would survive the onslaught if they got rid of attachments. How a well tuned sense gets rid of attachments?

1757.   Sun comes no more, moon goes no more…

1758.   Walking into a koan-trap feels like an insect nailed: still being able to move its wings though it can go nowhere. As the koan is cracked, no more nailing: on an icy ground even a Buddha needs an anchor.

1759.   As you go back to Mu, Mu says Mu to you! Want to play?

1760.   Thoughts laying: foreign eggs hurriedly hatched. In broad daylight the moon generates the ocean labor. The only thing that stands is Mu, propped up on the formless pillar. No longer an alien, not a friend either. Since none is going to talk, we'd understand each other while watching the gateless barrier.

1761.   There are ultimate truths trapped in commonplace truths. At any time one kind of truth can become the other kind and vice versa. Metaphysics has always a finger pointing to reality. When there is no right move, left move, ascent or descent, thing transcend. The last hatched egg on the hilltop cracked. No bird though. Did it transcend?

1762.   Side by side a lion and a rabbit watch the eclipse. As the eclipse loses shade…

1763.   The world-in-becoming abandons old customs. Old mirrors=Old odors! Old moeurs lose their meaning. New customs bring with them the revised form of emptiness in the proximity to the old ones.

1764.   The desire and its fulfillment are one.

1765.   The act of God was to make the appearance supercede the essence: like cloth covering a naked body or like mud covering a precious stone. Knock the shell, look inside! Under the skin a grain is still a grain. The subtlety is in the lack of anything else… As you go deeper and find nothing else but what it is, your moot point is the essence.

1766.   Paraphrasing John Cage: "I have nothing to say and I'm not saying anything; and that is Zen".

1767.   Worship the simplest God, like the Sun, for instance. Every day, its light would be moving along your path.

1768.   Organs are reusable, bones are reusable.

1769.   Diplomatic Zen has fewer words than regular Zen. If all mouths are in view words are all vanishing in a smile.

1770.   Any land is a promise, any Heaven is a hope.

1771.   What exists also dies. What dies also exist.

1772.   If you want to say a word it is just as good to write it down. Once you write it down it outlives your saying: "When moon rises swans reappear at the other side of the lake".

1773.   What is abruptly ending is abruptly beginning.

1774.   The poem about a fly would sound un-poetical if it wasn't for that battered frog…

1775.   Metaphysics are overlooking the transient. (Like you had an idea and you're just trying to remember it). The knobs of a bamboo stick…

1776.   If you read it carefully this Koan may trigger your Satori: What are you afraid of? Your heart cannot go into exile: It is rooted into your body. Your mind cannot go into exile: It is rooted into your skull. Your bones cannot pass through your skin. Though, as you walk through an undifferentiated landscape white bones are piercing through the earth's skin everywhere.

1777.   Drumming on a dinner table and waiting to fulfill the most natural comfort: eating. Mother says: stop doing that! And her voice resonates on the twilight streets till the appetite takes over.

1778.   In still water boats can't sail, birds' presence becomes uncertain. The poet chooses cautiously synonyms to replace a dead word.

1779.   Lately, my ailing horse befriended an ailing jockey. They're going to compete together in a race for life and win.

1780.   Doing nothing for days: only the crow on the tip of the flagpole keeps flapping her wings…

1781.   Dense noise as a flock of myriad of birds going south: out of silence, silence grows…

1782.   A glass of water can quench the thirst of one million flies.

1783.   The understanding is like a mouth filled with pain: no word can be spoken; no conceptualization can be locked away. The wall that separated Hell from Heaven, evil from good, East from West is now ashes.

1784.   Moonlight and sunlight: raining in a Southern place makes water soar in a Northern place.

1785.   If Satori doesn't appear act as if you're not interested in it. Light always comes to the blind as a see through.

1786.   A tiger catching a prey: "My wild body is restless though my wild mind is at peace".

1787.   Either stopping for asking or waking away and not answering are wrong. But neither answering nor avoiding it is right. Blessed are those living in seclusion for not having the chance to talk to themselves.

1788.   A door slams, a dog barks, a crow crows, an albatross shrieks: what a beautiful bunch of phenomena! On the yellow pad – bird drops… It starts to rain.

1789.   Silence leaks though the mill's grinding stones.

1790.   Going indoors when it rains, outdoors when it rains with hailstones.

1791.   Holding in my hand a bowl with water I succeeded to capture the moonlight. The star light is not getting in. Ultimately snows falls silently…

1792.   The icy heights of the enlightenment still let trees get barren and birds starve. Sometimes life has to settle in a warmer place. Though, a deep bow on the peak of the mountain can appease the sandstorms on thousand deserts.

1793.   Black scarecrows on a cotton field… Who is eating the cotton?

1794.   Nature is Zen and Zen is nature. That's why a fox's dream takes place in a forest and a fish's dream takes place in the ocean. The beauty of Zen is that if emptiness is the end of any journey the fish could end up in the same place with the fox: there is no clear who sees who. By Zen law, the eaten will enjoy the eating and vice versa.

1795.   I don't understand how DNA could demonstrate that a man is nothing but a variation of a mouse: not talking at all about similarities… Of course if I use Zen thinking I know that it is true.

1796.   Emptiness: the word and the thing cancelled one another.

1797.   The thinning layer of dust makes the stars look lifeless and the windy space threatening. Early morning the pigs gyrate in the street mud with no perception of the cosmic collapse. For a pig the universe stays indivisible…

1798.   Zen joke: Body nourishing a mind dream: this is a foolish desire. A Zen saying on it would be: a no-body nourishing a no-mind dream… Did you ever have an urge of screaming with an unexplainable joy? Zen doesn't have a place for it: instincts are crushed, urges are trampled, desires are flattened… Knowing no life is not going to help your suffering. So, if you have an urge to scream, do it, scream as if your mighty throat is using Buddha's lungs.

1799.   The one eyed lianas watching the endless path.

1800.   The dog says: "Once I was a man". Who's going to believe what the dog says? Adding a touch of Zen to this story, the dog starts barking: "Mu, Mu… I have Buddha nature. Lice have it too…" On the rock hill there is a den where stray dogs meet and spend secluded hours doing Zazen. Chao-Chou says: "Times change".

1801.   Naked but too prudish not to hide my true Self with my crossed hands…

1802.   When a shark locks its jaws the moon travels. When the shark opens its jaws the moon initiates high tidings. Parting jaws – acting reality: as long as you can bear…

1803.   The only physical principle that devises is the fire: ashes cannot be brought back as a tree…

1804.   A flower is indivisible…

1805.   Warning: Awakening is not going to spare your mind.

1806.   The moment when I saw suddenly what it meant: clawed clouds that climb up cliffs spawning sparks. The mighty rain…

1807.   The echo has one thousand ears; the shadow has two thousand eyes.

1808.   The body of reality is sunny during the day and starry during the night. If one sighs the breeze starts blowing. Cries of white monkeys in the cherry blossoms…

1809.   You could find in your surroundings the truth you're looking for while searching the infinite.

1810.   Stillness was never loud. Life was never silent. On long feet the wind says something about the departing clouds. In clay pot the interlocked weeds… Beyond this mountain the sun never ascends, the moon never descends.

1811.   Enlightenment as a very small vehicle: nothing to do when there's anything to think of…

1812.   Enterprising minds could one day succeed to help ordinary people fly like birds or walk like ghosts onto the air.

These accomplishments will still be phenomena. Zen teaches you why you shouldn't fly like a bird or walk onto the air.

1813.   Stimuli are made to stir phenomena for the living. A sensation that passes through the brain leaves a trail that teases other trails to come along and play. This entire explanation looks to me like soft barbed wire fences built around a rose to chase away the enlightenment. Or, isn't this just what we call being alive?

1814.   Hearing is a gift given to the one who listen.

1815.   When a question has no answer think of a river bottom on which pearls of water dance in a rainbow of sunny drizzles, or about the completeness of the letter "O", or about what MU would respond to it. If it doesn't say anything, your question invites a lie. If it responds "Attention!" Watch! Stockpiles of mountains crumble into the mirroring sea.

1816.   Thought=Act. When a thought is in total agreement with the act thousand stars on a scale measure a feather weight. The whole universe – floating like a breeze…

1817.   Hearing the unclasping of both hands.

1818.   The path to immortality is scattered with bones. On a myriad square miles not a single watchful eye…

1819.   The Bull Zen: Though they're perfectly equal and the manifestation of the perfect one, a freshly squeezed peach juice has more fragrance than a latrine rinse. In the world of discrimination a peach does not resemble a bull, and its juice is different than that of a latrine horned by it.

1820.   Words despite Zen's interdictions. Thoughts despite Zen's cold shoulder. If I'm here and now I can feel my mind. If I'm lost my mind is in exile. I can't turn it on when in exile, I can't turn it off when around. Meanwhile the awakening wants to use my no-mind and can't find it anywhere.

1821.   Weighing a thought on an immaculate footpath…

1822.   It is all acts, even listening to silence. Where is the yesterday's crowing? (Still traveling with the falling leaves?) Hard when it comes, soft as it goes away…

1823.   Bringing something you had forgotten back to your attention…

1824.   When one says that words are to the mind what legs are to the walk, what happens to the walk when the words are wiped out for some Zen benefit?

1825.   Taking awakening as a miracle and a divine gift is like taking your life as a mistake. Remember: life is being, awakening is ashes…

1826.   A toy boat sinks and one million voices yell for help.

1827.   As a flower gets formless its fragrance jumps at you with tiger claws…

1828.   Enlightenment in its absolute peace stirs sixteen billion years old memories…

1829.   If eyes were not a given what would we use instead? The moon passes overhead touching my hair…

1830.   Satori is not a big deal: the absolute presence shows to be an absolute absence. But the effort to attain it is! It teaches one to respect life and accept its outcome with serenity. And also one realizes that – once being there – there is not much left to learn of in this life. But watch: if everything originated out of nothing it doesn't mean that nothing gets a better appraisal than something: trees are still blossoming, maids are scrubbing the bath tubs, cell phones help hunters pinpoint their prey, clothes are hanged on ropes to dry in the sharp-cold air... The long awaited baby proves to be "twins"...

1831.   Voodoo Zen: When birth marks are seen on a dead white lamb, the roots of the elm tree burst with white blossoms, the silver moon returns and the would-be-clouds depart spilling fine laced curtains of water. The black crow opens its eyes in the world of the unseeing but cannot crow.

1832.   Emptiness is playing with the mind: opening the gates it spreads its cards. Kill your ideas. Play bridge with the inscrutable.

1833.   On a runaway boat to be at the oar is more important than meditating on a koan.

1834.   The cyclone tail kept drawing a circle while moving about. Inside – destruction, outside – destruction. It seems a circle means perfection only in the select world where natural phenomena are grounded.

1835.   To invoke a Buddha in a donkey? No poetry line would be able to put them together. Except the street dogs, barking at the full moon...

1836.   With every fish caught the water level is rising...

1837.   Time=Space equation could be understood by a calf while being brought forth. The separation from his mom cow invalidates the equation. The moral? Entering the world of experience initiates the differentiation. To humans, grasping space is more real than grasping time. For a rabbit running in front of a lion, time=space is as real as heaven=hell. Try to invoke the equation running for your life with a limping foot...

1838.   The bell without a clapper is like a donkey's back without a load... or like a talking doll without a tongue...

1839.   Light will never satisfy a snoozer. Silence will never satisfy a sharp tongue. Tossing and turning the whole night: The morning light arrives like a tumultuous sound of drums. As you point to the sun, that is where they come from. Pulling down the blinds to keep the sun out, you get sun inside your attention instead.

1840.   The rooster's song defeated by a morning moon eclipse...

1841.   As you see Buddha, bow and let him pass. As you don't see Buddha, bow deeper and let him pass. Intrepid men carry for their lives...

1842.   At the mountain's feet the light descends onto streams, cleansing the water...

1843.   Waves rising and falling... Water practices this dance for eons already. A life time is too short to try it. Instead, listen to the waves until they break through you: the serene lake, auspiciously...

1844.   Nothing is seen until brought in the view, though for ears things are different. Sounds find you while visions wait to be found.

1845.   You hear the rain falling and the water becomes a subject in your head. Though, seeing a waterfall you don't think of rain. There is this model of the mind, going from phenomena (rain) to the essence (water) that saves some of us from being taken as oxen.

1846.   Life and matter are aware of each other differentiation. The awakened one sees them both alike.

1847.   When the reality is undoubted, its knowledge is. Leaning on a shadow…

1848.   A hyperbolic Basho: "The old lake. An elephant jumps in. PLOP!"

1849.   Enlightenment is not appropriate to those who can afford to ride on the back of an ox named ignorance.

1850.   The one who is silenced by the guilt of knowing is more of a sinner than the one who is not.

1851.   The magpie replies: "Ay! Ay!" Often the true way arrives from what naturally comes into your mind. Bird calls and cues, hints and bird calls. Emptiness is coming for its "look-in" visit.

Inner-mind Zen, outer-life…

The fog carries out the abyss of the last shadows.
On the road, the sky still draws the remote phantom of the
morning rain. The air is lighter and lighter.
Flowers are blooming; fruits are falling onto the grass
separated from their sleep, like some frail
shadows.

And there she is, like spring's revival, a body in its
misty flight shivering words: love, love, love, restless and
endless echoes.

Where are the holy days of the past, the apple
trees in pink blossom, the river's valley wearing the
sleeping gown of the night until dawn?

Where are your words,
whispered into my ears, and our love, a too short awakening?
Or our dreams that mysteriously went away on the almost dead
sky?

Where are the whitened beams chasing away our minds' shadows,
and the orchard's leaves, rusting under the thin cloth of rain, and
the Heaven's smell, drifting away further and further...

You see, how slowly the death smacks, the road is empty, and on
the path to the woods the bunch of white bones and the small
indentations on the blackberry bushes.

To live in Heaven remote memories that
might exist and to appease your life with its triumphant return.
"Once upon a time you were an elf, a fairy adorned with flowery
brilliance, an angel who disobeyed its divine origins".

Oh, come,
day of tomorrow, the most beautiful, the most ennobled day, in
which the memory of a happy dream may come true! Let the sky
framing the color of the plain be more momentous than the days
that passed. Let the garden's shadow shelter the flight of the
Heaven's birds, let the grass stretch its path towards the spotless
thresholds of the everlasting shores bathed today in banqueting
chants.

God speaks secretly to the alive: let your days of life fly
as every other day, chainless, carrying above the hill crest the
watery harp of the pure love, awakened by the morning's wind,
like a flight of an undying bird over the temporal furrows.

Here is the day, at last: what did it seem like yesterday, in waiting?
An imperishable tam-tam, a light in an unending voyage, an
immune foreverness after which you must run. And now? What
remained after? A hope without glory, a thought fulfilled in a cold,
shadowy plain, its cherished words swept by the wind.

Man telling to himself:
'I'm still alive during my own life!' And, in the breeze of the
land, close to the mill's water hardly heated by sun, he heard
from far away the invincible song of the day passing in its death
through the flying grass thorns: peasants are leaving the fountain,
a bird enters the whitened flocks of the meadow, and then, the
silence comes, the mysterious peace still nailed in the childhood
world... A ragged sheaf, the lambs, playing, the shadow of the
singing rain. Flying stars seem whispering in the shade of the
wind, and the earth ripens in the darkness like the rush over the
water. This, thus...

That's the time when the song starts: 'During all sunset
your garden seems to open in the depth of the land. Love, that
begins with the cock's last song, words that seem to have no place
and no time: Your beautiful voice, your small ears, your skin made
to fathom unspoken words, groans stolen from sleep.

Where are your thoughts? Far away, near the celestial tree.
The fruit, you moisten your lips in, and your teeth: white flowers
like a wreath to the wind. Your hips like the moving sand. And
your belly, burning under the moon's rise; your breasts, a bunch of
heavy roses, your lips, a nest on a trembling branch.

From the ineffable light of the first day you understood the aim of
the immaculate songs: the sermon in bed, your eyes, appearing
more limpid then the early morning. An angel, at the window,
unchanged, wasting its flight for a look inside: halting... And, in
silence, you feel nothing but the wish to watch from above her
body falling under your body, and the wings of her arm's smell
rustling, subtle, unresting, and to hear her cries when feeling your
love coming closer and the ephemeral shore shining again.

'It's me', the bird says, 'it's me';

A cat leaping to catch a carnation in the dim lit window…

'It's me!' A tall bride with watchful eyes, and her groom, singing
his love to her watchful eyes: 'Your loving voice is a sob, your
belly's pain is a cry, your eyes, blackened dance in the air'.

'My soul is a blind bird deserted by God in the valley', she sings.

Mist and black branches fall on the morning's road: how bright are
the childhood's days, motionless smiles in the sighing sound of the
river;

The stars glitter above the road, as she sings, hiding under the vine, staring: in the silence of the dusk, chimeras... The sticks are fully wrapped in convolvulus, yellow bindweed; oh, hope, wander again along the path of the oak, caressed by light, blessed with love: summon me!

Forgotten steps, leaves which solemnly fall over the threshold...
On the path to the house, flowers torn by the wind.
The cracking of the pole under heavy rain; and, with the
sound of your steps, the chirp of a bird left behind by the sudden autumn. Near the garden, wrapped in smoke, the falcon, hurried master: just a sweet flight, and the short song stops, lost in the towering grass.

You see, as it happens in any voyage, you cannot part in
past for the days to come: the Heaven is lost. You're here now, and the days are clear. Tell me then, can you choose a road you dreamed about to a long, real journey? Your feet carry you wherever you like: you open the gate; the ephemeral shore of the day appears. Far away, the village seems caught in the moving shadows. The volute morning's light.

What love makes you utter still unheard the noise of the days to come? It's your breath like a ringing silver coin falling deeper and deeper in the immortal hollow of an apple tree.

Tomorrow... Will you be the exact image of the day which
yesterday roused in the hazy forest? What is there still warm in your heart, that makes you return to Earth on another day?

The eternal songs, the angels' flight over the shores: living the
beauty of a moment, a voice begs for love, and the answer, small words lighting a piece of a body in waiting. The river of kisses, like a warm fountain inside woman's breasts, murmuring songs, whispers that might mold appetites from ancient times: rains without fragrance, sounds from the depth of the forgotten days;

Sparrows fly through the bush in front of the window; frightening
winds blow... The sound of so many flights buried under the
shields of a stone, found yesterday in the towering grass.
Look at the morning mist, its shadows, held by hands
which had once been warm.

The organ of the horizon, in which day by day, other and
other shadows come to mow the grass: your bare breasts, steamed
by the sun, your wild black berries trembling in the humid grass.
You are like Mother Earth, a body nailing the time to its lips...

Fruitful hills, full of fruits bellies... The hill lighted by the
lightening. The mole, like a hollow echo! The watchman staring at
the mountain peak: it snows up there…

And repeatedly, nearer and nearer, the sound of rain as
if coming up from the depth of your breasts. Your hair, stretched
like a black wing in the air. The shadow eating from the hill,
biting: a strangled cloud, pouring out at the edge of the plain.

This is what your life is, in its way, loving: the slow murmur of
the rain, timelessly winding of a sense, as you sleep the sleep of
the great passage into the happening.

And there is again silence, like in a deserted world.

Your blood is a black dance and your
breast is the slow shaken light roofing the heated air. What afar
your mouth is, touching my bed with a drunken sweetness, singing
a misty song. In cherry trees, the light of your eyes awoke mildly,
like a bird blinded by lights in its flight through the darkness.

This is the door of the sunken memory, a basket filled with grape
and wild thyme... The moon is arching above the abyss. The wind
plays on a wild harp, the stars' fall upon us... Oh, that night, that

seem to wreck under the burn of the moon, and that cry, that cry, that cry:

Besides swallow nests, night comes hurried like a
prophet, reciting in holy whispers, the story of our forgotten joy:
allow me shadow to tear away thy dry branch!

 The warm earth seems Holy under so many flights. With every hour, the lamps on the street rise of so much illumination.

Let your feelings whirl up towards the vast sky glistening on the wild crest of the hill: it is the hour when barns are opened and cleared, the ticking of the windows is slumbering, mildly, like the penetration of the memory inside darkness.

Heat: the hand is searching for the taste of shade
of your sleeping breasts: your wild berries, covered with spicy ointments, and the dove, passing far, like an arrow through the top of the reddish elm; your breasts, a nest of white doves, flying on a darkened sky. Your hair, like a swallow's nest, suddenly scattered by a snow ball fallen from the thistle brush:

"The bite of the ephemeral pleasure: a hunter aiming at his target? No, an Echo!"

What day's today? The soot is falling, covering the
moonlight, making huge mysterious swarms, blown and scattered ashes on the deserted road: look, the huge wing of the nocturnal air. What a grand flight!

Detached from the loving word, you look for a companion star in the darkness. The icicles ring under the eaves like some deer horns left aside in the first spring day of the year. The moment of absence when the sunrise begins: far away, the village, sleeps, caught by the moving shadow. The sky lowers its high crests, undulating, the wandering stars still burning in the lost sight of nothingness.

Listen to your thoughts: the blind cadence of the wind carrying love words and love smells into your heart, the gleaming echo of the grass rising under the drying dew. The memory, a silence in which you walk. The far away moaning of the plain, never ceases.

Brewed together, the message of our bodies' love competes with the rattle of the shaking leaves... The past appears to you like your fear to live without love, not a single moment alone, every moment dying.

Tomorrow, how eternal this word seems: on ice steps, your dying love slides and falls, bitter waters carrying away the corpse of a history out of which I was banished.

A prayer only and the wind stops; a wish only, and, from the rustle of the ditch, the beak full of seeds appears again. To see your young age anchored in the threshold: the lizards moving their tails near the barn, the light's kiss lingering behind a bastard lost in the dark field. And you, singing the Heaven's song while lying in wait, eager to see if the doves will come again from the black fields, untouched by the rain.

The memory of the early morning when we went down by cart to the scorched pond, more and more rapidly. The slippery road, covered with carob, the wounded bird struggling to fly away from the tall grass; and then, suddenly, the summer rain whipping your breasts: white shadows in a deserted forest, heavy grapes sliding down to the root. I shall go to the orchard again; I shall pick the fruits you like, a sealed aloes your mouth savoring the wind, your hands falling down, like the white crowns of a mountain lily, fleeing your hair: an everlasting flight and without end. You smile now, and the moon's rays warm your eyes, and you fall over the grass, rolling like a stone thrown in a marsh of myrtle. Beauty, you cry, stay in the measure of a past misguidance! The hill under the sun's spears, two white shadows in a row, anchored near your belly, burning out, shouting at the sky: and the dike, losing with every hour a line at the horizon, as if broken by a secret rain.

This was the time when the most beautiful days on earth seemed to waste: the moon running away, frail and strange, passing over your eyes with every creak of a branch, the frozen snake of resin running on the oak tree, the Rotten furrow, stinking, the shadow of the antic elm
stirred by the owl.

Look, the dog's ghost behind the fence: it barks at me. In the morning, trembling with the frosty wind in the field, we began weeding: under your robe, your breast, awakened by a thistle, "Ouch!" waiting for the heat that suddenly came down in the thicket, near the furrow edge: it seems that your love comes from there, from the remote humming of the grass, from the smell of the woods, from the enchantment of the entire order of nature with perennial dreams: hark...

I hear the sound of your heart, which the sun never lighted, the vast veil of the world at birth, the flight of the bird chasing the shores away and the dark hill, bursting out from under the red sheath, which seems like life getting ready to guard body's awakening.

You'll lay and you'll kiss the old shade of the source, watching the flight of the mountain cock, enormous, passing through the abyss of the valley and, wildly crying, filling the hill with a rustling sound.

Oh, those days, how they still sleep, haunting the wavy grass of the plain with their blue glance.

Your life seemed divided in two: one part, still following the old song of a remote age, waiting for a sign: a hand troubling the light beam on a little breast, lips washed with wine for a night of kisses:

the other one, a road on which you seem lost in the immaculate garden of Heaven.

On the hill, near the road side, a young woman is awaiting for her man, near a fire of dry branches: the hour of knowledge! The first kiss, a delicate look at a red grape, white wilderness that seems to blossom near another shore.

Then the storm, the shore from which birds fly up away, as if at an order, stirring the sounds in her breasts, like an autumn day in a desert forest: your hand, stretching like the light, cradled by the yellow grass... a well with pure water, towards which light winds carry them straightly.

Love: when you will hear the wind stirred on the dark path of the garden, and you'll recognize yourself weak, torn apart by a fear which seems the very hard way of innocence, call your beloved: "Thou, the fleeting love, tell me, what moments will remain alive, from this early blossoming? Why your love, by making me merry, expels me, without warning, to the steadiness of my lonely past? Why, your love, the supreme delight of my body, and at the same time, with its supreme
pride, my death?"

When in the slow murmur of the early morning, heavy, you'll remain to grind fancies of a dream still unsealed from sleep, when in the perfume of the night you'll look for the color of the dawn, trying to escape in the daily voyage, call your beloved: "Thou, the endless love, tell me that in the hour of uncertainty of tomorrow, you'll remember your imperious duty to penetrate with your heart deep inside the immaculate songs". Love, perpetual quietness... But listen to this cry, overwhelming... My
beloved, my dove, awakened by tears, still sobbing in her sleep, tells her sad story: "I lost my body in a flight of a broken wing...".

White stars like milk in a bosom, filling with ivy my ocean of hay: her eyes, like the moving gravel over which water changes its face, clearing itself of illusion. Her lips, the taste of earth one feels when smelling a fountain's steam... Her lips, a cluster of red birds anchored in clay.

Summer seems still far: only the ravens, gathered in black packs fly among the carob trees, fighting. The street seems ashy. In the shade of a fountain the hunters are waiting for a better day. A man shouts down in the valley, shuffling his sandals towards the gate pole: a sheaf of dry flowers. And all things enter eternity again: the flocks descend to the river, reminding us that is still a spring morning in the gloomy sky.

My soul withdraws from the steps of the eternal night,
singing: "Your hair, so black, more black than the autumn leaves, your eyes, more misty than the fog carrying a bird in the air, your lips like a black queen in a white desert, your skin like a sandy wind, your nest like a black speech in a white magic dream".

The red cat is wallowing in the grass. Keeping a finger on a window pane, you wait to see it jumping, suddenly covered by the tumultuous haystack. Then the sound of the rain comes like an echo from the edge of the forest...

Once upon a time, the woman in front of me told me, once upon a time: "Look at my breasts, look at my shades, I am the distance seeking its place before disappearing, I am the ecstasy trying its cries in sleep, I am the expansion of the gracious words".

The mill merged into the pond water, and, by night, again, there was silence, and the embracing shadow, moving like a nun in a deserted church. You see, this is the drunken breath of the lips in prayer, the savage carving of the eyes of the self, the shut eyelids wickedly showing us what ecstasy is.

Loves! What are they? Dreams, looking for a migratory star; these forks throwing the grass into the time of the boundless dance, birds which flood over the water, spying the sky. The old fir tree fell on the grass bed which yesterday I sown; like a rustle, the forest vanished under the blue morning light, the sheep climbed the abrupt slope of the hill with leaps that seemed to scatter the bird nests.

Woman's arms at midnight, unforgotten woman's arms, sad sources of shadows and cries: was it her face? A flower drawing its move into solitude: memories, which the night has since long left in desert, became awake, and I asked myself, who could still laugh, who could cry? How does my love look today, under the heavy blows, my unforgotten love?

Nearly breathing, like a prolonged lightening... Your tears look like the morning dew, the spring water which seems to blossom near the sandy shore; your eyelids, like tortuous dust. And your tongue, singing the song of the days to follow: a strange voyage, where one sees the flowery grass still moving, the sweet quince tree branch still tapping the window, stiffened by the coals fire.

As you cover your voice, which, more deeply, in your dream, calls the endless love again: under your head, the heavy smell of the dry furrow, and the couple of hips, moving above.

Every summer starts in the field: the shores of a land on which unknown bodies descend, carrying laurel and myrtle in their hands; shores which, your body thinks, are appraised for by an unexpected voyage. Love seems an ocean moving beyond the passing time, vast rain under which eternal birds bind with their flights the heavily burdened constellations; your lips look for shelter in the tall grass, murmuring: "Oh, the Earth, under the falling sky!" Your hair, the wind touches no more, locked in my hands, like the pale sand beyond the woods' wall. Exhausted by love, you listen to the lazy rustling of the leaves at the edge of the forest: inaudible moans, which used to bring about the ecstasy of the first morning kiss: a mountain cock searching in the haystack the red little fruits, scattered by the midnight wind, and suddenly, the cry of merciless touch, bursting of agony, like fog rising from the dying storm, in the abyss.

The wind in the fog sighs warmly: your breasts, virgin roses on a bed used for offering. "I, bending my face, drinking water from your lips, according to the old habit which I have been parted from by sad feelings. And while I drink, here's the sky: oh, God, how many lonely nights I lived watching my wandering star among asters!"

Under the cellar's cover the swallow found yesterday is struggling to fly away; a sudden wing beating; two rounded eyes in the shade; then the frightened cry, tormented by the pain: a squirrel watching the happenings from a red thicket.

Listening to your blood: that gentle ticking which virgins devote to the heaven's memory.

The sweet tyrant of a lost childhood: the water pond near the fountain, ready to soothe the thirst of the little white birds. In the rye field, your dress hangs over the head. The sun is burning mildly. On the sky, flames cheerfully dance. Your naked body seems covered by milk, your naked breasts - two turtle doves, your tongue, a strawberry full of dew, praying to the sky.

I say: "I saw a little girl gathering red berries on the isle bank, and a fox carrying to a bush a bleeding bird". She laughs, young rows of white teeth sealed to any cry. She says: "I saw the high tower of the town hall, with its bent cock, getting bigger, cracking"; near the meadow there is a bed of flowers, on the bed, her unclad body, a misty skin full of incensed drops, a bird lengthening its wings for a short flight. Nearly breathing, her smile: like watering with virgin milk a grape, like a lily surrendering to the mighty wind: I say: "Come, thou, O my love, come...", as her breath begins swinging mildly at my slightest touch.

And then, I step in a hollow, and learn the song of heart: the call of the hill, its spicy smell of rain which I hardly feel... The wet leaves hanging on the hip tree, oh, how they moved to enlighten my melancholy... A black tiny flower, here and there, hanging under the bank of the moisten river bed. As if she'd be a dove, looking for feathers on her young hill, which is now open. She says: "My walk is troubled like never before; my mind is like caught by my body's sweetness;
my nest is bound in a spicy cloth".

You, everlasting love, you'll be among so many mornings, an omnipresent star, grass traveling through the frozen spaces of destiny. The heights die in the murmur of the sprinkled plain, the core of the past day goes rolling ahead, obscured by the fertile furrow, now full of seed. A fruit hidden in the shape of a flower, a deceiving illusion till birth: my love looks like the day of tomorrow, a bird unbound from the water, gently sliding on gravel.

What is Heaven? An ancient land, bound by the fleeting images of a body unwrapped from its mist. Your passion: a spring cry under the dark burrows in the hill; a meadow over which the eternal light opens its wings, passing like a wave among the sea bushes: a path that haunts me.

The sunrise looks like your heart uttering the secrets of love, a mouth singing what has not been uttered yet, rejoicing: A murmur opens the grass bunches in sleep. Oh, you star of the day, light the long, long route to the hill: it's dawn again, the sea breeze carries the mist away from the fence. You see, the whirlwind is stirring the red leaves near the fountain: soon, the hollow will open in front of the shadowy tree: listen to the plain's moans, the blind way of the plough tracing the hill face up to the sky.

He says: "Your hands, magic movements in sleep, your lips cover to the flowery tower". She sings: "Like the opening rose hurts the sky", she sings, "like blood tapestries...".

"Your eyes", he says, "Twin volcanoes dying out in the shadow of a spring bloom, your nest wild strawberry leaves coming to life, your tears like the morning dew piercing a flower's crown... Your murmur - a strange song for the struggling heart..."

What is the divine love? Everlasting! Her mouth closing the whispers of a sudden joy: "Oh, what a torrent, ah, too hurried cry, too hurried was it too, the mysterious rain".

Love - a harmless path to age. Far away, the cry
of the forest begins to spread... Here are your breasts, raised
like two haystacks near the field edge; and the rustle of your
berries darkening the wide valley. The wind's hands move along
the maze of straws, sensing the secret beat of life which burns the
time until overflowing.

A sudden flight over the hill, the clouds passing without echo over the vast plateau: dark stars in the pond, owls of the universe.

At sunset you invoke the sun, your eyes at peace with the sea shores, forgotten, your mind in the empire of so many dead prophecies. Your hands, asking for mercy: "Oh, night, guardian of the beings, tell me what is this morose echo of the last migration? The live stars, in swarms, lingering around my body, like a memory passing through merciless times..."

Pray to the water! The moon, like an eye in a thicket: the shore, like a warning: "no trespassing!" Far away, the stones on the hill hide the bird's long sleep. Red leaves in the lake's waters; the muddy field, slumbering. If you were alone! You shouted for a moment: "Who's there?" Daybreak of sacrifice, chained legs carrying burdens. Then the darkness cried and the winds scattered like a shadow.

Here is the shout awaken from its restless sleep: "Run, run, you, sun, don't stop..."

Kind words, uttered together with a cry, a voice in the sheep cote, counting lambs; among the weeds, the gate keeps moving, making its way out of the garden. The vine leaf seems bitten by goats.

Where are the two little sisters, dancing near the pond? A bird is struggling to reach the shore; with buzzing sounds, grass on which you tread as if deepened.

God is scrutinizing us with His water eye: where is miller's daughter? In the huge reality of your short awakening you said, startlingly: "I dreamed my own life!"

This love, whose deadly roaring... "The woman I love smiled at me in ruins of laurels, looking inside another heart": ice flowers overgrew the long night I was wandering in, lifting for ever their forest in air, drinking off...

The time is empty grinding.

The sun is still there, lying on the water, watching the horizon leaving its trace behind. A voice in the street is announcing the spring holidays. A wing beats noiselessly over the house. Tell me; what is the changeless time, if not the solitary thought of the dying?

The rustle of the monastic flags all around; and the dust, this offspring of the sluggish, heated day.

At the same crossing of roads, a woman gathers the hay scattered by the fox. The lambs are running, still undefeated by the grass gall; a cloud is chasing the heard from the distance. And there is silence... You can hear the old song of the man in the field: the hill, in its wake up, waving under the hay, heavy with dew. A girl with scratched hands searches for a nest

among leaves. A hunter makes traps on the same route, behind: "Ah, didn't I catch you, god dam fox?" Then, suddenly, the hills ignite, the yellow dust of the poplar rises back, above the footpath, the sun falls into the sea of grass: forgotten ecstasies, like a harbor lock, opened in a flesh of a body which grew old too soon.

"Your loving voice is a sob; your pain is a slow thought vanishing into the air". "My blood is a black dance", she sings, touching my body with a bitter drunkenness. How far the life is: I saw your eyes like shadows left in water, and your arms up, as if for prayer, and your lovely voice, like a smoke cup, I saw your body stripping, your sea weed hair on fire, your forehead like a white velvet sea, your opened lips, murmuring: "There, where oh!" The voluptuousness will vanish there, in sweet oases, looking for death.

A wild animal is sniffing the hay, rotten under dew. Listen to the pack of dogs barking at the face of the stranger woman who appeared near the fountain: Who's she? You didn't call her, yet she comes; "her breasts, falling like a black net over thy mouth; her breath, snowing over the deserted road".

The air is lighter and lighter; the ladder leaves a shadow like a black ring on the shiny skin of the pond. "Oh, tell me, who was there, beside me, the day when light, too much light carried my soul away?"

While rushing, I feel my limbs aching, my hands, stranger branches touching the shore. My mild beloved woman touches my shoulder: love, a more pure urge than a priestess carrying holy candles to a stone. The evening song starts, gently, her barren foot stamping the ground; the yelling, announcing the days of fast and forgetfulness: the village's fool talks of a black ghost: "Where is she?"

An adorned gate opening to the bride's household: fur footwear, silk tissues in the window; the girls are making the wild roses crown and the girdle; a black scarf is sown on the fence: let the years to come to be sang like a love song, and the lives to be lived in caress, a mirror of the lost Heaven, without return and without end...

How I used to call, from far away, the voice of the vineyard, and stare at the rustle of the forest in blossom, by autumn, and return the cry of the pond, imitating the owl. How I spied at the hill, oh, among tears how it would look now, with the stake of the old effigy in its bush, above time, as if carved in stone; the sky passed above the forest, repeating my cry in a short mimic.

Does the rock near the road, does it still let the moonlight
fall into the stream?

Near the strawberry bush a shadow appears: the wind runs
under the door like a sow. Is the air still carrying the herds of
angels, which you used to call before sleep? Look, the air guards
are there, wrapped in white. And on the hill, you could still hear
the sound of rain. The valley still harbors the greedy silence of the
fallen heights. A guideless flight, a heavy moan embracing the
black earth of the wild furrows. The plough lies rusty, wrapped in
cloth; the clouds descend like a giant column over the deserted
field, shadowing the hill's edge, white under snow.

Your life: a skylark in a thicket of thorns: it jumps, singing towards
the black sky: sfrr... The only companion, a flowery thicket,

knocking with its top branches at the window, sharply, like a belated call...

Oh, love! Where is the roar of the bees over the pasture? The sweet smell of your hands stretched in the wheat? The dew on your skin, and your mouth, in despair, murmuring chants you barely understood, and your swallow nest, reaching a strange ecstasy under rain's beatings. Where the blackbird is singing, heavy with seeds? The nut tree on which the snake, strangled by rain used to twist around; how you used to call the Heaven with your stubborn voice, hidden under the haystack: Do you see it? It came nearer...

Do you see it? A shadow passing shortly through the sunbeam... The sky is awakening again: swans pass like unreal spots on the lake, the earth in the furrow, opens like a corroded mirror; with fear you see the water's eye, its arrow unveiled by the ghostly wind;

Your black lips, steaming in the grass, like leaves scorched by drought in the wide horizon. The candle of the first stars and the bell sound of the hill vanish. You could hear just the water under the wooden floor: a word born dead, in the cry of the little blackbirds carried away by wind: the ripe hips giving away, the rustling dew, peacefully; a small beast rising on a wooden body at the shore; and the sun leaving the mill's entrance. An acacia leaf, falls in the cold wave of the pond. The shade stretches up the watchman's deserted tower. At last you hear the sad singing of the bastard;

The night embraces triumphantly the immensity of the plain. Like a torn tissue, a cloud glistens above the ceiling. The bees are buzzing in the moon rays: a strange serenity and a heavy calm;

The woman throws cedar seeds into the fire: last star! It can be seen behind the tree: a burning illusion. It was here that I experienced the passion and the curse of hunting: birds leaving behind bloody feathers up to the thicket of the isle, their wings opened, hanging above the burning charcoal, struggling between sleep and death. The dog cutting the path to the hawk, the sinister noise of the fallen cranes caught by storm at night.

And I began to deplore the frenzy of my body, hurriedly shuffling its feet among thickets, waiting and hunting. If under the vault, with so many stars betraying your sleep, you could find but for one moment, that wild, warm look of a girl searching in the isle thickets a sign of life, the collar of a dog chased from home: the Heaven's shores, covered by mist and dust... A love without boundaries, a sadness over which we throw ourselves: how the silent love renders with every moment, the secret of the days to come: "To be alive, just to live..."

The woman in black recites a lost poem: "Here is the door of the house you'll cross last", gently bending, "as if with the winter coming you'd still be alive, dead", her sharp voice, like the muffled croak of the crows from which my mother used to turn her face sighing: a gentle smile. Is it night, already? The leafless crossing lets the blue half of the moon pass through thistles; you could hear the strange breathing of the winds, which long ago, blew over your body, still living: the grass, the savage eye in the shadow, hiding the Great Death...

A butterfly flies in another world over your sad self, where love is gulped by the long shadow, where, under dark voices, the life's moan chokes and fades away dying: "You walked in sleep, one night full of passions, abandoning yourself, more than ever, to a bitter pride..." What was it yesterday? A feast? A mere announcement.

Near the shore, the hare, jumps from the reed, watching us. It might have been my grandfather, who's gone to the field. My mother comes holding a precious plate, filled with wild berries:

The fire cracks; you knew that hurting the shore with your feet, you'll die! Let the mole show you a hiding place: the moon is so clear, it looks like a huge coin, falling. The owl can be heard again, very close to you, in front of the window...

At last, you hear the wail of the mourners: first, the lambs are taken away; children can be heard striking the spoon in the door frame: the stars are black, as if dead in marsh. The time of vigil comes: three near the village's bridge, two hidden in the bushes, near the road, waiting for the black caravan. Would you like to come back here, and look at the hill's lightening?

It is morning in the bleeding forests. The dark bird of the pond rests on the hill, round and swollen, like an obscure star watching over the field; only the moon shines, breaking the silence with prophetical images. The green water whirls near the mill, murmuring like a moribund cry at dusk.

The amazing forests of the beautiful autumn are sleeping. "Wake me up, chant of the blossoming grass, wake me up you, beloved eyes of the innocence, staring at the whole world while passing...".

Those once lovely voices, leaving behind only red bilberry flowers; those eyes closed, resembling a piece of life, that slowly departed; oh, only a vague remembrance, foggy: a white butterfly descends in the rush; the marsh dresses in white and an unwieldy sound devastates the furrows; your lips, hiding in the dry blackberry bush, waiting, rustling: "the sound of sand which you throw over thy face, crying":

Where are my ears, listening to a song of the heart? My eyes are closed, under the roots of the ash tree, rising and lowering its branches, like thin nocturnal veins: I am a tree now, trying to live, shivering. The green leaves hide inside the thicket, my soul passed away, long time ago. The woodchopper taps the top of the dry fir tree; the wind whips the deserted hill, the pond water carries the cracking of the barn door to its exile. And you tell yourself: to my new face, which is watching, the beat of a bosom could return nothing but a flying shadow, some flowery grass lost in the hole of the endless night;

Like on the day I felt your warm breath telling words of love: your black eyes, brought hurriedly together with a whistle of the little bird: your breasts, seen like shades of the blackened sky, in the vast horizon.

It's midnight, the time when shy silences and secret dreams are awakened by a cry: the round eye of the moon shows on the top of the pole, in the haystack.

It is still daytime, what you see as midnight; listening to the void: only the singing sound of the water, poured off near the ditch; a woman, like a shadow, waters hesitantly a wild rose, near the window: a tiny thorn pierces her hand: a cry; the stone on the old footpath is heavy loaded with moss; young voices seem celebrating a strange, vain song:

"Tell me what moments will survive the secrets of this bloom?" My beloved tells a story: "Last night I almost died assaulted by dreams, and I found nothing in my memory but the rusted gate; near the gate, the weather worn armory: the light was still faraway, like a squirrel in the desert forest, rising its ears to the windless rain".

The hollow horizon moves the shadow of the mown grass and the world vibrate of too much eternity. The haystack is shaking again, torn by the wind. The rain falls over orchards, like an enormous bird, vaulting the water in the pond, with its lifeless song. What may this hour bring to the living? The limpid face of the plain shows itself, leaving a silky rust on the garden path.

And what will the by gone voice tell me, what its tongue will say, now, that the song of the heart dies wounded by alien echoes? I forbid you, night, to come nearer; the sky falls, torn apart, like the blackberry bushes by a pack of hounds urged to hunting! Here I am, with my fearful life, far off from the right road, in the strange garden of Heaven. The hill becomes darker, the plain moans in ecstasy again. Chainless again, as if penetrating the night with a source of light: did I hear the isle, the sugar cane moving towards the wooden threshold?

The red sun, like an enormous bell, appear from under the
dark gown of the horizon, making the grass move as if
under the weight of the mighty wind.

The earth fills with the undefeated song of the blackbird. What price shall I pay to live again a single day of my past, reviving from nothingness the cry of the wild love I chased, without loving.

I have fully lived famine, wars, and deaths: love –
a too solemn happiness.

Today I heard again the heavy sky, with its azure cape falling like a heavy bird nest over the hill: its sad song ended with the yells in the valley. The gray window of the shed, through which mother used to throw bread crumbs to the sparrows, always rubbing her hands over the fire: the resin, slowly burning and drying, the red moss on the oak tree; or the thistle I used to bind with hemp threads to the elm branches, and color for holidays.

The days seem to surface behind the hill. The barren trees blossom, the murmur of the water erupts near the pond, the moving face of the sky passes in abyss, covered by mist and smoke: one and the same look, another life; the wind no longer carries scents from the valley, the sun no longer travels over the hill, birds don't stop anymore in flight near the fountain.

The night is heavier, the same as yesterday, and the darkness of the flowery leaves is falling in the air. Your body, a bell tower entangled by the grass of death, leaving only the pudgy mole hills to penetrate from under the heap near the garden's path.

Come to the hazel tree meadow tonight! The plain appears cut from the shadow. The sky is like the sea deserting its vault: come, the light of the forest might hide the splendors of the past! On the dry road the leaves rise towards the forest; the restless lake frowns like your forehead, wearing the white crown of the spring rain; the rush smells of love; and there you are a gentle guide to the shadow!

The unknown sun of our last summer: the shore is empty. The light seems a fishing net thrown into the desert. A beggar is singing: "Days, endless days..." Here I am, soulless body, at my first encounter with the earth's holidays. Hay on the footpath, the wings of the stork fixed with nails on the threshold... And between wooden bars, the huge pumpkin, like a beautiful bucket close to a sheep which no longer gives milk. The evening chants, the dark birds so closely flying towards the marsh.

Every evening, you used to stare there: the hill
like an inflated canvas ready to be embroidered. The love hut looks like a sharp red stone carried by the stream to the bank. And, burning aimlessly, the brushwood fire near the hill foot... Where are our shouts, the heavy cry of the swallow, so many voices coming and going, leaving hurriedly the village at dawn...

The midwife coming every Sunday with bread rolls soaked in milk and spiced with rosemary and poppy seeds... And the witches sitting near the hill, watching the wild cocks falling in the autumn's drizzle...

"My dearest beloved, are thou tired of love? Are thou old? In front of the mill's tower which thou once climbed with dwarf elder crowns on your head, singing like an owl... who should appear? As if thou wandered along the paths of an old painting and then, rinse thy face in the rain, waiting for thy voice": the forest is leafless, the sunset colors are crushed, and, with an alert ear the deer scuttles away from the river: "Oh, how you used to run at that time, helpless, at the end of your strength, breathing with fervor..."

The carol singers wear bells at their girdles. The wind scatters again the hay near the fence. Then, the fairy queens appear, neither sunken, nor seen, around the silent hill, white shadows, looking for a broken piece of water, to see their faces: you have never been called there, you have never been allowed to go nearby: what are the fairy queens? Frozen dreams, tall ghosts like Unseen frozen shadows... Emptied bodies of what is seen or heard...

"Your wings are like weavers, throwing white cloth on the white and thin crust of the winter. Your crowing seems like night's try to drive away the luminous dawn".

The air is lighter and lighter. Will the branches be green again after passing through the deadly transparency of the ashy nights? Two shadows sit still, like the dead spirits at a burial site; the twilight, near the hill: the fountain wheel wails, set in motion by the sandy wind.

A candle lights in the hut: how much you wanted to weave the glowing grass in a crown, so as to stop the death, coming... Then, under the rain, running among thistles, afraid of your own shadow... How you threw the reed in fire, crying like a child: a few black feathers, left behind by ravens; the ghost, an emissary nobody knew until it arrived; "Oh, no, you'd have cried, how you would have cried!"

A stranger woman on the deserted isle, a strange crow in memory... The slow shadows are moving over the field. And the gloomy voice of the messenger resounds like an oracle: "I'm going to speak of the poetry of the deceased mind, since this is how the history of our species began, and I shall put down under the slab the two thousand words of the two thousand sayings... I see the sea, blossoming like a lute on the
dying man's bed, his troubled heart touched by grass, the night coming near him and piercing his voice with wild cries.

A call announcing the weeping which... announcing the pain which... announcing the fire which..." Why is this cry so far from the poor silence, and the silence the same?

The insistence of the immaculate song: the day, wounded by the ancient stubble, is still moving, moaning of tiredness; the reddish bushes, the endless dawn. The whole life lived once more!

What are those scorched faces, dissipating in the moon rays flooding the hut's door, left ajar? Is it that the day to come may hide the remorse of the past uttering? Or that the innocence of the days to come may die in the madness of the desert valley? The breath full of meanings talks to the quiet senses: call your mind, rejoice! The Heaven is here, the earth no longer wanders among stars: a plain with endless silences, united like an echo to the shadows of the blue lands...

The sun rises above the frail solitude of the road and wraps the whole nature in wonder. My beloved mind runs with wild feet through the high rains, shouting empty words: a cherry blossom, full of milk, sweet words uttered by a tongue, still alive... The gardens of the days to come: a fire near the furrow, a sheaf rolled down to the well: the hot singing of the blackbird.

And the future appears more pure, more shining than the sun heating the virginal water of the stream; a time when the ripe days give birth
to another days... After so many strange voyages here you are again, full of hopes, on your way to the hill.

The village seems severed from the outside world. The thin sunrise. In the shade, the bank near which the colts halted and, silent, the poisonous autumn smell falling on your lips. The cry in the meadow fades away, the deer, on their way to the mole, remain motionless.

The time in an everlasting expectancy. Some small birds rise in the air. And you don't know, what is there that overwhelms you out of the tempest of the enormous rain?

What is there that urges you to shout? The haystack scattered by the wind; no other thought but the one in which you see the death releasing the unspoken songs, your soul appearing under the smoky face of the moon, ready to warm a leaf carried shakily by the endless water...

In the thistles, a cluster of yellow birds, springing out, like a veil. The numberless nests. The snow fall, entangled by the wind. The white face of the miller, at the window: two fat hands shaking a sack; the midwife helps children to come to the world: a heart beating in the chest, ready to run away. The lighted window receives the wreath of the warm bread: old customs. Down, under the hill, the morning lights... The cock's riotous flight afar...

Short Glossary

Awakening (Enlightenment, Satori): Experiencing pure consciousness or the emptiness of "it". An enlightened one penetrates the mental and bodily walls to look into one's essential nature. The experience cannot be asserted though there are expressions that try to suggest what it is such as: "merging with the whole universe", "being embraced by the infinite", "experiencing the oneness", and "seeing and feeling something beyond what can be seen or felt". The experience cannot be apprehended either, in the same way as "death" cannot be apprehended before it happens. The awakening opens up the mind towards a different way of knowledge and knowing, by eliminating the distinction between known and knower, subject and object, relative and absolute, etc.

Buddha (An Enlightened One): A Buddha or an awakened one is the one who escapes from the "cycles of becoming" by taking possession of his cravings, his ego and his self building. A historic or a living Buddha accounts for such a journey to liberate oneself from attachments and, in this respect, for acquiring a pure and perfect body and mind that become the ideal vessels for the ultimate truth to manifest itself. To become a Buddha one has to observe certain spiritual practices, to obey unabatedly spiritual laws and stick to a mental discipline that could help one's being to attain the realization of an eternal and infinite truth that leads to omniscience.

Enlightenment – (see Awakening, Satori).

Meditation – Meditation is a practice that helps a practitioner acquire control of his/her mind in a way that could lead to the experience of awakening or enlightenment. There are various techniques one can use to meditate, some being more esoteric than others and so in need to a direction from a Zen teacher. Koan meditation is one of them, mantra meditation another.

Other methods could be experimented freely such as breathing, concentration on objects, forms, concepts, images. It is difficult to qualify and quantify which meditation technique brings faster results for it all depends on the mental affinities of the practitioner to the entire awakening process.

No-mind – If all that exist doesn't come from the mind then the only means to "look" into the essence of all is to drop the mind and contemplate the infinite of no-mind (mind emptied of concepts, definitions, knowledge). By cleansing the mind one could see one's own "self"-nature. The movement of the ordinary mind is therefore blocked in order to bypass the relative world in search of the absolute world.

One, One-ness – One cannot conceive an object or a process as being separate, independent of other objects and processes that occur in the universe. "A grain of dust that falls on the South Pole throws out a balance a mountain at the North Pole". Here there is something already known in quantum physics. In ordinary life this unity of the whole universe doesn't have an immediate effect. Every being feels like being above such a strict determination law. The feeling of one-ness or of unity is still a prerogative of the awakening moment. When one thinks of one-ness all objects and processes are inseparable and "the many" loses its meaning. As there are no many anymore the mental separation between interior and exterior, knower and known, etc. exists no more. The whole universe of mental dualities plunges into one-ness – the unified infinite depth.

Reality - Reality is what it is and what it is not, the presence and the absence, the evidence (proof) and the lack of evidence (empty signification), the truth and the false. In short, all that is conceivable or unconceivable is reality. In this respect what is not reality lies outside what is mind and no-mind. For instance, past is reality, though most subjects or objects that carried that past are gone. Buddha is gone, Jesus is gone, Napoleon is gone and Hitler is gone though they're all part of reality. Also, all living beings and inanimate objects are reality. The future is less reality every moment before it manifests itself. What's the difference between past that becomes absence and so it is part of a known reality and the future (the virtual absence) that becomes reality as it manifests itself? It seems that when time works on space (past, present) the space manifests itself; on the other hand, when space works on time (future) the time manifests itself. When time and space collapse in a moment of awakening the ultimate reality, non dual, unconditioned, unchangeable – the true nature of things reveals itself.

Satori – (Awakening, Enlightenment): Satori is the culmination of Zen meditation into a moment of total awareness. The verb *satoru* (to know) refers to a different "knowing" like for instance knowing what it is impossible to be known. Zen asserts that it is not possible to transpose this state into a philosophical (or any other speculative sort of) discourse. Some of the traditional expressions carried by various definitions of Satori are: "Seeing into one's original face", "Seeing into one's essential or true nature", "Seeing the ultimate truth". At the moment of awakening the knower and the known become one, that is, both the knower and the known are transcended. Such a unitary and indivisible state (oneness) is radically opposed to reasoning, that is to any discourse built on concepts and articulated by words (that carry with them duality, discrimination, dichotomy). In psychological/physiological terms one could presume that Satori is the coronation of the intuition's effort to coerce all the neurons specialized in awareness into performing a synchronous motion as a response to stimuli. It should be reminded to those who look at awareness with skepticism that consciousness (or super-consciousness) is still a state of the mind therefore it is a matter of neuronal activity. In a day to day state of mind only a limited number of neurons are fired up to entertain awareness. This number could vary depending on internal or external events that come to be acknowledged by the brain. Through meditation the awareness neurons get trained to remain in a wake-up state much longer than "needed" and, subsequently, to fire up additional neurons that come to entertain awareness for the sake of awareness itself. After a long Zazen or koan practice the awareness – that used to be a local function of the brain – expands more and more until it globalizes the brain. When all the awareness neurons of the brain get fired up to entertain awareness the awakening happens. In the awakened state the subject lives the experience of cosmic unity into emptiness. The whole reality is "seen" then beyond existence and non-existence and dissolves into the emptiness. The emptiness acts as a persistent, coherent and permanent reality. The awakening is a hypnotic moment – nonetheless – and serves essentially to make one's mind experience the reality in its true original and infinite state. Is this the ultimate truth or a superb illusion of a brain living a moment of synchronization with the universal flow? Awakening is sometimes seen as something that undermines reason and knowledge. In reality it should be taken more or less as being just a mystical experience that doesn't have any rapport – in theory or practice – with reasoning or knowledge per se. Knowledge will remain always open to what can be known while awakening will remain open to what is not and cannot rationally be known or expressed.

ZAZEN (Za- sitting, Zen – absorption: Sitting in Absorption): A "sitting" posture used by Zen practitioners to attain calmness and peace of mind. During sitting the practitioner tries to free his/her mind from concern about any aspect of thinking, and by doing so, to remove his/her mind from any sensory aspects of knowledge – thing, perception, representation, and thought-form. The aim of sitting in absorption is to overthrow the mind process (which is incompatible with the ultimate truth) and so break through the wall of thinking and "see" the essence of the "original face" or Buddha nature of the whole universe.

Zen – (Ch'an- meditation in Chinese). Ch'an became Zen when transposed into Japanese. The word Ch'an is derived from the Sanskrit word *dhyana* that defines an "absorbed" state of mind brought about by meditation and concentration techniques. Zen alludes to a state of super-consciousness that can be attended while one withdraws from ordinary life (bodily and mentally living) and commits his/her being to meditation. Through the practice of meditation the subject's mental attention moves from a body-and-mind universe onto a world beyond self-reference. Zazen is just one of many ways to meditate. In any meditation – instead of projecting the mind onto something, the mind projects onto itself. By doing that one discovers the ultimate truth, which is for a human being the self-nature without "self". The main characteristic of such a nature is that it is anonymous and universal and that it can be imagined as impregnating the whole universe. Call it emptiness or ether or whatever else it will remain unknown and unknowable to experience even after the awakening occurs. If awakening is a journey meant to provide a direct seeing into this original nature it is essential to look at it as something that could be found within. Then again, such an ultimate truth lies beyond a "meaning". A mind that is clear of rationalization might be able to "see" it. The awakened might witnesses its manifestation. Unfortunately, since this ultimate truth lies outside the reality of words – which is in Zen's view an artificial world conditioned by what body experiences as reality and the mind rationalizes as truth – one can't have a "feeling" for such ultimate truth until one gets awakened. In this ultimate truth there is nothing "true" but rather the annihilation of what true "means". As the ultimate truth reveals itself it shows that it deals with non-existent rather than existent. The manifestation of the universe of phenomena dissolves into a nothing-at-all entity, the emptiness. *As a sage would have said about such a revelation, "One needs an infinite number of words to express the inexpressible or rather one needs none".*

The end